Identities, Boundaries, and Social Ties

Identities, Boundaries, and Social Ties

Charles Tilly

Paradigm Publishers

Boulder • London

Copyright © 2005 by Paradigm Publishers

Published in the United States by Paradigm Publishers, 3360 Mitchell Lane Suite E, Boulder, Colorado 80301 USA.

Paradigm Publishers is the trade name of Birkenkamp & Company, LLC, Dean Birkenkamp, President and Publisher.

Library of Congress Cataloging-in-Publication Data

Tilly, Charles.
Identities, boundaries, and social ties / Charles Tilly.
p. cm.
Includes bibliographical references and index.
ISBN 1–59451–130–6 (hc: alk. paper)
1. Social structure.   2. Social networks.   3. Identity (Psychology)   4. Equality.
5. Democracy.   I. Title.
HM706.T55 2005
302.3'5—dc22

2005004921

Printed and bound in the United States of America on acid-free paper that meets the standards of the American National Standard for Permanence of Paper for Printed Library Materials.

Designed and Typeset by Straight Creek Bookmakers.

09 08 07 06 05
5 4 3 2 1

To Dean Birkenkamp, wise adventurer

Contents

Part V: Political Boundaries

Illustrations

Figures

Table

Preface

A FEW YEARS AGO, A PERPLEXED FRIEND ASKED MY OPINION OF A STRANGE experience. He had become a candidate for a major appointment in his academic field. When he gave his job talk at the new institution, he sensed some opposition, but still thought his chances for appointment remained good. He didn't get the offer. Later, someone told him what had happened at the institution's crucial meeting. Opponents had shown up at the gathering armed with documentation that he had committed a violation of academic virtue. His alleged dereliction involved practices that neither he nor I had previously recognized as a sin: self-plagiarism. Virtue's vigilant watchdogs showed that, without citing himself, my friend had repeatedly reused chunks of text in one publication that he had already employed in similar or identical form elsewhere.

I voiced my surprise. If self-plagiarism qualifies as an academic sin, hostile readers of my work will have no trouble using this volume as evidence of my utter corruption. Doubly so. First, most of this book's chapters appeared in print earlier in similar form, sometimes more than once. Second, favorite discussions repeat, sometimes using similar or identical words, from one publication to the next.

Take chapter 5, "Durable Inequality." In 1995, Phyllis Moen invited me to speak at a 1996 conference in Ithaca, New York, honoring my friend Robin Williams. I gladly accepted her invitation. On the conference day, despite heavy weather, I didn't have the sense to call the airline from my Manhattan apartment. A blizzard canceled my plane from New York City to Ithaca. Arriving at La Guardia Airport and learning the bad news, I rented a car at the airport and drove to Ithaca through heavy snow, arriving only minutes before my talk was scheduled to begin. I drew the talk from the current draft of a book I was then writing, which the University of California Press later published under the same title, *Durable Inequality* (Berkeley: University of California Press, 1998). But that book emerged from heavy reworking of lectures I had given at

UCLA from October to November 1995, when I was flying weekly round trips from New York to Los Angeles for my lectures after completing my week's classes at New York's New School for Social Research. In chapter 5, which text did I plagiarize?

Similarly, this book's chapter 10, "Chain Migration and Opportunity Hoarding," had its first public hearing as a lecture to the seminar on cultural diversity that Janina Dacyl and Charles Westin were running at the Centre for Research in International Migration and Ethnic Relations, Stockholm University. I was then serving as Sweden's Olof Palme Professor, based at Stockholm, during the winter and spring of 1996. Still working on *Durable Inequality,* I tried out the book's ideas about opportunity hoarding in the expert Dacyl-Westin seminar. I revised my text in light of the group's criticism. As often happens to collective volumes (including, alas, many I edit myself), it took several years before all the revised versions of papers from the Ithaca meeting and the Stockholm seminar were ready for publication. The collection that Phyllis Moen and her collaborators edited from the Ithaca papers didn't appear in print until 1999, and the Dacyl-Westin volume didn't appear until 2000. So which Tilly plagiarized from which Tilly?

During my 1996 sojourn in Stockholm, Peter Hedström and Richard Swedberg organized the conference on social mechanisms from which emerged their influential co-edited volume *Social Mechanisms. An Analytical Approach to Social Theory* (Cambridge University Press, 1998). The conference introduced me to Argentine-born physicist-philosopher Mario Bunge, whose understanding of social mechanisms and mine, we discovered, resembled each other. Without making much of the point, both of us had been offering mechanism-based explanations of social processes for years. We both presented papers on mechanisms at the Stockholm conference, but the editors chose not to publish them. For me, nevertheless, that encounter underlined the importance of clarifying how social mechanisms work, and identifying them with care. Every chapter in this book employs mechanism-based explanation, some more explicitly and polemically than others. Once again, the presentations borrow from each other, as well as from discussions I have published elsewhere.

Does all this repetition have a point? Many of my colleagues think mostly in articles: pursue complex research programs, but report ideas and findings via individual papers as ideas and findings come along. I think mainly in books: lay out inquiries that have beginnings, middles, and endings, but will if successful produce reports occupying a couple hundred pages. Many don't succeed, but still yield lectures, papers, or chapters that present their incomplete programs. Because I always keep several such books-in-the-making under way at a time and because ideas interconnect, I often transfer ideas, references, and language from one current text to another.

As a result, academic inquisitors who care about such things can easily detect repetitions within this book as well as between this book and other writings. If you read this book from cover to cover, for example, you will find several sermons that repeat in similar terms in separate chapters: distinctions among systemic, transactional, and dispositional explanations of social processes, definitions of mechanisms and processes, expositions of exploitation and opportunity hoarding, conceptualizations of democratization and de-democratization.

On balance, I consider that redundancy a benefit, not a cost. The book as a whole presents the chief ideas and phenomena on which I worked during the decade starting in the mid-1990s: certainly the identities, boundaries, and social ties of the book's title, but also mechanisms, processes, democratization, de-democratization, citizenship, inequality, collective violence, stories, social movements, and trust. Although each of these ideas and phenomena gets more sustained attention elsewhere—hence the perhaps excessive self-citation that recurs through the text—here cross-connections among them become clearer. The book identifies, for example, connections between inequality and de-democratization, between identities and inequality, between citizenship and identities. I won't claim that fifteen papers produced over a decade constitute a seamless whole. I will claim that, read together, they offer a distinctive, coherent account of social processes.

How so? From several different angles, the book's chapters treat interpersonal transactions as the basic elements of social processes. They show how interpersonal transactions compound into identities, create and transform social boundaries, and accumulate into durable social ties. They claim that individual and collective dispositions result from interpersonal transactions. Resisting the focus on deliberated individual action, furthermore, the book repeatedly gives attention to incremental effects, indirect effects, environmental effects, feedback, mistakes, repairs, and unanticipated consequences. Yes, social life is complicated. But, the book shows, social life becomes comprehensible once you know how to look at it.

Part I

Introduction

Chapter 1

Ties That Bind . . . and Bound

LIAH GREENFELD HAS NAILED UP FIVE CHALLENGING THESES about the social sciences on the highly visible virtual doors—the websites—of Boston University. Theses 2 and 3 castigate the social sciences for taking physics as their scientific model, and for organizing disciplines around political and ideological concerns. The remaining theses read as follows:

1. Even though the human sciences were meant to study humanity, they focus on social structures, which, far from being distinctively human, are essential in the lives of all animals, hence are best addressed by biology. What separates humanity from the rest of the animal kingdom is not society or social structures, but the transmission of social order via symbolic means, i.e., culture, rather than by genes. Symbolic or cultural processes take place primarily in people's minds. Instead of being unconscious subdisciplines of biology, the social sciences should be sciences of culture and the mind.

4. Quantification and mathematical modeling, applied to the study of social "structures," tended to treat them as if they evolved mechanically. Mental reality, in turn—i.e., the meaning that people assign to their actions—was postulated to be a mere reflection of these structural processes, and therefore was grossly under-researched.

5. The problems of this paradigm are seen in the failure of social-scientific predictions, and the inability of social science to provide useful solutions to social problems. It is also reflected in the fact that, while sophomores

3

in physics have left Newton far behind, the writings of Weber, Durkheim, even Plato and Aristotle, often seem more adequate than many contemporary social-scientific studies for understanding the world in which we live (Friedman 2004: 144–45; see also BU 2004).

Greenfeld's five theses propose culturally informed phenomenology as the proper alternative to the mechanical representations that have, in her view, held back the social sciences.

In terms that will appear repeatedly through the rest of this book, Greenfeld is fostering dispositional explanations of social processes in opposition to their chief alternative: transactional explanations. (As chapter 2 declares, social theorists have historically given plenty of attention to a third alternative—explanation by reference to self-sustaining social systems—which currently attracts few supporters, and which in any case Greenfeld also rejects.) But within dispositional accounts, she is also rejecting those views of human consciousness that treat it as rationally calculating and/or closely bound to physiology. She calls for social scientists to center their attention on the pursuit of meaning by cultured minds. Thesis 4 states the point explicitly: mental reality consists of "the meaning that people assign to their actions."

In her own research, Greenfeld follows the creed. Greenfeld's explanations center on transformations of culturally informed consciousness. Her first book laid out a comparative history of nationalism centering on the birth and diffusion of a peculiar but potent set of beliefs (Greenfeld 1992). Her more recent *Spirit of Capitalism* assembles comparative histories of England, the Netherlands, France, Germany, Japan, and the United States to expand her previous claims (Greenfeld 2003). Nationalism, for Greenfeld, exists when people subject to a common political authority share consciousness of belonging to a distinctive sovereign community. In the earlier book, the timing and form of nationalism, thus defined, accounted for distinctive subsequent political orientations in England, France, Russia, Germany, and the United States.

In her more recent book, Greenfeld proposes an aggressively dispositional explanation. She argues that similar changes in consciousness caused people to overturn millennia of suspicion as they committed themselves to a belief in economic growth as desirable and natural. They did so because identification with the nation promoted a shared sense of dignity, efficacy, and relative equality among the nation's members, hence a new willingness to undertake economic effort whose outcome depended on the efforts of distant others. Changed beliefs, according to the argument, then caused sustained economic growth to occur, country by country.

Greenfeld prudently denies that nationalism causes reorientation to economic growth wherever it occurs. She also allows that the capabilities assigned center stage in most economists' accounts of economic growth affect how and how fast growth occurs. She accordingly distinguishes between economists' stories of *how* and her—motivational—story of *why*. Greenfeld's story self-consciously pits nationalism against Weber's Protestant Ethic, while retaining Weber's general causal logic: new cultural forms generate new forms of consciousness, which in turn shape economic activity.

Against arguments locating the conditions of economic growth in proper market mechanisms, appropriate mixes of economic resources, technological innovations, and/or disciplined, achieving cultures in the style of Max Weber's Protestants, Greenfeld's analysis offers something new and intriguing: a stress on identifications with communities of fate as promoters of costly collective action. (This book's chapter 4 takes up that very issue.) Like Margaret Levi's analysis of popular compliance with state demands, Greenfeld's treatment of nationalism draws our attention to the crucial importance for collective enterprises of arrangements that increase the probability—or at least the perception—that others will join the common effort, and that authorities will impose public obligations more or less uniformly (Levi 1988, 1997).

For such an argument to gain credibility, nevertheless, Greenfeld's international comparisons must show that the sequence 1) nationalism 2) belief change 3) economic growth recurred both within countries and across them. The within-country component calls for a demonstration that national consciousness did, indeed, alter whole populations' commitments to economic activity, and that altered commitments did, indeed, fuel sustained growth. The across-country component requires earlier nationalism in England than elsewhere, absence of sustained economic growth in Tokugawa, Japan, and so on. It implies that both nationalism and economic commitment eventually transformed the United States even more profoundly than its predecessors. It also necessitates brushing off objections that economic growth in the Netherlands, China, or elsewhere either preceded or caused that of England.

Fully aware of these logical requirements, Greenfeld sets up the book as a series of single-country analyses in roughly chronological order. She precedes the country-by-country reviews with a pithy introduction and follows them with a thoughtful epilogue concerning the (very mixed) future of economic growth, especially in her native Russia. Readers should therefore ask three questions of the book: Do the treatments of individual countries adequately describe their experiences with nationalism, alteration of mentalities, and economic growth? Do within-country and cross-country sequences correspond to the argument's logical requirements? Do the proposed causal processes hold up to empirical and logical scrutiny?

On the first count, Greenfeld concentrates so heavily on ideological transformation that historically informed readers will constantly find themselves calling up unmentioned and unanswered alternative explanations. In the case of England, for example, I could not suppress thoughts about how the 16th century shift from wool to cloth production signaled England's integration into the continental economy, especially that of the Low Countries and northern France. On the second count, the dismissal of the early-developing Netherlands, although well informed, looks like special pleading: the nonnationalist Dutch Republic, Greenfeld tells us, poses no objection to the general thesis because its economy probably contracted during the later 17th century, a contraction that disqualifies it as a case of sustained economic growth. On the third count, the dual processes by which first awareness of a shared nation spreads and then that awareness motivates economic effort remain underspecified and mysterious.

Greenfeld's linking of economic growth to nationalism has many virtues: boldness, serious engagement with history, systematic use of national comparisons, grappling with serious problems. If my line of argument holds, however, her adoption of a dispositional account dooms the effort to failure.

Later chapters present my own view of nationalism and offer different descriptions of several countries that Greenfeld takes up, notably England and France. What matters here, however, is the claim to explain. You can't get there from here, I argue: however finely etched, the quickening awareness of whole peoples that they belong to a sovereign nation cannot explain their country's takeoff into economic growth. In principle, any such explanation must account for realignment among the major factors of production: capital, labor, land, and technology. It is at best implausible that parallel shifts in national consciousness caused that realignment in country after country (Kohli 2004, Mokyr 2002, Pomeranz 2000). Even if that implausible effect occurred, we would still need to know how it produced realignments of capital, labor, land, and technology. Here the how *is* the why.

Greenfeld's arguments provide a helpful specification of the position against which this book rebels from beginning to end: the claim that individual and collective dispositions explain social processes. The pages that follow do not deny that individuals have consequential dispositions, or that ambient culture informs those dispositions. Nor do they endorse physics as a model for the social sciences. They make the case, however, for interpersonal transactions as the basic stuff of social processes. They show how interpersonal transactions compound into identities, create and transform social boundaries, and accumulate into durable social ties. They claim that individual and collective dispositions result from interpersonal transactions.

Resisting the focus on deliberated individual action, furthermore, this book repeatedly gives attention to incremental effects, indirect effects, environmental effects, feedback, mistakes, repairs, and unanticipated consequences. Doing so, it heeds Mustafa Emirbayer's call for a newly relational social science (Emirbayer 1997). But it also harks back to Robert Merton's insistence on mechanism-based explanations of social processes (Merton 1968: 43–44).

Strictly speaking, we observe transactions, not relations. Transactions between social sites transfer energy from one to another, however microscopically. From a series of transactions we infer a *relation* between the sites: a friendship, a rivalry, an alliance, or something else. (Without being too rigid about it, in general, I will call those connections "ties" when referring to their durable characteristics, and "relations" when talking about their dynamic interactions.) Cumulatively, such transactions create memories, shared understandings, recognizable routines, and alterations in the sites themselves. In the pages that follow, I will sometimes speak of transactional perspectives but of relational mechanisms. Most of the time, however, I will save words by lumping the two together as "relational."

Relational mechanisms figure prominently throughout the book. Some chapters simply pit them against dispositional explanations, as in my imagined debate with Liah Greenfeld. Others place them ontologically, claiming that transactions and relations provide a firmer ground for analysis than do social systems or disposition-propelled actors. Still other discussions concentrate on the logic of explanation as such; they distinguish covering law accounts, specifications of necessary and sufficient conditions, variable-based searches for correlations, location of elements within systems, imputations of dispositions, and explanations involving mechanisms and processes (see Stinchcombe 2005). In the latter case, transactional mechanisms and processes typically combine with their environmental and cognitive counterparts.

Figure 1-1 provides a sample of the reasoning you will encounter repeatedly in later chapters. Overall, it analyzes the transformation of collective identities: shared answers to the questions "Who are you?" "Who are we?" or "Who are they?" Such identities, it indicates, center on boundaries separating us from them. On either side of the boundary, people maintain relations with each other: relations within X and relations within Y. They also carry on relations across the boundary: relations linking X to Y. Finally, they create collective stories about the boundary, about relations within X and Y, and relations between

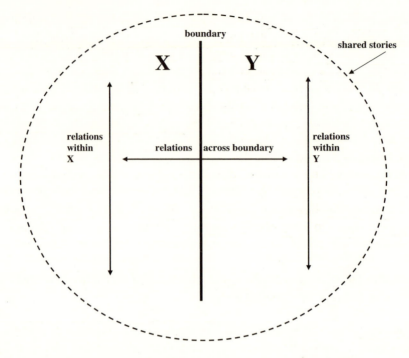

Figure 1-1. Boundaries, Ties, and Identities

X and Y. Those stories usually differ from one side of the boundary to another, and often influence each other. Together, boundary, cross-boundary relations, within-boundary relations, and stories make up collective identities. Changes in any of the elements, however they occur, affect all the others. The existence of collective identities, furthermore, shapes individual experiences, for example, by providing templates for us Croats and distinguishing us from those Serbs.

Here we face an important choice, the same choice posed by Liah Greenfeld's work. We can, like most analysts, treat identities as characteristics of individual consciousness: how you think of yourself. Or, with relational analysts, we can observe that:

- identities reside in relations with others: you-me and us-them
- strictly speaking, every individual, group, or social site has as many identities as it has relations with other individuals, groups, or social sites
- the same individuals, groups, and social sites shift from identity to identity as they shift relations

- every political process includes assertions of identity, including definitions of relevant us-them boundaries
- such assertions almost always involve claims about inequality—our superiority, our subordination, their unjust advantages, and so on
- nevertheless, profound social processes affect which identities become salient, which ones remain subordinate, and how frequently different identities come into play
- political institutions incorporate certain identities (for example, "citizen" or "woman") and reinforce the relations on which those identities build
- struggles over and within political institutions therefore regularly involve conflicting claims over what political identities have public standing, who has rights or obligations to assert those identities, and what rights or obligations attach to any particular identity
- of course, all such processes have phenomenological components and effects, but give and take among individuals, groups, and social sites—including political contention—create the regularities in identity expression that prevail in any particular population

Identities, Boundaries, and Social Ties unpacks these arguments in detail. Parts 4 and 5 of the book ("Boundaries" and "Political Boundaries") deal most extensively with these identity processes. But they underlie the book's reasoning from beginning to end.

Part 2 ("Relational Mechanisms") focuses on political processes: collective violence, democratization, and sacrifice for collective causes. Within those processes, however, it seeks out recurrent causal mechanisms that produce alterations in connections among social sites: relational mechanisms. Without denying the significance of other sorts of mechanisms—cognitive and environmental—it thereby makes the case for placing relational mechanisms at the base of any effort to explain social processes.

Part 3 ("Inequality") adopts the same approach to explanation but applies it to inequality in general, not just political inequality. It concentrates on the formation and transformation of unequal categories in the manner of figure 1-1. It treats inequality as a special form of collective identity, one in which people on one side of a boundary enjoy advantages over people on the other side. Singling out the relational mechanisms I call exploitation, opportunity hoarding, emulation, and adaptation, it moves from a general account of categorical inequality to reflections on unequal access to knowledge, especially scientific knowledge.

Part 4 ("Boundaries") builds on the two previous sections. Ideas about relational mechanisms and inequality clear the way to explaining how boundaries form, change, activate, and de-activate, and thus shape social interaction. It includes a general account of boundary processes (chapter 9: "Social Boundary Mechanisms"), a closer look at migration processes that have already come up in chapter 9 (chapter 10: "Chain Migration and Opportunity Hoarding"), and a wider-ranging historical exploration of citizen-noncitizen boundaries as paired forms of inclusion and exclusion (chapter 11: "Boundaries, Citizenship, and Exclusion").

The book's final section (part 5: "Political Boundaries") draws together strands from all the earlier sections: relational mechanisms, inequality, and boundaries as well as this introduction. It wraps them around citizenship as a general phenomenon, connections between inequality and democratization or de-democratization, political identities as historical products, and historical transformations of the means that people use in making social movement claims. More so than the book's earlier sections, part 5 reveals the worried concern for democracy that motivates most of the book: documented worries that democracy remains vulnerable to reversal, that blatant inequality threatens democracy, that withdrawal of trust networks from public politics likewise diminishes democracy's chances, and that the populist forms of collective expression embodied in social movements may disappear with new forms of inequality, exploitation, and opportunity hoarding.

Readers who persist to the end may not close this book convinced that relational mechanisms explain social processes in the ways that I claim, or even that transactional accounts provide a surer grip on social processes than their dispositional and systemic competitors. But engagement with the following chapters should at least clarify the stakes of the competition. For the explanation of boundaries, identities, stories, inequality, public politics, and everyday social relations, dispositional and transactional accounts compete with each other fiercely. On that point, at least, Liah Greenfeld and I can agree: the stakes are high.

Part II

Relational Mechanisms

Chapter 2

Violent Conflict, Social Ties, and Explanations of Social Processes

Shortly before his premature death in 2003, the brilliant political analyst Roger Gould completed a superb, coherent, vivifying book while undergoing intensive treatment for cancer. As a cancer victim who survived, I read Gould's *Collision of Wills* (2003) with triple interest: as evidence of my good fortune, as a tribute to his courage, and as a memorial to his intellectual contribution.

Reading *Collision of Wills* brings home how much we have lost with Gould's departure. In plain, well-crafted prose the book lays out an original, persuasive account of social processes that generate small-scale lethal conflicts. It accomplishes much more than that, presenting forceful views of good and bad social science, offering a serious challenge to the (widely prevalent) attribution of uniform propensities to collectivities, and fashioning a remarkable theory of group differences in past-, present-, and future-orientation. Now that his cancer-delayed edited volume, *Rational Choice Controversy in Historical Sociology*, has finally appeared, a much wider range of readers will recognize that Gould was becoming not only a widely admired craftsman of social scientific research but also a distinctive major voice in criticism and synthesis (Gould 2005).

In writing *Collision of Wills*, Gould recurrently wore his heart on his sleeve, striking out against social scientific confusions and errors: dangers of insisting that explanations of behavior rely on the categories that the actors themselves employ, risks of imputing coherent interests and identities to collectivities, fallacies of composition, and much more. He often used foot-notes for reflections, critiques, and extensions of this sort. Students and fellow social scientists can therefore profit from three rather different readings of the book: the first for argument and evidence, the second for asides and critiques, the third for reflection on general explanations of social processes. This essay concentrates on the third point: general explanations.

Crudely speaking, general descriptions and explanations of social processes divide into three categories: systemic, dispositional, and transactional. *Systemic* accounts posit a coherent, self-sustaining entity such as a society, a world-economy, a community, an organization, a household, or at the limit a person, explaining events inside that entity by their location within the entity as a whole. Systemic descriptions and explanations have the advantage of taking seriously a knotty problem for social scientists: how to connect small-scale and large-scale social processes. They have two vexing disadvantages: the enormous dif-ficulty of identifying and bounding relevant systems, and persistent confusion about cause and effect within such systems.

Dispositional accounts similarly posit coherent entities—in this case more often individuals than any others—but explain the actions of those entities by means of their orientations just before the point of action. Competing disposi-tional accounts feature motives, decision logics, emotions, and cultural tem-plates. When cast at the level of the individual organism, dispositional descrip-tions and explanations have the advantage (*pace* Liah Greenfeld!) of articulating easily with the findings of neuroscience, genetics, and evolutionary analysis. They have the great disadvantage of accounting badly for emergence and for aggregate effects.

Transactional accounts take interactions among social sites as their starting points, treating both events at those sites and durable characteristics of those sites as outcomes of interactions. Transactional accounts become relational—another term widely employed in this context—when they focus on persistent features of transactions between specific social sites. (The rest of this book uses the terms "transactional" and "relational" interchangeably.) Transactional or relational descriptions and explanations have the advantage of placing com-munication, including the use of language, at the heart of social life. They have the disadvantage of contradicting common sense accounts of social behavior, and thus of articulating poorly with conventional moral reasoning in which entities take responsibility for dispositions and their consequences.

Systemic, dispositional, and transactional approaches qualify as metatheories rather than as directly verifiable or falsifiable theories. They take competing ontological positions, claiming that rather different sorts of phenomena constitute and cause social processes. The three therefore generate contradictory lines of explanation for social processes. (As chapter 3 takes up explanatory strategies, indeed, I will distinguish skepticism, covering law, systemic, dispositional, and mechanism-based approaches, arguing that the five items—which combine ontology, epistemology, and logic—better describe the types of explanations social scientists currently employ in actual practice.) In the nature of the case, however, sustained competition between social scientific explanations usually takes place *within* one of these ontological lines rather than across them; systemic explanations compete with other systemic explanations, and so on.

Take the widely discussed process of democratization and its less widely discussed reversal, de-democratization. Systemic accounts of democratization and de-democratization typically identify the society or polity as the relevant unit of analysis, stressing the dependence of democratic institutions and practices on such aggregate characteristics as wealth, cultural homogeneity, and level of civic participation; controversies concern which aggregate characteristics of political systems make the difference. Dispositional accounts of democratization and de-democratization (which dominate current discussions of the subject) center on attitudes and incentives that promote or inhibit willingness of different actors to play the democratic game; controversies concern which attitudes and incentives make a difference, and how they do so. Transactional accounts of democratization and de-democratization characteristically feature the sorts of relations among major political actors that promote their sustained participation in competitive public politics; controversies concern which relations matter, and how they work.

When it comes to the more immediately relevant question of collective violence, systemic accounts often trace the character or intensity of violence to mismatches of societal elements, for example between the general ethos and the opportunity structure. Dispositional accounts (which, as with democratization and de-democratization, prevail these days) commonly highlight incentives and opportunities available to individuals who already have violent propensities. Transactional accounts, in their turn, often center on trajectories of negotiations between individuals or groups.

Of course, absolutely pure versions of systemic, dispositional, or transactional accounts rarely appear in serious social scientific work. My own preferred descriptions and explanations of social processes avoid systems and assign a fundamental place to transactions. But they also recognize that transactions endow social sites, including persons, groups, and social ties, with information, codes, resources, and energies that shape the participation of those sites in subsequent transactions.

As matters of priority, nevertheless, systemic, dispositional, and transactional accounts point social scientific work in different directions. From the mid-19th to the mid-20th century, systemic thinking preoccupied major social analysts from Auguste Comte to Talcott Parsons, only to lose considerable ground during the later part of the 20th century. Dispositional thinking held its own from the utilitarians onward, but became even more prevalent as systems lost their social scientific sway and the prestige of a very dispositional economics grew. Transactional thinking never dominated 19th- or 20th-century social science, but the names Karl Marx, Georg Simmel, George Herbert Mead, and John R. Commons recall its long-term presence as a minority alternative.

As the 20th century drew to a close, furthermore, transactional accounts of social processes enjoyed something of a renaissance. Richer and more dynamic forms of network analysis in sociology, institutionalism and constructivism in political science, plus the increasing prominence of organizational, institutional, and transaction-cost analyses in economics illustrate the trend. Gould's *Collision of Wills* contributes significantly to the revival and renewal of transactional accounts in social science. Peter Bearman's preface to the book puts the point nicely:

> In this book Gould develops an original framework for making sense of what appears on the surface to be senseless violence between individuals and small groups. Taken at face value, most accounts of interpersonal violence suggest that violence erupts because of the most trivial things. One idea prevalent in the literature is that violence is about trivial things because all people encounter opportunities for conflict at some time, that most of these opportunities are about silly things, and that some people are simply prone to violence, so in the end, most violence is about things that don't matter much. Gould challenges this idea and shows that interpersonal violence is a property of relations, not persons. (Gould 2003: xi–xii)

In my own more ponderous language, Gould's analysis avoids system accounts, criticizes dispositional accounts, and adopts a mainly transactional account of collective violence at the small scale.

Except in its final chapter, the book's analysis centers on common properties of crucial social relations across a wide variety of lethal conflicts: bar fights in Renaissance Flanders, vengeance in 19th-century Corsica, homicide in 20th-century American cities and elsewhere, killing in response to witchcraft in a number of different times and places, still more instances in footnotes and asides. Leaving aside the book's many polemics and sermons, the main argument concerns situations in which at least one party is claiming deference from another in the absence of well-established supports for that deference in the form of previously established relations between the parties, widely available definitions of the relationship, or third-party enforcement of the claim for deference.

No social setting establishes perfect stability or consistency in these regards, Gould points out, so that a) all social relations involve some asymmetries that are open to contestation and b) small-scale struggles over deference claims occur all the time. But such struggles become more frequent and more destructive, he argues, when established relations among parties are changing, conflicting definitions of relations are becoming more salient, and third-party supports are uncertain or ineffective.

The last line of analysis allows Gould to formulate one of his most striking arguments: that in times of political crisis crimes of violence rise not (or at least not exclusively) because people get caught up in political conflict but because such crises destabilize supports for existing deference patterns. Although one might give a systemic gloss to this final argument, it clearly centers on transactions. It raises serious doubt that any dispositional account could predict the involvement in collective violence of Flemish barflies, Corsican stiletto carriers, American urban murderers, or observers of witchcraft across the world.

The general argument also implies that:

1. Conflict occurs more frequently in symmetrical than in asymmetrical relationships.
2. Violent conflict occurs especially in relatively symmetrical but inconsistent relationships.
3. Instability in adjacent relationships increases the likelihood of conflict in the relationship at hand.

Much of the book consists of sequences in which Gould lays out some portion or implication of this general argument with exquisite care, fends off frequent confusions and/or competing arguments, then presents a simple but telling body of evidence to support the argument. The most extended treatment concerns homicide in 19th-century Corsica, but similar care goes into such analyses as the treatments of homicide's annual fluctuations in Corsica, France, Italy, and Finland.

The final chapter breaks with this mode in a remarkable series of reflections on two linked topics: how social settings that set a high value on masculine honor actually operate, and what difference it makes to social life (including conflict) whether people have strong investments in a) maintaining their past selves, b) gratifying their present selves, or c) ensuring their future selves. In Gould's stimulating view, willingness—or obligation—to sacrifice past and present selves on behalf of future selves encourages people to accept subordination within well-defined hierarchies, and dramatizes acts of rebellion in which the rebels renounce benefits that prudence or submission would guarantee for their future selves.

Like the best social science, Gould's analysis of violence in small-scale interpersonal confrontations immediately suggests analogies, extensions, and applications outside its immediate empirical range. Many observers of violent entrepreneurs such as Mafiosi have argued, for example, that protection services, however illegal, commonly provide ways of securing advantageous outcomes to risky, consequential transactions where trust is in short supply; the mechanisms involved in that supply of trust look like the same mechanisms that generate lethal encounters in Gould's account, but now reversed.

Willingness to accept current subordination in anticipation of fulfillment for future selves also directly parallels a major conundrum in the study of democracy: under what conditions and how people accept current sacrifices ranging from military service and heavy taxes to having one's party lose an election, yet instead of fleeing or subverting the regime they persist in participating. Long career ladders in which people abandon their pasts and climb the steps though years of subordination deserve Gouldian attention. We might even apply Gould's insights to careers in social science, including the deference and respectful citation required of junior scholars.

"Call to arms"

We survivors and heirs of Roger Gould should not let the matter rest there, with simple celebration and dutiful citation of an insightful book. We can do more. Let's return to the explanation of collective violence, but now think about the larger scale. In sociology, political science, economics, and journalism, prevailing analyses of collective violence rely heavily on dispositional accounts. The relevant actors range from genes to persons to groups to whole civilizations. Relevant dispositions vary from ideas to impulses to calculations of advantage. Across all variants, however, one dispositional understanding prevails: explaining collective violence means singling out the crucial actors and identifying their dispositions to violence. In a dispositional mode, analysts who abhor the violence in question then hope to alter violent dispositions, reduce incentives or circumstances that currently activate those dispositions, block their realization, or divert them to harmless outcomes.

Gould's transactional account challenges all such prescriptions. It points instead toward alterations in social relations as the effective means of reducing violent encounters. Such alterations might include stabilizing deference patterns, reducing the inconsistency of those patterns, separating parties to uncertain deference relations, inserting third-party monitors or mediators, reducing access of the parties to lethal weapons, and increasing opportunities for those who accept today's subordination to ensure their future selves.

Collision of Wills leaves a large agenda for transactional analyses of collective violence. Considered in terms of total deaths, wounds, and property damage, the great bulk of collective violence does not occur in the small-scale encounters on which Gould's book properly concentrates. Militias, gangs, armies, disciplined villagers, ethnic activists, dealers in contraband and other organized groups specializing in coercion figure widely in larger-scale collective violence. We might, of course, conclude that such violent specialists and the deference-contesting pairs described by Roger Gould inhabit such different causal worlds that Gould's insights do not apply. We might even conclude that for all the value of transactional explanations in cases of interpersonal rank ambiguity, large-scale collective violence requires systemic or dispositional explanations. After all, the existing literature on ethnic conflict, civil war, interstate war, and related phenomena overwhelmingly adopts systemic and/or dispositional accounts. Why not just ride the mainstream?

That would be a mistake. The approach sketched by Roger Gould has powerful implications for the analysis of larger-scale collective violence. To take only the most obvious extension, the same sorts of contests over ambiguous social rank that set Gould's individuals at each other's throats also operate between categories and groups: interacting castes, neighboring villages, rival gangs, competing militias, members of adjacent racial categories, and more. Further afield, Gould's approach suggests ways of thinking about the largest puzzles in the study of collective violence:

1. Why does collective violence, unlike suicides and individual homicides, concentrate in large waves, often with one violent encounter appearing to trigger the next, then subside to low levels for substantial periods of time?
2. How and why do people who interact without doing outright damage to each other shift rapidly into collective violence, then back (sometimes just as rapidly) into relatively peaceful relations?
3. In particular, how and why do people who have lived with their categorical differences (often cooperating and intermarrying) for years begin devastating attacks on each other's persons and property?
4. Why do different kinds of political regimes (for example, democratic and authoritarian regimes) host such different levels and forms of collective violence?

5. How and why do peacekeeping specialists such as police and soldiers so
   regularly and quickly switch between violent and nonviolent action?

I do not claim that we can read out answers to these five pressing questions
directly from the pages of Gould's book. But I do make two claims: first, that
systemic and dispositional answers to the questions, which are legion, have not
proven very satisfactory; second, that the very sort of transactional reasoning
we find in Gould leads to fruitful programs of theory and research in all five
regards.

Changes in uncertainty about interactions across established us-them boundaries, for example, exert strong effects on switching between violent and nonviolent collective interactions. Uncertainty commonly increases when:

- overarching political authorities lose their ability to enforce previously con-
  straining agreements binding actors on both sides of the boundary (example: subordination of Catholics weakens in 18th-century Ulster as a pros-
  pering linen industry alters patterns of inequality, and Protestant-Catholic
  conflict intensifies)
- those same authorities take actions that threaten survival of crucial connecting structures within populations on one side of the boundary while
  appearing to spare or even benefit those on the other side (example: between 1829 and 1835, British authorities expand Catholic political rights
  while banning both the Catholic Association and the Protestant Orange
  Order, thus threatening Protestant hegemony)
- the declining capacity of authorities to police existing boundaries, control
  use of weapons, and contain individual aggression facilitates cross-boundary opportunism, including retaliation for earlier slights and injustices (example: police withdraw from black neighborhoods during early stages of
  Los Angeles and Detroit confrontations of the 1960s, then both looting and
  attacks on ostensibly white property spread)
- leaders on one side of the boundary or the other face resistance or competition from well-organized segments of their previous followers (example:
  Algerian Islamic purists turn simultaneously against secular leaders and
  defecting villagers, engaging in widespread massacres of Muslims in the
  process)
- external parties change, increase, or decrease their material, moral, and
  political support for actors on one side of the boundary or the other (example: French revolutionary authorities send troops to the Vendée in sup-

port of beleaguered Patriots, thereby threatening the rural people who are harassing the Patriots)

You will not find these causes of rising relational uncertainty, hence of collective violence, listed explicitly in *Collision of Wills*. No doubt Roger Gould, never an easy sell, would have rejected, resisted, respecified, or modified some of them. I may have gotten them wrong. Nevertheless, the main point remains: well outside the small-scale world of lethal one-on-one confrontations, the sort of description and explanation Gould has bequeathed to us promises to improve our understanding of conflict processes at large.

Nor did he contribute to studies of conflict alone. Taken as a whole, the work of Roger Gould provides a model for the renewal of transactional analyses across social science. Its combination of rigor, ambition, originality, and skepticism can only inspire us survivors.

Chapter 3

Mechanisms in Political Processes

Early in their careers, students of social science commonly learn an exercise resembling the scales and arpeggios every beginning violinist must master: essential for gaining a sense of the discipline, but by no means the heart of virtuoso violin performance. The exercise consists of identifying a phenomenon—nationalism, revolution, balance of power, or something else—then lining up two or three ostensibly competing explanations of the phenomenon. An effective performer of the exercise then proposes to adjudicate among competing positions by means of logical tests, crucial cases, observations of covariation across cases, or perhaps a whole research program whose results the newcomer can report in a doctoral dissertation.

Although scales and arpeggios appear intermittently in concert pieces, no soloist who played nothing but scales and arpeggios, however skillfully, would last long on the concert circuit. Those of us who teach the social science equivalent of scales and arpeggios generally recognize the exercise's limitations even if we continue to employ it ourselves for limbering our (and our students') mental sinews. Rarely can (much less does) a single inquiry offer definitive proof or disproof for any particular social-scientific theory of nationalism, revolution, balance of power, or any other political phenomenon. To assemble evidence that one's chosen opponents might recognize as definitive generally requires moving far onto the opponents' preferred epistemological, ontological, and methodological terrain. An opponent worth opposing, furthermore, usually commands a sufficiently rich array of ideas that minor adjustments in a refuted argument rapidly generate new arguments that have not yet suffered falsification. Veteran performers therefore usually learn to make their cases cumulatively, and on stages of their own choosing.

The worst, however, is yet to come. Behind many ostensibly theoretical disputes in social science lurk disagreements about the nature of valid explanations. Confrontations among advocates of realist, constructivist, and institutionalist approaches to international relations, for example, concern explanatory strategies rather more than directly competing propositions about how nations interact. Similarly, rampant debates about nationalism more often hinge on specifying what analysts must explain, and how, than on the relative validity of competing theories. Within social science as a whole, wrangles over the value of rational choice models no doubt offer the most vigorous and visible recent examples; despite challenges to specific arguments and empirical claims, the most serious of those disputes pivot on the character of valid explanations.

Rational choice advocates assume that intentional human decision making causes social processes; therefore that explanation consists of pinpointing contexts and rationales of human decisions. Some critics of rational choice accept choice-theoretic criteria of explanation but reject standard characterizations of how choices occur. Many others, however, reject the whole enterprise as beside the point. The latter are not simply proposing alternative theories; they are reaching for other criteria of explanation. They are at best engaging in metatheoretical debates.

Competing Views of Explanation

What, then, is at issue? Not just competing explanations. Recent debates about democratization, for example, concern not only the choice of explanatory variables but also the very logic of explanation. To clarify the issues and point to possible resolutions, this chapter locates mechanism- and process-based accounts within the range of competing approaches to explanation, drawing especially on analyses of democratization. It also urges the significance of environmental and relational mechanisms as they interact with the cognitive mechanisms that have prevailed recently in social scientists' uses of mechanistic explanations.

As in history, five views of explanation compete for attention within social science: skepticism, covering laws, and dispositional, system, and mechanism-based accounts. The competing views involve varying combinations of ontology—the systems, transactions, and dispositions of earlier chapters—with differing views of knowledge itself.

Skepticism considers political processes to be so complex, contingent, impenetrable, or particular as to defy explanation. In this view, investigators can perhaps reconstruct the experiences of actors undergoing what they or others call democratization, but attempts at generalization will inevitably fail. Short of an extreme position, nevertheless, even a skeptic can hope to describe, interpret, or assign meaning to processes that are complex, contingent, particular, and relatively impenetrable. Thus skeptics continue to describe, interpret, and assign meaning to the Soviet Union's collapse without claiming to have explained that momentous process.

Covering law accounts consider explanation to consist of subjecting robust empirical generalizations to higher-and-higher-level generalizations, the most general of all standing as laws. In such accounts, models are invariant—work the same in all conditions. Investigators search for necessary and sufficient conditions of stipulated outcomes, those outcomes often conceived of as "dependent variables." Studies of co-variation among presumed causes and presumed effects therefore serve as validity tests for proposed explanations; investigators in this tradition sometimes invoke John Stuart Mill's Methods of Agreement, Differences, Residues, and Concomitant Variation despite Mill's own doubts of their applicability to human affairs.

The rules of causal inference proposed by the standard political science methods text of King, Keohane, and Verba (1994) do not require general laws, but they belong to this tradition (Ragin 2000: 14; see also Abell 2004; Brady and Collier 2004; Stinchcombe 2005). In principle, either democratization occurs in similar ways everywhere under specifiable necessary and sufficient conditions or the elements of democratization (e.g., creation of representative institutions) conform to general laws. The covering law analyst's job is to establish empirical uniformities, then to subsume them under such generalizations.

Dispositional accounts consider explanation to consist of reconstructing a given actor's state at the threshold of action, with that state variously stipulated as motivation, consciousness, need, organization, or momentum. With the understanding that certain orientations of actors may be universally favorable or even essential to democratization, to explain democratization thus entails reconstructing internal conditions of efficacious actors immediately preceding and during transitions from nondemocratic to democratic regimes. The actors in question may be individuals, but analysts often construct dispositional accounts of organizations or other collective actors. Explanatory methods of choice then range from sympathetic interpretation to reductionism, psychological or otherwise. Thus many students of democratization seek to characterize the attitudes of major actors in democratic transitions, then to verify those characterizations through interviews, content analyses, or biographical reconstructions.

Although authors of covering law and dispositional accounts sometimes talk of systems, systemic explanations strictly speaking consist of specifying a place for some event, structure, or process within a larger self-maintaining set of interdependent elements, showing how the event, structure, or process in question serves and/or results from interactions among the larger set of elements. Functional explanations typically qualify, since they account for the presence or persistence of some element by its positive consequences for some coherent larger set of social ties or processes. Nevertheless, systemic accounts can avoid functionalism by making more straightforward arguments about the effects of certain kinds of relations to larger systems.

Within the realm of democratization, system accounts typically argue that only certain kinds of social settings sustain democracy because democratic institutions serve or express powerful values, interests, or structures within those settings. Thus analyses in the mass society tradition, now largely abandoned, once treated totalitarianism and democracy as stemming from different degrees and forms of integration between ordinary people and society as a whole.

Mechanism- and process-based accounts select salient features of episodes, or significant differences among episodes, and explain them by identifying within those episodes robust mechanisms of relatively general scope (Barbera 2004; Bunge 1997; Coleman 1990; Elster 1989, 1999; Hedström and Swedberg 1998; Padgett and Ansell 1993; Stinchcombe 1991, 2005). Similarly, they search for recurrent concatenations of mechanisms into more complex processes. As compared with covering law, dispositional, and system approaches, mechanism- and process-based explanations aim at modest ends: selective explanation of salient features by means of partial causal analogies. In the analysis of democratization, for example, such mechanisms as brokerage and cross-class coalition formation compound into crucial recurrent processes such as enlargement of polities. Later I will propose an array of mechanisms and processes that figure widely in democratization.

Mechanisms, too, entail choices. A rough classification identifies three sorts of mechanism: environmental, cognitive, and relational. *Environmental mechanisms* mean externally generated influences on conditions affecting social life; words like "disappear," "enrich," "expand," and "disintegrate"—applied not to actors but their settings—suggest the sorts of cause-effect relations in question. *Cognitive mechanisms* operate through alterations of individual and collective perception; words like "recognize," "understand," "reinterpret," and "classify" characterize such mechanisms. *Relational mechanisms,* finally, alter connections among people, groups, and interpersonal networks; words like "ally," "attack," "subordinate," and "appease" give a sense of relational mechanisms.

Some advocates of mechanistic explanation (e.g., Hedström and Swedberg 1998) not only privilege cognitive mechanisms but also conceive of explanation as necessarily moving to a lower level of aggregation—explaining war, for example, by identifying mechanisms that operate at the level of the individual or the small group but aggregate into larger-scale effects. The common distinction between microfoundations and macroeffects springs from such a conception of explanation. That intellectual strategy has the advantage of remaining close to the main line of social science explanations, and the disadvantage of ignoring a wide range of significant cause-effect connections. In fact, relational mechanisms (e.g., brokerage) and environmental mechanisms (e.g., resource depletion) exert strong effects on political processes without any necessary connection to individual-level cognitive mechanisms.

Causal mechanisms do, to be sure, make appearances outside of mechanism-centered analyses. System theorists have often appealed to equilibrating mechanisms, although those mechanisms have proved notoriously difficult to specify and observe. Dispositional explanations often incorporate cognitive mechanisms such as satisficing and rationalizing. Satisfactory covering law accounts require not only broad empirical uniformities but also mechanisms that cause those uniformities. To the extent that mechanisms become uniform and universal, furthermore, their identification starts to resemble a search for covering laws.

Yet two big differences between covering law and mechanism-based explanations intervene. First, practitioners of mechanistic explanation generally deny that any strong, interesting recurrences of large-scale social structures and processes occur. They therefore doubt that it advances inquiry to seek law-like empirical generalizations—at whatever level of abstraction—by comparing big chunks of history.

Second, while mechanisms have uniform immediate effects by definition, their aggregate, cumulative, and longer-term effects vary considerably depending on initial conditions and on combinations with other mechanisms. Thus the mechanism of brokerage operates uniformly by definition, always connecting at least two social sites more directly than they were previously connected. Yet the activation of brokerage does not in itself guarantee more effective coordination of action at the connected sites; that depends on initial conditions and combinations with other mechanisms.

As represented by manuals, courses, and presidential addresses, approved social science doctrine generally favors some combination of dispositional and covering law explanations: to explain political action means not only to recon-struct accurately the state of an actor—especially, but not exclusively, inten-tions of a cogitating individual—at the point of action, but to locate that state as a special case of a general law concerning human behavior. Such a doctrine rests on an implausible claim: that ultimately all political processes result from extremely general uniformities in the propensities of human actors, especially individual actors. Despite more than a century of strenuous effort, social sci-entists have securely identified no such uniformities. But they have, in fact, recurrently identified widely operating causal mechanisms and processes. Rather than continuing to search for disposition-governing covering laws, it would therefore make sense to switch wholeheartedly toward specification of mecha-nisms and processes.

Mechanisms, Processes, and Episodes

Let us adopt a simple distinction among mechanisms, processes, and episodes:

Mechanisms form a delimited class of events that change relations among specified sets of elements in identical or closely similar ways over a variety of situations. Thus brokerage—joining of two or more previously less connected social sites through the intervention of third parties—constitutes a political mechanism of extremely general scope.
Processes are frequently occurring combinations or sequences of mechanisms. Thus scale shift—alteration in the range of sites engaging in coordinated ac-tion—regularly results from concatenation of brokerage with the mechanisms of diffusion, emulation, and attribution of similarity.
Episodes are continuous streams of social life. Thus, depending on analyti-cal purposes, we can adopt the Mexican presidential election of 2000, the 1999–2000 campaign leading to that election, or the entire period of opposition mobilization from 1988 to 2000 as the episode under examination.

Episodes sometimes acquire social significance as such because participants or observers construct names, boundaries, and stories corresponding to them: this revolution, that emigration, and so on. The manner in which episodes acquire shared meanings deserves close study. But we have no *a priori* warrant to believe that episodes grouped by similar criteria spring from similar causes. Students of episodes therefore face three logically distinct problems: 1) delin-eating episodes so that they provide material for coherent comparisons; 2) grouping episodes according to causal similarity and dissimilarity; and 3) explaining how some episodes acquire politically significant names and meanings.

Social scientists have invested considerable energy in the first of these enterprises. Analysts often chop continuous streams of social life into episodes according to conventions of their own making, thus delineating generations, social movements, fads, and the like (Almeida and Lichbach 2003; Azar and Ben-Dak 1973; Beissinger 2002; Brockett 1992; Cioffi-Revilla 1990; Diani and Eyerman 1992; Favre, Fillieule, and Mayer 1997; Franzosi 1998a, 1998b; Gerner et al. 1994; Hug and Wisler 1998; Mohr 2000; Mohr and Franzosi 1997; Oliver and Myers 1999; Olzak 1989; Ragin and Becker 1992; Rucht and Koopmans 1999; Rucht, Koopmans, and Neidhardt 1998; Shapiro and Markoff 1998; Tilly 2002b; White 1993). Students of democratization have frequently lined up ostensibly comparable episodes in different countries and periods as their means of establishing generalizations concerning preconditions, transitions, or democratic consolidation (e.g., Anderson, Fish, Hanson, and Roeder 2001; Bermeo 2003; Bratton and van de Walle 1997; Collier 1999; Inkeles 1991; Lafargue 1996; López-Alves 2000; Mueller 1997; Ramirez, Soysal, and Shanahan 1997; Rueschemeyer, Stephens, and Stephens 1992; Stephens 1989; Tilly 2004b; Whitehead 2001).

In general, analysts of mechanisms and processes regard the coherence and significance of episodes as something to be proven rather than assumed. They reject the common view that the episodes people call revolutions, social movements, or democratic transitions constitute *sui generis* phenomena each conforming to a coherent internal logic. For them, uniformly identified episodes provide convenient frames for comparison, but with an eye to detecting crucial mechanisms and processes within them. Choice of episodes, however, crucially influences the effectiveness of such a search. It makes a large difference, for example, whether students of generational effects distinguish generations by means of arbitrary time periods or presumably critical events.

Democratization as a (Major) Case in Point

To clarify the stakes of choices among skepticism, covering law accounts, dispositional explanations, system ideas, and mechanism-process explanations, it will help to narrow our empirical focus. Instead of reviewing international relations disputes, rational choice controversies, and similar well-defined sites of competing paradigm exercises across social science, the remainder of this chapter concentrates on a field of energetic inquiry where disputes over explanatory principles have not yet achieved such sophistication. The study of democratization invites attention because some of social science's brightest ideas concern democratization, yet specialists in the subject generally proceed as if they were engaged in well-joined comparisons of competing theories. (That happens, I speculate, especially where competing practical proposals lie close at hand; ostensibly competing *explanations of* democratization link to competing *programs for* democratization.) In fact, skepticism, covering law accounts, dispositional analyses, system ideas, and mechanism-process explanations all jostle for space within the zone of democratization. Explanatory choices faced by specialists in democratization pervade most of social science and history. Thus we can observe the whole world in a fairly small pond.

Rather than surveying alternative approaches to democratization, let me focus on exemplary recent works by Ruth Collier and Deborah Yashar. Reflecting on other political scientists' attempts to explain democratization, Ruth Collier writes as if alternative theories were competing. She concludes that recent analyses have concentrated excessively on deliberate elite decisions at the expense of social processes and popular actors. Classical theorists of democracy from Aristotle onward stressed either broad historical processes or necessary structural and cultural conditions for democratization, but those classical traditions have given way to quick specifications of favorable conditions followed by extensive analyses of elite agency:

> The dominant framework used in theoretical and comparative accounts, then, has not only adopted an actor-based rather than a structural perspective, but it has tended to privilege certain kinds of actors: individual elites rather than *collective* actors, strategically defined actors rather than *class*-defined actors, and state actors more than *societal* actors. (Collier 1999: 8)

More than competing explanations confront each other here. Collier is describing alternative *principles* of explanation, and therefore alternative specifications of what students of democratization must explain. In the accounts she criticizes (but, in a nice irony, ultimately joins), explanation consists of specifying the motivations and actions of those power holders that proposed and enacted democratizing reforms during moments of relatively rapid and definitive movement into democratic terrain.

The field's current emphasis on strategic elite decision making marks a decided shift from once prevalent analyses of political culture, social structure, and institutional processes. Much earlier work conceived of explanation as identifying durable features of polities that caused democratization to begin, succeed, or fail. Scholars, such as Stein Rokkan and Barrington Moore Jr., once offered long-term political process explanations of democratization and its alternatives (Rokkan 1969, 1970; Moore 1993 [1966]; see also Immerfall 1992; Skocpol 1998; Stephens 1989; Torsvik 1981). By self-consciously criticizing, extending, and modifying the Moore-inspired analysis of Rueschemeyer, Stephens, and Stephens (1992, 1993), Collier gestures toward that earlier tradition.

Yet Collier herself implicitly accepts most of the recent shift away from long-term explanation; she pleads mainly for inclusion of workers as sometime-advocates and agents of democracy. Her concentration on temporally compact "democratic episodes" during which polities passed from nondemocratic to democratic regimes draws attention away from the long-term processes dear to Rokkan, Moore, and their followers. Collier's systematic comparison of thirty-eight such episodes in twenty-seven countries demonstrates how often organized workers did, indeed, participate directly and consequentially in transitions to more democratic regimes.

Collier concludes that in (mainly European) episodes of democratization occurring between 1848 and 1931, workers played a less central part than previous analyses—especially those of Rueschemeyer, Stephens, and Stephens—have suggested. In (mainly Latin American) episodes from 1974 to 1990, however, workers figured more centrally than today's transitologists have generally allowed. Thus Collier challenges elite-centered analyses, but adopts their conception of explanation: in Collier's book, explanation consists of correctly attributing agency to crucial actors at the point of transition.

Not all challengers to elite-centered explanations travel in quite the same direction. Deborah Yashar joins Collier in stressing the limits of both necessary-condition and elite-centered analyses. Like Collier, furthermore, she rejects attempts to build one-size-fits-all general theories of democratization:

> Grand theorizing at one time attempted to do so, by focusing on structural patterns of agrarian capitalism, industrialization, levels of development, and international capital. Subsequent middle-range theorizing maintained an emphasis on structural patterns but focused on particular sets of cases. While these grand and middle-range theories delineated general patterns that were particularly inimical to or supportive of democracy, they were less clear about the process and causal mechanisms by which particular democracies were founded. More recently, scholars have attempted to redress these problems by focusing on the particular actors involved in founding and overthrowing democracies. These agency- and process-oriented explanations, however, have assumed a largely

descriptive cast and have proven less than successful in explaining the conditions under which newly founded democracies endure. (Yashar 1997: 2)

So saying, however, Yashar begins to break with Collier's analysis of democratization. She constructs a historically grounded comparison of democratization and its failures in Costa Rica and Guatemala from the 1870s to the 1950s. Both countries installed authoritarian regimes in the 1870s; both regimes resisted popular mobilization for reform during the 1930s; both installed left-populist governments in the 1940s; and in both cases the critical transition to divergent democratic and authoritarian regimes began with concerted, armed opposition to those left-populist governments. Yashar seeks to explain both a) divergent outcomes to similar crises and b) subsequent survival of distinctly different regimes. So doing, she switches away from necessary conditions and elite strategies toward the operation of very general causal mechanisms within historically specific settings.

Yashar addresses two distinct questions: 1) during the period 1941–54 (more precisely 1941–48 in Costa Rica, 1944–54 in Guatemala), why did a democratizing coalition come to power in Costa Rica but not in Guatemala? 2) Subsequently, why did Costa Rica continue a process of democratization while Guatemala veered into repressive authoritarianism? Her explanations center on the mechanisms that caused Costa Rica's reform coalition of the 1940s to survive and Guatemala's to splinter, both in the face of determined opposition from armed forces and members of the agrarian elite.

Yashar's answer does not lie in the more peaceful proclivities of Costa Rican elites. While a military invasion followed by a coup did initiate Guatemala's definitive swing toward authoritarianism in 1954, it was not incremental adjustment but civil war that initiated Costa Rica's definitive swing toward democracy in 1948. The fact that the United States backed Guatemala's 1954 invasion and coup, Yashar shows, by no means explains the different fates of the two countries. Similar domestic political processes, permuted in subtly different organizational contexts, yielded dramatically disparate outcomes.

After the critical period of 1948–54, Guatemala and Costa Rica struck off in nearly opposite directions. Backed by the United States, the Guatemalan government built up its military strength. It sought to penetrate and subdue the countryside through military and paramilitary force. During the thirty years of civil war that followed, Guatemala suffered some 100,000 deaths and 38,000 disappearances (Stanley 1996: 3). Meanwhile, Costa Rica's 1949 constitution abolished the army and established civilian-controlled police forces, thus initiating a transition to relatively nonviolent domestic politics after the civil war of 1948. Government assistance programs and political party mobilization integrated Costa Rican rural dwellers into national politics. After 1954, divergences between authoritarian Guatemala and democratic Costa Rica only sharpened.

Minimizing international demonstration effects, Yashar argues that similar processes produced different outcomes in the two countries:

> First, a publicly expressed division within the elite in the context of rising popular demands for political and economic inclusion precipitated the formation of democratizing reform alliances. Second, the Liberal period shaped the reform strategies deployed and the alliances formed. Third, the balance of power within the reform coalition determined the stability of the reform coalition itself. (Yashar 1997: 70)

More concretely, in both countries agrarian elites mobilized against city-based reform governments during the 1940s, but the crucial mechanism of coalition formation produced different outcomes in Costa Rica and Guatemala.

In Costa Rica, a split in the governing coalition left middle-class opponents of the previous populist-reformist regime in control of the governmental apparatus. Those new governors outflanked both the previous labor-communist-populist coalition and the agrarian opposition by nationalizing Costa Rican banks, imposing an emergency tax, and dismantling the army. Their government then proceeded to solidify its rural support by means of welfare programs, market controls, and party-based political mobilization. Both flanks reluctantly but durably accepted integration into the new regime.

Despite having followed a trajectory parallel to Costa Rica's into the 1940s, Guatemala later pursued a startlingly different path. As in Costa Rica, a left-populist government came to power in Guatemala during the 1940s and generated widespread elite opposition. A 1947 labor code and a 1952 agrarian reform, both liberal in conception, further stimulated antiregime mobilization by the rural oligarchy. Unlike its politically divided Costa Rican counterpart, the Guatemalan Catholic hierarchy generally aligned itself with the opposition to organized labor and to what the Church denounced as communism. Middle-class activists split among labor advocates, moderate reformers, and anticommunists.

Within a deeply fragmented opposition to the regime, the military offered the strongest connections and the greatest capacity for collective action. With U.S. backing, a small "liberation army" invaded from Honduras in June 1954. Although that force remained close to the Honduran border, within ten days the Guatemalan Army—likewise with U.S. support—had assumed power. In telling these two contrasting stories, Yashar makes a strong case that coalition-shaping mechanisms caused crucial differences between authoritarian Guatemala and democratic Costa Rica.

Making the same comparison after the fact, other analysts have frequently pointed to supposedly durable national differences in political economy or political culture as causes of the contrasting outcomes. Pursuing a larger comparison among El Salvador, Nicaragua, Guatemala, and Costa Rica, for example, Jeffery Paige stresses differences between positions of the Guatemalan and Costa Rican coffee elites:

> The Guatemalan elite was overwhelmingly landed and agrarian, with a relatively weak agro-industrial fraction. Debt servitude, serfdom, and other forms of legal bondage created class relations similar to those of the European feudal manor . . . Although these relations began to change with the post–World War II rationalization of coffee, before the 1970s institutions of coerced labor inhibited popular mobilization and created a strong interest in authoritarian political structures to control the unfree population . . . The most striking contrast with the Guatemalan elite was that of Costa Rica, in which the agrarian fraction was relatively weakly developed because it lost control over substantial amounts of land to a persistent class of family farmers . . . The Costa Rican elite was overwhelmingly an elite of processors. Class relations revolved around the relationship between these processors and the small holders, not between the landowners and their laborers . . . Politics revolved around the gentlemanly disagreements between large and small property owners, and the elite soon found that such conflicts could be easily managed by the gradual extension of the franchise to rural property owners and the establishment of democratic institutions. (Paige 1997: 87)

Despite his book's later concessions to the recent influence of neoliberal ideologies, Paige generally depends on durable features of class structure for his explanations of democratization or its absence. In his accounts, divergences of the 1940s and 1950s sprang from structural differences established decades before then.

In contrast, Yashar insists on considerable similarities between the political economies and governmental regimes of Guatemala and Costa Rica up to the 1940s. Although differing political arrangements laid down by previous history strongly affected the postwar political realignments of Guatemala and Costa Rica, Yashar demonstrates dramatically widening divergences between the two polities *during and after* the struggles of 1941–54.

Yashar conducts her analysis soberly, leading carefully to the conclusion that in the two cases at hand the longer-term outcomes of struggles over property distribution and control of the countryside—struggles not fought out explicitly between advocates and opponents of democracy as such—fundamentally affected subsequent democratization and its failures. She argues sensibly that both kinds of struggle matter more generally in democratization, and urges deep historical investigations of similar causal processes elsewhere. Her account of democratization stresses a search for robust causal mechanisms rather than for general models, universally applicable necessary and sufficient conditions, or analyses of agency at crucial points of transition.

Mechanisms of Democratization

How might a full-fledged reorientation of explanation to causal mechanisms and processes facilitate the study of democratization? Let me sketch an illustrative mechanism-based argument. Democracy, for present purposes, consists of *protected consultation*: relations between agents and subjects of a government in which a) different categories of subjects enjoy relatively broad and equal access to those agents; b) governmental disposition of persons, activities, and resources within the government's purview responds to binding consultation of subjects; and c) subjects receive protection against arbitrary action by governmental agents. Democratization is any move toward protected consultation, de-democratization any move away from protected consultation.

How and why do such moves occur? Figure 3-1 summarizes the argument's broadest terms. For the sake of clarity, it erases the distinction between transitions to democratic regimes and survival of democratic regimes, on the bet that the same mechanisms and processes explain transition and survival. Except for the "shocks" and "regime environment" at the diagram's top, the scheme stresses proximate causes: those that either constitute or immediately precipitate moves toward protected consultation.

Democratization, runs the argument, emerges from interacting changes in three analytically separable but interdependent sets of social relations: public politics, inequality, and networks of trust. In the course of democratization, the bulk of a government's subject population acquires binding, protected, relatively equal claims on a government's agents, activities, and resources. In a related process, categorical inequality declines in those areas of social life that either constitute or immediately support participation in public politics. Finally, a significant shift occurs in the locus of interpersonal networks on which people rely when undertaking risky long-term enterprises such as marriage, long-distance trade, membership in crafts, and investment of savings; such networks move from evasion of governmental detection and control to involvement of government agents and presumption that such agents will meet their long-term commitments. Only where the three sets of changes intersect does effective, durable democracy emerge.

Behind those proximate causes operate further changes that frequently activate them. These changes recurrently activate the proximate causes in the scheme of figure 3-1:

1. increases in the sheer numbers of people available for participation in public politics, for example as industrialization expands the number of free laborers
2. increases in the connections among those people, for example, as massive military efforts connect citizens in the war effort, as members of military units, and then as veterans
3. equalization of resources and connections among those people, for example, as mass media make communications more widely available
4. insulation of public politics from existing inequalities, for example, as dissident elites form cross-class movements against regimes
5. integration of interpersonal trust networks into public politics, for example, as union- or government-backed systems of social security and health care grow

None of these constitutes or even guarantees democratization, since none of them directly affects relations between governmental agents and citizens. All of them, however, commonly promote shifts toward broad, equal, consultative, and protective relations between governmental agents and citizens through their activation of some crucial, recurrent causal mechanisms. For the sake of simplicity, figure 3-1 bundles the five background changes together in "regime environment."

What causes what? As represented in figure 3-1, a variety of changes here bundled together as "regime environment" activate mechanisms that in turn generate incremental alterations in public politics, inequality, and networks of trust. Changes of inequality and of trust networks have independent effects on public politics. Regime environment also produces occasional shocks in the form of conquest, confrontation, colonization, or revolution. Such shocks accelerate the standard change mechanisms, thus causing relatively rapid alterations of public politics, inequality, and networks of trust.

Whether incremental or abrupt, those alterations interact. Under rare but specifiable conditions those alterations produce democratization. Democrati-

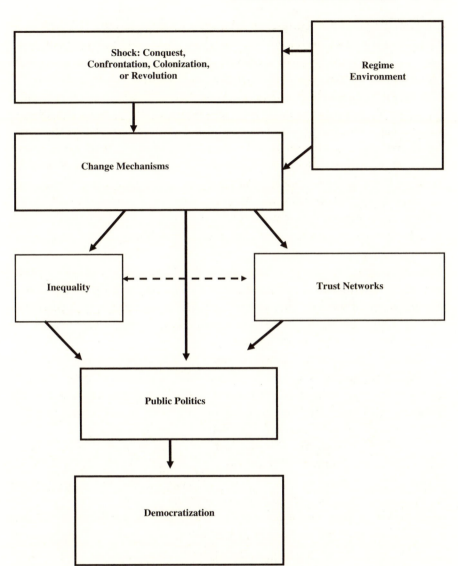

Figure 3-1. Causal Sequences in Democratization

zation is not a product but a special condition of public politics. Although these ideas emerged from my effort to explain variations in democratization and its failures across Europe since 1650, they coincide nicely with the arguments we have seen Deborah Yashar applying to the experiences of Costa Rica and Guatemala.

What mechanisms produce the changes in question? Table 3-1 lists likely suspects. It includes both individual mechanisms and robust processes—sequences and combinations of mechanisms that recur over a wide range of circumstances and produce substantially similar immediate effects. Following the idea that democratization consists of changing relations between subjects and governments, the list concentrates on relational mechanisms and processes. A fuller account would include more cognitive and environmental mechanisms, for example: a) shifts in beliefs about the likelihood that governmental agents will meet their commitments and b) increases or decreases in the government's resource base. Since previous treatments of democratization have stressed cognitive and/or environmental mechanisms, however, it seems useful to bring out the likely importance of relational mechanisms in this discussion.

Table 3-1 groups mechanisms and processes into three categories: those affecting relations between categorical inequality and public politics, those affecting relations between trust networks and public politics, and those operating chiefly within public politics. For the sake of clarity, it excludes negative complements of these mechanisms and processes—for example, fortification (rather than dissolution) of coercive controls supporting current relations of exploitation and opportunity hoarding.

The causal account therefore proceeds at three levels. First, any changes that increase insulation between nongovernmental inequalities and public politics, integrate interpersonal trust networks into public politics, and push public politics itself toward protected consultation promote democratization wherever they occur. Second, particular mechanisms and processes favor insulation of inequality, integration of trust networks, and transformation of public politics. Third, confrontation, colonization, conquest, and revolution promote democratization, when they do so, by accelerating the very same mechanisms and processes that promote incremental democratization.

As stated, parts of this argument are deliberately tautological. To say that transformation of public politics in the direction of protected consultation promotes democratization merely restates the definition of democracy adopted here. The tautologies, however, serve important purposes. They specify what students of democratization must explain. They thereby focus the search for explanations on proximate causes of those explananda—mechanisms that directly alter connections between trust networks and public politics, for example, and other mechanisms that shift the intersection between governmental and nongovernmental inequalities. As Collier's analysis encourages us to believe, proximate causes certainly include cognitive mechanisms and processes. But they also emphatically include relational and environmental mechanisms.

Table 3-1. Sample Mechanisms and Processes Promoting Democratization

1. Inequality
- dissolution of coercive controls supporting current relations of exploitation and opportunity hoarding
- education and communication that alter adaptations supporting current relations of exploitation and opportunity hoarding
- education and communication that supplant existing models of organization, hence alter emulation of inequality in formation of new organizations
- equalization of assets and/or well-being across categories within the population at large
- insulation of existing categorical inequalities from public politics

2. Networks of Trust
- creation of external guarantees for government commitments
- incorporation and expansion of existing trust networks into the polity
- governmental absorption or destruction of previously autonomous patron-client networks
- disintegration of existing trust networks
- expansion of the population lacking access to effective trust networks for their major long-term risky enterprises
- appearance of new long-term risky opportunities that existing trust networks cannot handle
- substantial increase of government's resources for risk reduction and/or compensation of loss
- visible governmental meeting of commitments to the advantage of substantial new segments of the population

3. Public Politics
- coalition formation between segments of ruling classes and constituted political actors that are currently excluded from power
- brokerage of coalitions across unequal categories and/or distinct trust networks
- central co-optation or elimination of previously autonomous political intermediaries
- bureaucratic containment of previously autonomous military forces
- dissolution or segregation from government of nongovernmental patron-client networks
- imposition of uniform governmental structures and practices through the government's jurisdiction
- mobilization-repression-bargaining cycles during which currently excluded actors act collectively in ways that threaten survival of the government and/or its ruling classes, governmental repression fails, struggle ensues, and settlements concede political standing and/or rights to mobilized actors
- extraction-resistance-bargaining cycles during which governmental agents demand resources under control of nongovernmental networks and committed to nongovernmental ends, holders of those resources resist, struggle ensues, and settlements emerge in which people yield resources but receive credible guarantees with respect to constraints on future extraction

France vs. Britain

A quick comparison of France and the British Isles from 1650 to 2000 will concretize the program of theory and research that follows. First, we must decide on the units of observation. Neither polity had constant boundaries over the entire period. Even disregarding the fact that in 1650 the Fronde deprived young Louis XIV and his government of control over much of their nominal territory, the France of that time lacked Roussillon, much of Provence, Corsica, Savoy, Franche-Comté, most of Alsace-Lorraine, and significant sections of the north. Even after 1800 France's territory expanded and contracted several times.

Nor did the British polity remain constant. A traveler through the British Isles in 1650 would have seen a Scotland rebelling openly against English hegemony and a Scottish military force in northern England backing Charles Stuart's claim to succeed his father Charles I; just the previous year, England's contentious revolutionaries had united temporarily to decapitate King Charles. In Ireland, Catholic leaders were battling not only each other but also the English invading force of Oliver Cromwell. Nor—as current struggles in Ulster make clear—did territorial uncertainty cease with the Glorious Revolution of 1688–89. To trace democratization and its failures in "France" and the "British Isles" over the 350-year period requires frequent readjustment of the governments, territories, and populations at risk.

These specifications made, some important puzzles arise: why the French created some of the world's most widely emulated democratic institutions, yet fluctuated rapidly between relatively democratic and undemocratic regimes in 1789–93, 1829–32, 1847–51, 1868–75, and 1936–46; why the same British who struggled their way to fairly stable democracy in Great Britain after 1815 were never able to perform the trick in Ireland; why some French and British colonies ended up fairly democratic and others quite authoritarian, and so on. The very questions make it clear that confrontation, conquest, colonization, and revolution all affected the prospects for democracy in France and the British Isles multiple times since 1650.

The mechanism-based program laid out earlier suggests answering such questions by tracing alterations in trust networks, categorical inequality, and their intersections with public politics year by year over the entire period. That procedure will not explain anything, but it will specify what must be explained. In 19th-century France, for example, connections between public politics and workers' trust networks as represented by mutual aid societies, trade networks, and migration systems clearly waxed and waned in rhythm with the rise and fall of protected consultation; how and why those connections changed deserve close attention from anyone who seeks to explain French democratization.

Table 3-1's roster of mechanisms suggests looking closely at disintegration of existing trust networks as well as governmental absorption and destruction of previously autonomous patron-client networks. France's tumultuous movement into less undemocratic institutions between the later Second Empire and

World War I, for example, resulted in part from the decay of vast clandestine artisanal networks and their replacement by legal workers' organizations integrated into public politics by means of political parties, recognized labor unions, and such institutions as Bourses du Travail.

On the British side of the Channel, the equally tumultuous 1830s provide a splendid opportunity for examination of democratizing mechanisms at work. In surprising parallels to the democratizing processes described by Deborah Yashar, the British government then twice quelled insurrection by engineering compromises that produced democratic consequences. First, after repeated earlier failures of campaigns for Catholic political rights, Wellington's government forced through Catholic Emancipation (1829) in response to an enormous Irish mobilization despite strong anti-Catholic organization within Great Britain itself. Then Grey's government responded to vast agitation within Great Britain—agitation inspired by and built in part on the organizational webs of Catholic Emancipation—by passing a Reform Bill (1832) over the initially fierce opposition of the king, the House of Lords, and substantial portions of the national power structure. That the 1832 bill excluded most of the workers who had participated in mobilization for Reform and thereby contributed to the subsequent rise of worker-based democracy-demanding Chartism only confirms the importance of examining the actual mechanisms by which democratization occurs.

Agenda

Adoption of mechanistic explanations has strong implications for research and analysis in social science. Let me single out four of them: 1) simultaneous downgrading and upgrading of contentious episodes as objects of study; 2) reorientation of explanations from episodes to processes; 3) comparative examination of mechanisms and processes as such; 4) integration of cognitive, relational, and environmental mechanisms.

Simultaneous downgrading and upgrading of contentious episodes as objects of study. The downgrading consists of denying *sui generis* reality to such episodes. As conventional or arbitrary entities, events we call revolutions, nationalist mobilizations, wars, and episodes of democratization take shape as retrospective constructions by observers, participants, and analysts. They do not have essences, natural histories, or self-motivating logics. Moreover, they intersect with more routine processes—even more reason to avoid segmenting their study.

Episodes also require upgrading, however. Once we recognize that we have snipped them from their historical and social contexts, we must make explicit the

procedures and criteria that mark their beginnings, ends, boundaries, and participants. That calls for the development of expertise in delineating comparable events
(Tilly 2002b). The process by which a given episode acquires the standing
of revolution, social movement, war, strike, or something else has political
weight and content; such designations affect, not only how subsequent analysts explain them, but also how participants behave and how third parties
react to them. Thus the social processes that label and bound episodes belong
on our agenda.

We must also notice that choices of scale—for example, the choice among
particular elections, electoral campaigns, and whole transitions from nondemocratic to democratic regimes as the unit of observation—significantly affect
both the nature of comparisons among episodes and the likely relative prominence of various mechanisms and processes. Many mechanisms and processes
operate at multiple scales; disintegration of trust networks often produces
changes in small groups as well as in whole countries. But others occur much
more frequently at one scale than another: commitment occurs at the scale of
the individual and produces collective action at an interpersonal scale. Tactical
innovation happens mainly at a local scale, followed by diffusion (a cognitive-
relational process) to broader scales.

Democratization, in contrast, depends by definition on the presence of government and polity and thus occurs at scales from community to world region.
A major challenge that remains is to examine how the mechanisms and processes that characterize contention at one scale affect it at another: for example,
between the local and the global in democratic transitions (Markoff 1996b,
1999).

Reorientation of explanations from episodes to processes. Although recent analyses point to retention of comparable episodes as units of observation, they also
recommend abandonment of efforts to explain all salient features of whole
episodes. They thereby rule out the common procedure of matching episodes
to general models in order to demonstrate that the model does not fit some
salient feature of the episode, then modifying the general model to increase the
fit. Recent studies of democratization do not offer much hope of gaining explanatory leverage by matching whole episodes with invariant general models
of mobilization, transition, or consolidation, much less with invariant general
models of democratization in all its varieties.

Instead, social scientists should concentrate their explanations on selected
features of episodes (for example, why rapid shifts in identity occurred) or on

recurrent processes in families of episodes (for example, how and why cross-class alliances frequently create or expand revolutionary situations). In either mode, explanation consists of identifying crucial mechanisms and their combination into transforming processes.

Comparative examination of mechanisms and processes as such. Far beyond the zone of democratization, the sorts of mechanisms and processes enumerated in table 3-1 deserve comparative analysis for their own sake. Bureaucratic containment of previously autonomous military forces, for example, appears to come close to a necessary condition for democratization, but it also has significant effects on the capacity of government, the likelihood of civil war, the level of domestic violence, and even the prospect that a given state will engage in international war. Without abandoning close examination of historical episodes, it would advance political inquiry to encourage comparative research into the mechanisms of bureaucratic containment. Similarly, social science could only gain from superior comparative knowledge concerning mechanisms and processes that connect or disconnect inequalities within and outside public politics.

Integration of cognitive, relational, and environmental mechanisms. Proceeding from the view that recent theorists of political phenomena, including democratization, have slighted relational processes, this chapter deliberately emphasizes relational mechanisms. Nevertheless, my concrete analyses have repeatedly invoked combinations of relational with cognitive and/or environmental mechanisms. The mechanism called "insulation of existing categorical inequalities from public politics," for example, inevitably includes a cognitive component defining boundaries among categories. Changing conceptions of racial, ethnic, gender, religious, or class differences therefore affect that insulation or its failure. Such shifts, furthermore, often result in part from changing balances of resources among people on opposite sides of categorical boundaries, for example, disproportionate increase of numbers or wealth on one side of the line.

In such circumstances, it is not clear in principle whether we are observing two or three distinct mechanisms that frequently conjoin, or have discovered a sufficiently invariant combination of cognitive, relational, and environmental changes to justify treating the complex as a single robust process. Nor can we decide in general and in advance how the elements interact—whether, for example, cognitive shifts always precede relational changes, or vice versa. Interaction among cognitive, relational, and environmental mechanisms presents urgent problems for theory and research on political processes.

Back to Familiar Ground

Social scientists should not find the analysis of mechanisms and processes alien. Aristotle's treatment of democracy and its ills, after all, specified mechanisms and processes by which transitions from one sort of regime to another occurred. Aristotle recognized distinctions within his major types of regime, for example, five types of democracy, of which the fifth

> is that in which not the law, but the multitude, have the supreme power, and supersede the law by their decrees. This is a state of affairs brought about by the demagogues. For in democracies which are subject to the law the best citizens hold the first place, and there are no demagogues; but where the laws are not supreme, there demagogues spring up. For the people becomes a monarch, and is many in one; and the many have the power in their hand, not as individuals, but collectively . . . this sort of democracy is to other democracies what tyranny is to other forms of monarchy. (Barnes 1984: II, 2050–51)

In these circumstances, furthermore, demagogues often stir up the rabble to attack the rich and thereby seize power for themselves. In this way, democracy turns into tyranny. Aristotle proceeded repeatedly from ostensibly static categories to dynamic causal processes. In thinking through the effects of different military formats, for example, he offered a shrewd causal account:

> As there are four chief divisions of the common people, farmers, artisans, traders, labourers; so also there are four kinds of military forces—the cavalry, the heavy infantry, the light-armed troops, the navy. When the country is adapted for cavalry, then a strong oligarchy is likely to be established. For the security of the inhabitants depends upon a force of this sort, and only rich men can afford to keep horses. The second form of oligarchy prevails when a country is adapted to heavy infantry; for this service is better suited to the rich than to the poor. But the light-armed and the naval element are wholly democratic; and nowadays, where they are numerous, if the two parties quarrel, the oligarchy are often worsted by them in the struggle. (Barnes 1984: II, 2096–97)

Amid the specification of favorable conditions for different sorts of regime, we find Aristotle identifying struggle-centered mechanisms by which transitions from regime to regime actually occur. A short version of my sermon therefore reads as follows: emulate Aristotle.

Chapter 4

Do Unto Others

AFTER THE FACT, CIVIL RIGHTS ACTIVISTS CALLED JUNE-AUGUST 1964 Freedom Summer. On June 21, the second group of volunteers for Mississippi voter registration drives and related educational projects was arriving in Oxford, Ohio, to receive training before entering the field. Near Philadelphia, Mississippi, that same day, first-batch volunteer Andrew Goodman joined staff members James Chaney and Michael Schwerner to investigate a church bombing. Local police arrested the three on traffic charges, detained them past nightfall, and then released them. The three civil rights workers disappeared. The next day, passersby found their incinerated station wagon near a swamp.

The public would not know until August that someone had murdered Chaney, Schwerner, and Goodman, and then buried their mangled bodies beneath an earthwork dam. But the Oxford volunteers sensed that their co-workers in Mississippi had met foul play. They could hardly have received a more vindictively violent warning of dangers to come. People a lot like them had died in the line of duty. What was more, Mississippi's violence continued. "In just the first two weeks of the summer project," Charles Payne reminds us, "in addition to the murder of Mickey Schwerner, James Chaney, and Andrew Goodman in Philadelphia, Mississippi, there were at least seven bombings or fire-bombings of movement-related businesses and four shootings and a larger number of serious beatings" (Payne 1995: 301).

On 26 June, volunteer Stuart Rawlings wrote in his journal:

> What are my personal chances? There are 200 COFO [Council of Federated Organizations] volunteers who have been working in the state a week, and three of

them have already been killed. I shall be working in Forrest County, which is reputedly less violent than Neshoba County. But I shall be working on voter registration, which is more dangerous than work in Freedom Schools or Community Centers. There are other factors which must be considered too—age, sex, experience, and common sense. All considered, I think my chances of being killed are 2%, or one in fifty. (McAdam 1988: 70–71)

Shocked and frightened, some volunteers left Oxford for home. Most, however, stayed with the group. "And with the decision to stay," reports Freedom Summer chronicler Doug McAdam, "their commitment to the project and attachment to the 'beloved community' grew as well" (McAdam 1988: 71).

Why did they stay? More generally, why do people incur serious costs—here including the risk of beating, bombing, and death—on behalf of other people's welfare? Stated as an individual choice to act before the deliberated action occurs, figure 4-1 clarifies what we have to explain. (Later sections of the chapter, however, will point out how this very statement of the problem as individual choice *ex ante* misleads us.) What differentiates situations in which a given actor a) gains benefits while another actor sustains harm (**egoism**), b) gains benefits while another actor likewise gains benefits (**cooperation**), c) sustains harm while another actor likewise sustains harm (**destruction**), or d) sustains harm while another actor gains benefits (**altruism**)?

Egoism and cooperation have attracted enormous attention in the form of public goods problems, prisoners' dilemmas, and the like (Shubik 1993). Steadfast rational action theorists (e.g., Hardin 1995) have typically sought to show that actions appearing to qualify as cooperation, destruction, or altruism actually reduce to egoism once we detect the incentives to which actors respond. Within the zones of interstate war, civil war, industrial conflict, and interethnic conflict, rational action theorists (e.g., Lake and Rothchild 1998) have often argued that destructive **outcomes** characteristically stem from initial situations of egoism in which participants fail to recognize that their interaction will lead to losses for all. In such cases, better advance information about likely outcomes would presumably prevent the conflicts from occurring at all.

Rational action theorists have often found allies among evolutionary biologists (e.g., Clutton-Brock et al. 1999) who interpret ostensibly altruistic animal behavior as a form of individual self-preservation. (For contrary views among evolutionary biologists, psychologists, and economists, however, see, e.g., Sober and Wilson 1998; Haidt and Joseph 2004; Bowles and Gintis 1998.) Clear thinking institutionalists (e.g., Greif 1994; Ostrom 1998) have commonly joined rationalists in denying the existence of destruction and altruism but have also insisted that certain normative, institutional, and network arrangements pro-

[handwritten margin note: Individual Choice of action is misleading]

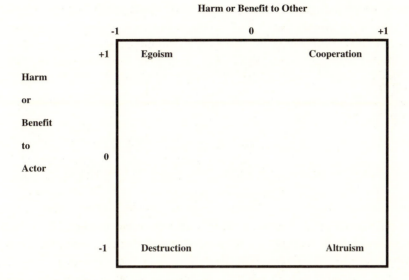

Figure 4-1. Individual Choices Among Harm and Benefit for Actor and Other

mote cooperation even in cases where strictly self-seeking behavior would yield greater short-run benefits. They thereby interpret short-term altruism as long-term egoism or cooperation.

In the statement that put "resource mobilization" in play as a way of analyzing social movements, Mayer Zald and John McCarthy (1977) distinguished between *beneficiary* and *conscience* constituents of movement organizations. By definition, conscience constituents contribute resources to an organization's actions but gain no resources from realization of the organization's goals; superficially, then, they resemble our altruists. Speaking of contemporary American social movement organizations, Zald and McCarthy describe conscience adherents as generally more affluent and well connected than beneficiaries. Conscience adherents therefore prove attractive to social movement entrepreneurs. But they also pose risks for organizations and entrepreneurs because of their propensity to withdraw support from the cause when the going gets rough or new interests come along. Although Zald and McCarthy never quite explain why conscience constituents participate at all, they imply strongly that a) their participation costs them relatively little and b) they participate because (and only so long as) it gives them self-satisfaction. They actually participate for net benefits. Thus Zald and McCarthy, too, end up converting altruism—at least this mild form of altruism—into egoism or cooperation.

Similarly, students of volunteer work (e.g., Wilson and Musick 1999) generally assume or argue that providing care for others under the auspices of churches and voluntary organizations (as distinguished from care given within households and kin groups) falls under our heading of cooperation: when working properly, it gives net benefits to donor and recipient alike. After acknowledging that some volunteers harm themselves by overdoing it, Robert Wuthnow offers advice:

> Millions of Americans, as we have already seen, provide useful services to the needy *and* gain a sense of personal enrichment and fulfillment from it. The trick is to develop skills that allow us to show compassion and at the same time take care of our own needs. (Wuthnow 1991: 193)

"Personal enrichment and fulfillment," then, constitute net benefits for most volunteers. Indeed, Wuthnow calls his book *Acts of Compassion,* but subtitles it *Caring for Others and Helping Ourselves.*

For analyses of thoroughgoing destruction and altruism, we must therefore turn away from students of voluntary organizations and back to students of contentious politics. Even there, destruction and altruism have received much less attention than have egoism and cooperation. But they are the two locations we must describe and explain.

Genuine cases of destruction and altruism exist. They include the range of contention that Doug McAdam calls "high risk activism" and others call "sacrifice for the cause" (Fernandez and McAdam 1988; Hirsch 1990; Loveman 1998; McAdam and Paulsen 1993). They also include terrorism and the sort of activism—usually lower risk—elicited by environmental movements (Bárcena, Ibarra. and Zubiaga 1995; Broadbent 1998; Diani 1988, 1995; Giugni and Passy 1997; Hanagan 1998; Hellman 1995; Lowe and Rüdig 1986; Mason 1989, 2004; Mason and Krane 1989; Passy 1998; della Porta 1995; Sant Cassia 1993; Walter 1969). Although terrorists' enemies often label them as egoists on the ground that the terrorists gain pleasure or profit from other people's harm, much mayhem ends up as net loss for its perpetrators (Tilly 2004e).

Terrorists and self-immolators typically declare that they are sacrificing themselves in order to benefit other members of their cause. During such campaigns as antislavery, ecology, and animal rights, campaigners may gain self-satisfaction, revenge, or spite, but on the whole they incur significant costs for benefits reaped chiefly by others—or perhaps by no one at all (d'Anjou 1996; Drescher 1986, 1994; Swedberg 1999). If they actually occur, destruction and altruism deserve close attention because they challenge individual-level cost-benefit accounts of participation in contentious politics.

Let us narrow our focus to the special cases of destruction and altruism in which action of Actor X **causes** detectable consequences for both the actor and for some distinct other. Destruction then refers to collective action in which an actor inflicts net losses on another actor while enduring net losses itself, regardless of possible benefits or losses for third parties. Altruism refers to collective action in which an actor produces benefits for another actor while enduring net losses itself, again regardless of possible benefits or losses for third parties.

These are, of course, matters of degree. An action qualifies as just barely altruistic by imposing small net losses on the actor and causing small net gains for the beneficiary, as when activists attend a few too many meetings in moderately effective expressions of support for prisoners' rights. It qualifies as extremely altruistic by imposing large net losses (for example, death or exile) on the actor while producing large gains (e.g., liberation) for the beneficiary. To clarify the issues, let us concentrate on relatively clear cases of destruction and altruism, cases where the actor bears significant costs.

How is it that some participants in some kinds of contentious politics (e.g., suicide bombers) end up simultaneously producing harm for themselves and others? How is it that other actors (e.g., self-sacrificing protectors of endangered species) end up taking losses while producing benefits for others? The most commonly available answers run as follows:

1. **Secret Satisfaction**: X is actually receiving net benefits because participation, sacrifice, and/or the other's welfare provides X with satisfaction
2. Side Benefits: X is receiving selective incentives that compensate for visible losses
3. **Social Security: X sustains short-term losses in support of relationships that promise benefits over the long run**
4. **Ideology**: Commitment to a cause, belief, and/or illusion leads X to disregard costs of risky actions and/or provides intrinsic rewards
5. **Group Pressure: Collective processes obscure or override X's computation of likely costs and benefits from various possible courses of action**
6. **Habit**: X obeys customary authorities and/or continues customary routines without calculation of outcomes
7. **Accident**: Net losses to X result from unlikely or unpredictable consequences of X's action

Except for Habit, Accident, and some versions of Group Pressure, these common explanations all assert that destruction and altruism are actually egoism and/or cooperation in disguise. For Freedom Summer volunteers who went to Mississippi despite the Goodman-Chaney-Schwerner killing and other warnings of danger, someone might argue accordingly that 1) they gained self-satisfaction from the experience, 2) solidarity with other volunteers more than made up for danger, 3) they were buying into a way of life for which the current risk was a reasonable cost, 4) they were self-selected zealots, heedless of cost, 5) they shamed each other into staying, 6) college had taught them to conform, or 7) they failed to see connections between Mississippi violence and their own futures.

To be sure, these explanations do not exclude each other; one can easily argue, for example, that ideologues (case 4), unlike habitual conformists (case 6) derive direct satisfaction (case 1) from sacrifice. All seven declare that, *ex ante,* the diagram's bottom half is empty: no actor will deliberately undertake action whose foreseeable consequence is net loss. But the cases that interest us here are precisely those in which participants do sustain losses in contention, and not by inadvertence. Such episodes as Freedom Summer establish that genuine cases inhabit our diagram's lower reaches: even if explanations 1 through 7 apply in part, we find significant instances in which—by any ordinary assessment of costs and benefits—actors bear major costs from which they benefit little or not at all, while others stand to gain substantially.

Why, then, would anyone ever choose a costly action from which someone else would be the sole beneficiary, or from which no one would benefit at all? The last few decades' work on collective action and contentious politics identifies the very question as seductive but misleading. The question is seductive because it maps so neatly into the short-run individualistic explanations of social processes that prevail in everyday stories about political life. It is misleading for exactly the same reason. Looked at closely, contentious politics turns out to include very few moments of stark, make-or-break individual choice between helping self and helping others. Like social life in general, it involves many unanticipated consequences—processes in which participants would never have engaged if they had made cool decisions beforehand with respect to the outcomes that actually occurred (Tilly 1996). It includes many situations in which relations to other actors make all the difference. Relations to third parties, furthermore, often matter more than relations between the actor and the action's immediate object.

Figure 4-1 therefore identifies a challenging range of phenomena after the fact, but obscures our explanatory problem. It assumes that people make individualized yes/no choices in anticipation of predictable costs and benefits. In order to explain destructive and altruistic forms of contentious politics, however, we must look for relational processes that promote self-sacrifice—whether or not participants recognize the risks they face at the outset. This chapter pursues such a search.

If this chapter does its work well, it will:

- establish that genuine cases of destruction and altruism exist, and thus require explanations other than that they are really egoism or cooperation in disguise
- raise doubts whether individual-level cognitive causal mechanisms alone can explain participation in destruction and altruism
- make a case for the impact of relational causal mechanisms on propensities of different groups to sacrifice on behalf of others
- show that individual decision-making mechanisms articulate closely with such relational mechanisms
- relate sacrifice-inducing processes to network structure and political identity formation
- argue that destruction and altruism occur through similar causal processes, the difference between them depending chiefly on relations of actor and object to third parties
- suggest (but not argue or demonstrate) that the same sorts of mechanisms also explain egoistic and cooperative forms of contention

In order to accomplish those objectives, it will wander a bit among topics that at first glance connect poorly with destruction and altruism: compliance, stories, identities, conscription, mutiny, war, revolution, strikes, and contentious politics in general. By the end, connections among these disparate topics should be clear.

Margaret Levi's Contribution

Despite reasoning mainly in an individualistic mode, Margaret Levi has recently made an important contribution to answering our questions about sacrifice. She astutely chooses to analyze resistance to and compliance with military conscription—a quintessential case in which individuals face the choice of bearing large costs on behalf of benefits they will share little or not at all, and to which their participation will make little difference. Conscription does not make it all the way down into our diagram's destruction or altruism corners because conscripts ordinarily belong to the citizenry on whose behalf they serve. (Levi makes valuable observations on how military service qualifies people for citizenship and thereby reshapes citizenship itself; see also Tilly 1995.) Conscripts therefore stand to benefit, however slightly, from their own military service. But the case comes close enough that we might hope to learn from Levi about destruction and altruism.

Levi self-consciously builds her analysis on game theory (Levi 1997: 7–8). She thereby commits herself to single-actor explanations of social behavior: individuals make decisions that affect other individuals in response to incentives operating within constraints. She moves beyond bare rational actor formulations, however, in two significant ways. She first identifies relations with others as significant constraints on individual decision making and, second, sketches histories of the institutions that shape constraints, including relations with others. Repeatedly, as a result, she reaches beyond the self-imposed limits of her models to examine interactive processes such as continuous bargaining. Concretely, she analyzes situations in which potential soldiers, governmental agents, and other subjects of the same government bargain out consent to military service or resistance to that consent.

Levi's model of "contingent consent" states that individual citizens are more likely to comply with costly demands from their governments, including demands for military service, to the degree that

1. citizens perceive the government to be trustworthy
2. the proportion of other citizens complying (that is, the degree of "ethical reciprocity") increases, and
3. citizens receive information confirming governmental trustworthiness and the prevalence of ethical reciprocity (Levi 1997: 21)

More loosely, Levi argues that citizens consent to onerous obligations when they see their relations to governmental agents and to other citizens as both reliable and fair. Fairness and justice matter (Eliasoph 1998; Jasso 1999; Moore 1979; Shklar 1990; Vermunt and Steensma 1991; Young 1990). Levi does not specify what mechanisms produce these effects; she treats them as empirical generalizations to verify or falsify. She implies, however, that the effective mechanisms are individual-by-individual calculations concerning likely consequences of compliance or resistance. "Contingent consent requires," she declares, "that an individual believe not only that she is obliged to comply but also that others are or should be obliged to comply" (Levi 1997: 205). Like other rational action theorists, she centers her explanations on cognitive processes.

Counterhypotheses Levi means to refute include 1) habitual obedience, 2) ideological consent, and 3) opportunistic obedience (Levi 1997: 19). Each of these identifies a different cognitive orientation of subjects to authorities. Opportunism, as Levi defines it, can respond to a variety of incentives including secret satisfaction, side benefits, and social security; the only two of the seven explanations enumerated earlier Levi ignores are therefore group pressure and accident. (In fact, as we will see, she eventually incorporates group pressure as well.) Her evidence from the United States, Canada, the United Kingdom, France, New Zealand, Australia, and Vietnam concerns differential compliance with demands for military service according to period, population segment, and character of war. Observed differentials challenge habit, ideology, and opportunism accounts while confirming Levi's empirical generalizations summarizing contingent consent: on the whole, compliance with conscription was greater in situations of relatively high trust, and so on.

Institutions, organizations, and social relations enter Levi's explanations as background variables—not as direct causes of compliance but as shapers of the perceptions and information that themselves explain compliance. Thus Canada's sharp division between Anglophones and Francophones helps explain both readiness of the Anglo majority to impose conscription on the entire country and greater resistance of the French-speaking minority to military service (Levi 1997: 163–64). Institutions, organizations, and social relations also affect available courses of action and their relative costs. Thus French history, with its long establishment of the nation in arms and its weak development of pacifist sects, made conscientious objection much less available to draft resisters in France than in Anglo-Saxon countries (Levi 1997: 191–92).

Toward the end of her analysis, Levi offers a larger opening to social structure: she argues that third-party enforcement strongly affects the actual likelihood of other people's compliance, hence any particular individual's perception of fairness (Levi 1997: 213). Governmental coercion of potential defectors significantly affects not only those recalcitrants themselves but also others who become more willing to serve when they know that others will have to serve as well. At this point in Levi's analysis, networks of interpersonal commitment start playing a significant and fairly direct part in the generation of social action. Levi offers another opening to social structure by recognizing how significantly governmental performance affects compliance; poorly or erratically performing governments receive less compliance. (This very problem led Albert Hirschman to distinguish exit, voice, and loyalty as alternative responses to governmental failure, but Levi does not follow up that lead.) By this point, interactive processes are doing an important part of Levi's explanatory work.

Levi's two overtures to social structure deserve a whole opera. We have, for example, some evidence that in wartime workers strike more frequently and soldiers desert in larger numbers when their country's military forces show signs of losing badly (see, e.g., Lagrange 1989). For North Carolina's Confederate forces in the American Civil War, Peter Bearman (1991) has shown that ordinary individual-level characteristics tell us little or nothing about propensity to desert, but that collective properties of fighting units made a significant difference. Early in the war, locally recruited companies tended to stick together, while geographically heterogeneous companies suffered relatively high rates of desertion. As the war continued, however, the pattern reversed: after the summer of 1863, members of geographically homogeneous companies became more likely to desert the cause. "Ironically," notes Bearman, "companies composed of men who had the longest tenures, who were the most experienced, and who had the greatest solidarity were most likely to have the highest desertion rates after 1863" (Bearman 1991: 337).

Bearman plausibly accounts for this surprising shift as the result of a relational process: Confederate recruiters originally concentrated on forming companies locally, but deaths and tactical reorganization eventually made some companies geographically heterogeneous. Early in the war, commitment to a locality and commitment to the Confederate cause as a whole aligned neatly. As the war proceeded, however, overall losses introduced increasing discrepancies between national and local solidarity; collective connection to the same locality simultaneously activated commitments to people at home and facilitated collective defection from the national military effort.

Variable desertion connects closely with another phenomenon: a tendency of strikes, rebellions, and revolutionary situations to concentrate in immediate postwar periods (Tilly 1992, 1993a). One Levi- and Bearman-style component of these phenomena seems to be the following: governments pursue major wars by imposing tightened central controls and accumulating large debts, but by so doing they also expand their commitments to all collaborating parties. During the war, signs that governments are losing capacity to meet those commitments induce collaborators in the war effort to press claims for immediate advantages and/or to withdraw their effort. After the war, few governments actually retain the capacity to meet their wartime commitments; in Levi's terms, they suffer declines in trustworthiness. The worse their losses in war, the more they lose capacity and suffer discredit (cf. Schumpeter 1947: 354). Disappointed political creditors respond by accelerating their demands and/or withdrawing their compliance with the government's own demands. These are not mere mental events; they involve genuine changes in relations among important actors within a regime. Levi gives us two structural processes to examine seriously: 1) alterations in networks of interpersonal commitment, 2) changed relations between governmental agents and citizens.

These processes become all the more interesting when we recognize how crucially they affect prospects for democracy. Consider trust, defined as the placing of significant enterprises and resources at risk to other people's malfeasance, mistakes, or failures. However we define democracy, it depends on two kinds of trust: 1) that significant others, including governmental officials, will meet their current commitments, and 2) that if a political actor loses in the current round, it will get another chance (Przeworski 1997; for more general discussions of trust and its political impact, see Besley 1995; Burt and Knez 1995; Edwards and Foley 1998, 1999; Elster 1999; Feige 1998; Gambetta 1993; Granovetter 1995b; Greif 1994; Landa 1994; Ledeneva 1998; Paxton 1999; Rotberg 1999; Seligman 1997; Shapiro 1987; Solnick 1998; Tilly 2004d; Woolcock 1998; Yamagishi and Yamagishi 1994).

Less obviously, democracy depends on a degree of articulation between public politics and networks of interpersonal commitment organized around trade, religious practice, kinship, and esoteric knowledge. In networks of these kinds, people carry on long-term, high-risk activities whose outcomes depend significantly on the performances of others; in that sense, they qualify as trust networks. Through most of human history, subjects of states insulated all such networks from political interference as best they could. Where subjects succeed in protecting their trust networks, they fight off state intervention, subvert state capacity, offer minimum consent to state demands, and withdraw effort from production of public goods under state auspices. Sympathetic to insulation and protection of trust networks, James Scott (1985) calls many of these strategies "weapons of the weak." A necessary (if by no means sufficient) condition of democracy, however, is enough state capacity to meet governmental commitments, defend constituted political actors, and enforce agreements among them. If the weak prevail in this regard, paradoxically, democracy suffers.

Well-insulated trust networks erect almost insuperable barriers to state capacity. In Reformation Europe, for example, the formation of ties among ordinary Protestants greatly inhibited the rule of princes who did not convert themselves or make firm compacts with Protestant leaders (te Brake 1998: 81–90). In 19th-century Switzerland, only the weakening of separate trust networks embedded in Protestant and Catholic congregations provided an opening to democratization in a country racked repeatedly by civil war between 1798 and 1847. Democratization always involves the formation of new *modi vivendi* between trust networks and governmental agents, whether directly or through powerful political actors such as parties, churches, and special interest associations.

Levi's formulations brush against these phenomena but do not quite capture them. In all of them, locations within interpersonal networks, rather than unmediated relationships between individuals and authorities, significantly affect people's commitment to collective enterprises. The effect is even more general. We have good reason to believe that collective action on a large scale depends heavily on commitment to subgroups within the acting population rather than directly on the enterprise as a whole (Sandell 1998). That is, of course, the implication of Doug McAdam's findings concerning the effects of network integration on participation in Freedom Summer.

From Social Interactions to Destruction and Altruism

Let us take advantage of these openings to think more generally about destruction and altruism. We continue to assume that cognitive mechanisms affect individual compliance in the manner that Levi argues. But we shift (as does Levi herself) from Levi's initial terrain of individual compliance to the overlapping territory of contentious politics: the collective making of claims that would, if realized, significantly affect the interests of others. We investigate the dynamics of relations that appear as static constraints in Levi's initial consent model.

Accepting provisionally Levi's account of individual-level mechanisms that promote compliance, we can inquire into interpersonal processes that facilitate or activate the mechanisms in question. Under what conditions, why, and how do social interactions encourage people to take significant losses—individual and/or collective—in pursuit of collective claims? Does it make any difference whether those losses are shared with objects of claims (destruction) or taken exclusively by the claimant while some other party benefits from the claims (altruism)? Does the existence of ties that participants regard as reliable and fair promote readiness to engage in destruction or altruism?

These ways of putting our question make clear that with her moves toward "group pressure" Levi has opened up three promising lines of explanation for destructive and altruistic forms of contention:

1. outright coercion by other parties
2. mutual coercion within an acting group
3. by-product commitments

Take coercion first. Levi rightly argues that no polity operates entirely by means of harm and threats of harm. Yet some do a great deal of their work that way. Vast Mongol empires, for example, maintained themselves for centuries through large applications of coercion (Barfield 1989; Johnston 1995; Morgan 1990; cf. Stanley 1996; Scott 1998; Tilly 1999b; Wolf 1999). More generally, exploitative systems make involuntary altruists of their victims. As seen from the victim's side, exploitation consists of taking losses for another's benefit. Exploitation always depends, at least in part, on coercion (Bottomore 1983: 157–58; Roemer 1982; Stinchcombe 1995; Tilly 1998c, ch. 4). Under a wide range of circumstances, coercion produces compliance and loss.

Mutual coercion, furthermore, occurs within acting groups. With high exit barriers and little opportunity for communication among disgruntled members, many a sect or conspiracy maintains control over its members even when numerous participants privately prefer rebellion or escape (Gamson, Fireman, and Rytina 1982; Zablocki 1980). Similarly, Roger Gould (1999, 2003) identifies a process by which clans whose individual members would much rather stay alive engage in self-destructive feuding as internal coercion augments in response to external threat. Mutual coercion promotes a wide variety of destruction and altruism.

By-product commitments probably play an even larger part in collective destruction and altruism than does coercion. Social ties entailing significant rights and obligations grow up from a wide variety of activities: birth, common residence, sexual relations, mutual aid, religious practice, public ceremonial, and more. Some of those ties ramify into networks of identity and trust: sets of social ties providing collective answers to the questions "Who are you?" "Who are we?" and "Who are they?" as well as becoming sites of high-risk, long-term activities such as reputation building, investment, trade in valuables, procreation, and entrance into a craft. Trade diasporas, Landsmannschaften, credit circles, lineages, religious sects, and journeymen's brotherhoods provide salient cases in point.

Networks thus formed and reinforced acquire strong claims over their members. Gossip, shaming, and threats of expulsion multiply their effectiveness in such networks. Since the very connections among members become crucial resources, external threats to any member become threats to the high-risk, long-term activities of all members. As a result, external repression operates on networks of identity and trust in two rather different modes. It damps collective action when it concentrates on raising the cost of any new action but incites collective resistance when it threatens survival of the network and its associated identities (Goldstone and Tilly 2001; Khawaja 1993; Lichbach 1987; Olivier 1991). Collective resistance, furthermore, can easily turn into collective aggression, or into simultaneous damage of self and other, in the course of strategic interaction.

Lest these observations seem distant from the questions about destruction and altruism with which we began, consider the process Charles Payne describes:

> Mrs. Annie Devine played a crucial role in the movement in Canton, Mississippi. CORE's Rudy Lombard speaks of a meeting where "She looked me in the eye and said 'Rudy, I *know* you won't deny us your talents in Canton this summer. I'm depending on you.' I knew I was trapped. No way I could turn that woman down." The organizers and the local people who took to them were in a positive feedback loop, in which the courage and humanistic values of one side encouraged a like response from the other. "They were gentlemen," said Mr. Larry of the McComb organizers, "and around them we were gentle." That would be even more true in reverse. (Payne 1995: 239–40)

Rudy Lombard implies that without Mrs. Devine's moral pressure he never would have run the risks he actually ran on behalf of the cause. But Mrs. Devine's moral authority did not depend on personal charisma alone; it operated within a previously established network of mutual awareness and commitment. It depended, at least in part, on Lombard's and Devine's relations to third parties. Through just such interactive processes by-product commitments promote sacrifice. Models of self-directed individuals who respond to incentives within constraints may capture crucial instants of decision or indecision, but they misrepresent the interactive social processes that generate and transform such instants. They cannot deal with the dynamics of interpersonal commitment.

Notice where we are going. Within contentious politics, actions that observers and participants retroactively interpret as consequences of deliberate individual choice almost always turn out to result from interactive processes. Some of those processes occur abruptly (for example, one person's shouting "Fire!" and other people's running), and some of them proceed quite incrementally (for example, day-by-day modulation of an acquaintance from distant to friendly). In order to explain destructive and altruistic contention, we must make four related moves in our representation of social processes:

- from individuals to networks
- from individual beliefs to shared stories
- from personal cognition to conversation
- from action to interaction

Participation in contentious politics consists of conversational interaction within networks in the context of collectively constructed stories. Although individual mental events explain some aspects of contentious conversation, much of its dynamics results from alterations in networks, stories, or the course of conversation itself (Auyero 2003; Emirbayer 1997; Emirbayer and Goodwin 1994; Emirbayer and Mische 1998; Goodwin et al. 1999; Polletta 1998a, 1998b, 2005; Somers 1992, 1994; Tilly 1998b, 1998d, 1999a, 2002a).

Here we encounter a major difficulty in contemporary analyses of contentious politics (see Cerulo 1997: 393–94). This is the difficulty: Humans live in flesh-and-blood bodies, accumulate traces of experiences in their nervous systems, organize current encounters with the world as cognitions, emotions, and intentional actions. They tell stories about themselves in which they acted deliberately and efficaciously or were blocked from doing so by uncontrolled emotion, weakness, malevolent others, bad luck, or recalcitrant nature. They tell similar stories about other people. Humans come to believe in a world full of continuous, neatly bounded, self-propelling individuals whose intentions interact with accidents and natural limits to produce all of social life. In many versions, those "natural limits" feature norms, values, and scripts inculcated and enforced by powerful others—but then internalized by self-propelling individuals.

Closely observed, however, the same humans turn out to be interacting repeatedly with others, renegotiating who they are, adjusting the boundaries they occupy, modifying their actions in rapid response to other people's reactions, selecting among and altering available scripts, improvising new forms of joint action, speaking sentences no one has ever uttered before, yet responding predictably to their locations within webs of social ties they themselves cannot map in detail. They tell stories about themselves and others that facilitate their social interaction rather than laying out verifiable facts about individual lives. They actually live in deeply relational worlds. If social construction occurs, it happens socially, not in isolated recesses of individual minds.

The problem becomes acute in descriptions and explanations of contentious politics. Political actors typically give individualized accounts of participation in contention, although the "individuals" to which they attribute bounded, unified, continuous self-propulsion are often collective actors such as communities, classes, armies, firms, unions, interest groups, or social movements. Even such sensitive analysts of political interaction as Doug McAdam and Charles Payne generally cast their accounts one actor at a time. Analysts and participants alike attach moral evaluations and responsibilities to the individuals involved, praising or condemning them for their actions, grading their announced identities from unacceptable (e.g., mob) to laudable (e.g., martyrs). Accordingly, strenuous effort in contentious politics goes into contested representations of crucial actors as worthy or unworthy, unified or fragmented, large or small, committed or uncommitted, powerful or weak, well connected or isolated, durable or evanescent, reasonable or irrational, greedy or generous.

Meticulous observation of that same effort, however, eventually tells even a naïve observer what almost every combat officer, union leader, or political organizer acknowledges in private. Public representations of political identities and other forms of participation in struggle proceed through intense coordination; contingent improvisation; tactical maneuvering; responses to signals from other participants; on-the-spot reinterpretations of what is possible, desirable, or efficacious; and strings of unexpected outcomes inciting new improvisations. Interactions among actors with shifting boundaries, internal structures, and identities turn out to permeate what in retrospect or in distant perspective analysts portray as actor-driven wars, strikes, rebellions, electoral campaigns, or social movements. Hence the difficulty of reconciling individualistic images with interactive realities. Margaret Levi's valuable analysis of consent never quite escapes the difficulty.

Interactive Political Identities

In response to that difficulty, let us stress social interaction as the locus and basis of contention. Let us recognize that political identities consist of public representations of relationships: us to them and us to us. Let us further recognize that much of contentious politics directly involves identity claims: we speak as X, we claim a certain relationship to Y, our being Xs gives us the right to Z, and so on. We can then draw on analogies between political contention and argumentative conversation, which follows a dynamic that is irreducible to the initial intentions of the conversationalists (see, e.g., Duneier and Molotch 1999). Above all, let us break with the common assumption that intentions—or, worse yet, reasons given by participants after the fact—explain social processes. Yet, ironically, we will end up observing that assertions of unitary actors and performances to validate those assertions play central parts in a great variety of contentious politics. The assertion of self-propelled unity turns out to be both a socially organized illusion and a profound truth of contention.

Who, then, are the actors? What sorts of people are likely to engage in contentious politics? What sorts of people, that is, are likely to make concerted public claims that involve governments as objects or third parties and that, if realized, would visibly affect interests of persons outside their own number? In principle, any connected set of persons within a given polity to whom a definition of shared stakes in that polity's operation is available qualifies. In practice, beyond a very small scale every actor who engages in claim making includes at least one cluster of previously connected persons among whom have circulated widely accepted stories concerning their strategic situation: opportunities, threats, available means of action, likely consequences of those actions, evaluations of those consequences, capacities to act, memories of previous contention, and inventories of other likely parties to any action.

In practice, furthermore, such actors have generally established previous relations—contentious or not—to other collective actors; those relations have shaped internal structures of the actors and helped generate their stories. In practice, finally, constituent units of claim-making actors often consist not of living, breathing whole individuals but of groups, organizations, bundles of social ties, and social sites such as occupations and neighborhoods. Actors consist of networks deploying partially shared histories, cultures, and collective connections with other actors. The volunteers who trained in Oxford, Ohio, during June 1964 were joining and transforming a well-articulated network of activists.

Such actors, however, almost never describe themselves as composite networks. Instead, they offer collective nouns; they call themselves workers, women, residents of X, or United Front Against Y. They attribute unitary intentions to themselves, and most often to the objects of their claims as well. They recast social relations and network processes as individuals and individually deliberated actions. What's going on? Identities in general consist of social relations and their representations, as seen from the perspective of one actor or another. They are not durable or encompassing attributes of persons or collective actors as such. To bear an identity as mother is to maintain a certain relation to a child. The same person that bears the identity mother in one context easily adopts the identities manager, customer, alumna, and sister in others.

A crucial subset of identities is categorical; it pivots on a line that separates Xs from Ys, establishing distinct relations of Xs to Xs, Xs to Ys, and Ys to Ys. black/white forms an important pair in the United States, but so do male/female, Jew/Gentile, worker/boss, and welfare recipient/social worker. Each pair defines not only a boundary but also a locally variable set of relations across that boundary.

Seen as social relations and their representations, all identities have a political side, actual or potential. Whether husband/wife or black/white, each categorical pair has its own historically accumulated forms of deliberation and struggle. Much identity-based deliberation and struggle raises questions that, when generalized, become problems of the common good: questions of inequality, of equity, of right, of obligation. Public debates and private identities often interact, as when women and men enact in their daily lives the issues and terms of great public struggles over gender inequality.

Finally, all polities leave room for some claim making on the basis of shared identity, and all polities build some identities explicitly into public political life; demands in the name of a religious minority illustrate the first phenomenon, installation of legal distinctions between citizens and aliens the second. Recognizing the ubiquity of identity politics in some senses of the term, we can nevertheless call identities explicitly **political** when they qualify in one or both of these last two regards: when people make public claims on the basis of those identities, claims to which governments are either objects or third parties.

Identities are political, then, insofar as they involve relations to governments. Obvious examples are official, military veteran, citizen, imprisoned felon, and welfare recipient. Identities such as worker, resident, and woman likewise become political in some regimes, either where governments actually rule by means of such identities or where any set of people who subscribe to the same program have the right to voice collective demands. Over the long run, American political struggles inscribed the identity pair black/white more definitively into public politics than was the case in Brazil, although not so comprehensively as in South Africa (Marx 1998; see also Fredrickson 1997). But in all three countries black activists have repeatedly divided over whether they should make demands in their capacity as blacks, as citizens, as workers, as women, or perhaps as some combination of these categories (see, e.g., Jenson 1998; Seidman 1993, 1999).

Or consider the politics of Hindu/Muslim divisions in India. One of the most hotly debated questions in current Indian politics is whether, if it came to full power, the increasingly influential Bharatiya Janata Party (BJP), with its origins in Hindu nationalism, would inscribe religious categories into the previously secular Indian national governmental structure. In the present Indian system, people who share routine religious identities already have the right to form parties of their own, so long as they represent themselves as embodying distinctive cultural traditions rather than creeds as such. Authorities currently contest any such right in Turkey, Algeria, Tanzania, Afghanistan, and parts of the former Soviet Union. To that extent many religious identities are already political identities in India.

Indeed, in some regards the Hindu/Muslim pair operates across South Asia chiefly in relation to government rather than as an organizer of everyday social relations; in routine social interaction, caste, class, community, and gender tend to prevail (see, e.g., Brass 1994, 1996, 1997; Copland 1998; Tambiah 1996, 1997; Varshney 2002). Hindu/Muslim designates a political distinction rather than separating two well-defined, unitary, transcendental worldviews from each other. To an unknown but probably large degree, shared orientations of category members result from, rather than cause, recurrent political relations between members of different categories (Laitin 1999; cf. Turner 1982: 69–70).

Over the course of contentious politics, actors take action in the names of identities. Identities define their relations to specific others. Their actions actually consist of *inter*actions with those others, interactions that center on claim making. They put on a performance of mutual, public claim making by paired identities. In the name of their asserted collective identity, interlocutors for actors demand, command, require, request, plead, petition, beseech, promise, propose, threaten, attack, destroy, seize, or otherwise make claims on assets that lie under someone else's control. When interlocutors for others reply in the name of their own political identities, an episode of contentious politics has begun.

As the process continues, relevant identities often modify. From the perspective of local power holders, COFO volunteers arrived in Mississippi as alien invaders; although they never became friends of the white power structure, they and their staff organizers became significant actors in local politics. One way or another, clusters of civil rights activists established recognized, collective, identity-framed relations with local and national holders of power. That those relations were rarely cordial does not gainsay the point. Warfare and strike activity, after all, also involve contentious politics among well-defined parties.

Dynamics of Altruism and Destruction

Armed with an interactive, identity-based understanding of contentious politics, let us return to the explanation of altruism and destruction. Recall that destruction refers to collective action in which an actor inflicts net losses on another actor while enduring net losses itself, regardless of possible benefits or losses to third parties. Altruism, then, refers to collective action in which an actor produces benefits for another actor while enduring net losses itself, again regardless of possible benefits or losses to third parties.

Several different mechanisms promote one variety of self-sacrifice or another. The first is outright external compulsion. As in Levi's cases of mass conscription, a government's readiness to coerce reluctant soldiers drives unwilling individuals to undertake lethal risks. The second is mutual coercion within a network, a process that gains efficacy with high barriers to private communication and exit, as well as with prior organization of that network as the site of high-risk trust and wide-ranging identity.

Following Levi's analyses, we can reasonably suppose that mutual coercion will also gain efficacy with:

- public enforcement of fair treatment within networks of potential activists
- third-party enforcement of previously made public commitments
- guarantees of network durability
- guarantees of mutual support among network members
- signaling of determination among potential participants in risky actions
- central coordination of identity-sustaining action within trust networks

To the extent that these mechanisms converge, we can even expect suffering to become a badge of worthiness, a proof of commitment, in some respects a reward in itself.

We must move beyond Levi's analyses, however, to recognize the significance of two other causal mechanisms that promote destruction and altruism. One is the activation of shared stories with which defection is incompatible (McAdam and Paulsen 1993; Polletta 1998b, 2005). As we have seen, people integrate political identities with shared stories about those identities. Such stories crystallize answers to these sorts of questions: Who are we? What are our rights and obligations? What do we intend? Who are they? What are their rights and obligations? What do they intend? Those stories constrain participants in contention thrice: by setting limits on what sorts of joint interaction they consider, by influencing their collective self-presentation, and by embodying standards of proper individual performance. If stories about who "we" and "they" are include imputations of courage, shared fate, and exposure to hostile outsiders, those stories in themselves raise the self-imposed costs of self-seeking behavior. They increase estimated costs of alternatives to mutual defense.

The other causal mechanism is external threat to survival of shared identities and trust networks. To the extent that people have invested their futures in such networks and cut themselves off from opportunities to exit, external threats to any part of the network become threats to the whole. Thus people will die defending their networks against heavy odds. Freedom Summer volunteers joined a beleaguered minority of activists in hostile territory. Each threat to their collective survival increased the salience of their shared identity and reduced the likelihood of individual defection. To be sure, reversal of the other crucial mechanisms in the form of panic among leaders, sharp division within the cause, or open challenges to shared stories raises the probability of helter-skelter exit. But over a wide range, activation of external threats to shared identities and trust networks promotes common defensive efforts, even to the point of substantial net losses for participants.

These arguments finally bring us to distinctions between destruction and altruism. One version of destruction resembles altruism: where a shared identity and trust network come under serious external threat, under some circumstances a set of actors incurs large costs for itself and inflicts large costs on others for the benefit of third parties with whom it shares identity and trust network. Thus some objects of genocide attack the perpetrators in order to distract their attackers from other family members. A second version involves even more general losses, as cornered members of a trust network destroy themselves and their attackers rather than submit to the subjugation or defilement that is likely to follow their surrender. In both scenarios, relations to third parties make a large difference: in the first case, because third parties of similar identity stand to gain from destructive action; in the second case, because the absence of third-party monitors with relations to both parties increases the likelihood of destruction.

Altruism, by the same reasoning, becomes more feasible in the presence of 1) identity-trust ties to the object of self-sacrificing action, 2) threats that relatively limited actions can reduce, and 3) third parties that are likely to intervene on the beneficiary's behalf once self-sacrifice alerts them to the threat faced by the trust network at large. Conversely, in the absence of extensive identity-trust ties both destruction and altruism should be rare or nonexistent. The line of reasoning brings us back to a kind of agreement with rational action skeptics about destruction and altruism: cases of apparent self-sacrifice for unlike others—trees, the environment, endangered species, and unknown foreigners—will ordinarily turn out to depend on mechanisms operating within groups of activists. Mutual coercion, third-party enforcement, and other mechanisms from Margaret Levi's well-stocked tool kit will explain those cases. In the final analysis, they will not involve isolated individual decisions to take substantial net losses for the benefit of others. Instead, they will result from by-product commitments and interactive processes.

If these sorts of arguments apply to destruction and altruism, they ought likewise to account for egoism and cooperation. In egoism and cooperation, by definition, actors receive (or at least can anticipate receiving) net benefits from their interactions with others. Straightforward satisfaction-seeking therefore probably plays a part in egoism and cooperation that it does not in genuine destruction and altruism. Yet here, too, we should find that relations to immediate others, as distinguished from the cause as a whole, significantly affect participation and its satisfactions (see Bowles and Gintis 1998; Goldstone 1994; Hechter 1987; Nesse 1999).

No doubt full analyses of egoism and cooperation would also require identification of further mechanisms. We should, for instance, search out mechanisms that make it possible for an egoistic actor to benefit by inflicting harm on others and other mechanisms altering the categorical distinctions and relations currently available to participants in contention (see Tilly 1998c). For the moment, however, it will suffice to examine how well this chapter's analyses apply to concrete cases of destruction and altruism.

Assertion is not proof. Single-actor accounts of contentious politics have held such sway in recent years that we have far too little evidence to assess the plausibility or implausibility of my speculations. At least those speculations have the virtues of concreteness and novelty. Where, then, do we stand? We have identified these clusters of causal mechanisms as likely contributors to collective destruction and collective altruism:

1. application of straightforward coercion by outsiders
2. application of mutual coercion within preexisting networks, especially where barriers to exit and to private internal communication are high
3. public enforcement of fair treatment within networks of potential activists
4. third-party enforcement of previously made public commitments
5. guarantees of network durability
6. guarantees of mutual support among network members
7. signaling of determination among potential participants in risky actions
8. central coordination of identity-sustaining action within trust networks
9. activation of shared stories with which defection is incompatible
10. external threats to survival of trust networks

Let no one misunderstand: such a list of ten extremely general relational mechanisms falls far short of constituting an all-purpose explanation for altruism and destruction. In any particular case, we should expect to find different combinations and sequences of such mechanisms, hence significantly different trajectories and outcomes. The list simply points explanations of altruism and destruction in a certain direction: away from elementary *ex ante* decision matrices toward relational processes.

The proposed mechanisms have the virtues of being observable and being widely documented in actual accounts of high-risk contentious politics. Doug McAdam sums up his network-oriented interpretation of Freedom Summer:

Activism depends on more than just idealism. It is not enough that people be attitudinally inclined toward activism. There must also exist formal organizations or informal social networks that structure and sustain collective action. The volunteers were not appreciably more committed to Freedom Summer than the no-shows. Their closer ties to the project, however, left them in a better position to act on their commitment. Those volunteers who remain active today are distinguished from those who are not by virtue of their stronger organizational affiliations and continued ties to other activists. Attitudes dispose people to action; social structures enable them to act on these dispositions. (McAdam 1988: 237)

McAdam's summary moves in the direction of this chapter, but from the vantage point of the individual participant rather than the collective process. We need to know more about collective processes that generate commitment, collaboration, and sacrifice. My conclusion, then, is simple: the ten mechanisms we have uncovered provide crucial causal connections among individual experiences, social structures, and high-risk contentious interaction. Their convergence sets altruism or destruction in operation. They probably play significant parts in lower-risk egoism and cooperation as well. The challenge is to detect those mechanisms, examine their sequences, concatenations, and outcomes, and then determine exactly how they work.

Part III

Inequality

Chapter 5

Durable Inequality

Mᴏꜱᴛ ᴠɪᴠɪᴅ ᴀᴄᴄᴏᴜɴᴛꜱ ᴏꜰ ɪɴᴇQᴜᴀʟɪᴛʏ ᴇᴍᴘʟᴏʏ ᴛʜᴇ ɪᴍᴀɢᴇ of a giant ladder on which individuals or groups occupy rungs higher or lower than all the rest. Let me make the case for inequality as a maze in which clusters of people wander separated by walls they have built themselves, not always knowingly. Let us not ask "What causes human inequality in general?" but "How, why, and with what consequences do long-lasting, systematic inequalities in life-chances distinguish members of different socially defined categories of persons? How do categorical inequalities form, change, and disappear?" Since all social relations involve fleeting, fluctuating inequalities, let us concentrate on durable inequalities, those that last from one social interaction to the next, with special attention to those that persist over whole careers, lifetimes, and organizational histories.

Let us concentrate, furthermore, on distinctly bounded categories such as female/male, aristocrat/plebeian, citizen/foreigner, religious affiliation, ethnic origin, or race rather than continua such as rich/poor, tall/short, ugly/beautiful, and so on. Bounded categories deserve special attention because they provide clearer evidence for the operation of durable inequality, because their boundaries do crucial organizational work, and because categorical differences actually account for much of what ordinary observers take to be results of variation in individual talent or effort.

As Max Weber noted almost a century ago, the creation of what he called "social closure" forwards efforts by the powerful to exclude less powerful people from full benefits of joint enterprises, while facilitating efforts by underdogs to organize for the seizure of benefits denied (Weber 1968: I, 43–46, 341–48; Parkin 1979: 44–116). A relationship is likely to be closed, Weber remarked,

> in the following type of situation: a social relationship may provide the parties to it with opportunities for the satisfaction of spiritual or material interests. If the participants expect that the admission of others will lead to an improvement of their situation, an improvement in degree, in kind in the security or the value of the satisfaction, their interest will be in keeping the relationship open. If, on the other hand, their expectations are of improving their position by monopolistic tactics, their interest is in a closed relationship. (Weber 1968: I, 43)

Organizations such as firms and corporate kin groups use closure by drawing complete boundaries around themselves, then monitoring flows across those boundaries with care.

Contrary to Weber, however, I argue that at a scale larger than a single organization completely bounded categories are rare and difficult to maintain, that most categorical inequality relies on establishment of a partial frontier and defined social relations across that frontier, with much less control in regions distant from the frontier. Yet in other regards the analysis resonates with Weber's discussion. It builds a bridge from Max Weber on social closure to Karl Marx on exploitation, and back. My analysis concerns social mechanisms—recurrent causal sequences of general scope—that actually lock categorical inequality into place.

The central argument runs like this: Large, significant inequalities among human beings correspond mainly to categorical differences such as black/white, male/female, citizen/foreigner, or Muslim/Jew rather than to individual differences in attributes or propensities. Even where they employ ostensibly biological markers, such categories always depend on extensive social organization, belief, and enforcement. Durable inequality among categories arises because people who hold power in reward- and punishment-allocating organizations solve pressing organizational problems by means of categorical distinctions. Inadvertently or otherwise, those people set up systems of social closure, exclusion, and control. Multiple parties—not all of them powerful, some of them even victims of exploitation—then acquire stakes in those solutions. Variation in the form and durability of inequality therefore depends chiefly on the nature of the organization(s) involved, previous social locations of the categories, character of the organizational problems, and configurations of interested parties.

Through all these variations, nevertheless, we discover and rediscover paired, recognized, organized, unequal categories such as black/white, male/female, and citizen/noncitizen. The dividing line between such categories usually remains incomplete in two senses: 1) some people (persons of mixed race, transsexuals, certified refugees, and so on) do not fit clearly on one side of the line or the other, and 2) in many situations the distinction does not matter. Still, where they apply, paired, unequal categories do crucial organizational work, producing marked and durable differences in access to valued resources. Durable inequality depends heavily on institutionalization of categorical pairs.

Since the argument is unfamiliar and complex, it may help to lay out its major elements and their causal connections even before defining crucial terms. The list will serve as a preliminary map of the wilderness this chapter will explore:

1. Paired unequal categories consisting of asymmetrical relations across a socially recognized (and usually incomplete) dividing line between interpersonal networks recur in a wide variety of situations, with the usual effect being unequal exclusion of each network from resources controlled by the other.

2. Two mechanisms we may label **exploitation** and **opportunity hoarding** cause durable inequality when their agents incorporate paired unequal categories at crucial organizational boundaries.

3. Two further mechanisms we may title **emulation** and **adaptation** reinforce effectiveness of categorical distinctions.

4. Local categorical distinctions gain strength and operate at lower cost when matched with widely available paired unequal categories.

5. When many organizations adopt the same categorical distinctions, those distinctions become more pervasive and decisive in social life at large.

6. Experience within categorically differentiated settings gives participants systematically different and unequal preparation for performance in new organizations.

7. Much of what observers ordinarily interpret as inequality-creating individual differences are actually consequences of categorical organization.

8. For these reasons, inequalities by race, gender, ethnicity, class, age, citizenship, educational level, and other apparently contradictory principles of differentiation form through similar social processes and are to an important degree organizationally interchangeable.

Whatever else it accomplishes, my presentation should make clear what is at issue in such an organizational view of inequality-producing mechanisms. At a minimum, it will challenge other analysts to clarify causal mechanisms implied by their own preferred explanations of durable inequality, then to search for evidence that those causal mechanisms are actually operating.

Although the word "organization" may call to mind firms, governments, schools, and similar formal, hierarchical structures, I mean the analysis to encompass all sorts of well-bounded clusters of social ties in which occupants of at least one position have the right to commit collective resources to activities reaching across the boundary. Organizations thus include corporate kin groups, households, religious sects, bands of mercenaries, and many local communities. Durable inequality arises in all of them, and all of them at times incorporate categorical distinctions originating in adjacent organizations.

Humans invented categorical inequality millennia ago and have applied it to a wide range of social situations. People establish systems of categorical inequality, however inadvertently, chiefly by means of two causal mechanisms:

first, where powerful, connected people command resources from which they draw significantly increased returns by coordinating effort of outsiders whom they exclude from the full value added by that effort; call this mechanism **exploitation**

second, when members of a categorically bounded network acquire access to a resource that is valuable, renewable, subject to monopoly, supportive of network activities, and enhanced by the network's *modus operandi*; name this mechanism **opportunity hoarding**

The two mechanisms obviously parallel each other, but people who lack great power can pursue the second if encouraged, tolerated, or ignored by the powerful. Often the two parties gain complementary, if unequal, benefits from jointly excluding others.

Two further mechanisms cement such arrangements in place: **emulation**, the copying of established organizational models and/or transplantation of existing social relations from one setting to another; and **adaptation**, elaboration of daily routines such as mutual aid, political influence, courtship, and information gathering on the basis of categorically unequal structures. Exploitation and opportunity hoarding favor the installation of categorical inequality, while emulation and adaptation generalize its influence.

A certain kind of inequality therefore becomes prevalent over a large population in two complementary ways. Either a) the categorical pair in question—male/female, black/white, citizen/noncitizen, etc.—operates in organizations that control major welfare-affecting resources and its effects spread from there, or b) it repeats in a great many similar organizations, regardless of their power.

In the first case, work-producing and coercion-wielding organizations—corporations and states, plantations and mercenary forces, textile mills and drug rings, depending on the context—take pride of place because they ordinarily control the largest concentrations of deployable resources within large populations. In some settings of ideological hegemony, nevertheless, religious organizations and their own categorical distinctions have similar effects on inequality around them.

In the second case, households, kin groups, and local communities hold crucial positions because within a given population they a) form and change according to similar principles and b) strongly influence biological and social reproduction. Gender and age distinctions, for example, do not ordinarily separate lineages from one another, but their repetition in many lineages lends them influence throughout the population. The basic inequality-generating mechanisms, nevertheless, operate in similar fashions over a wide variety of organizational settings.

Categorical inequality represents a special case of categorical relations in general. It is a particular but spectacularly potent combination within a small set of network configurations that have reappeared millions of times at different scales, in different settings, throughout human history. No one has codified our knowledge of these configurations. Provisional nominees for the basic set include the **chain**, the **hierarchy**, the **triad**, the **organization**, and the **categorical pair**:

1. The chain consists of two or more similar and connected ties between social sites—persons, groups, identities, networks, or something else.
2. Hierarchies are those sorts of chains in which the connections are asymmetrical and the sites systematically unequal.
3. Triads consist of three sites having similar ties to each other.
4. Organizations are well-bounded sets of ties in which at least one site has the right to establish ties across the boundary that bind members of internal ties.
5. A categorical pair consists of a socially significant boundary and at least one tie between sites on either side of it.

(We might actually reduce the basic set to three, since a hierarchy is simply a special type of chain and, as we shall see, an organization is an overgrown categorical pair; for present purposes, however, it helps to distinguish all five.) Figure 5-1 schematizes the five elementary forms.

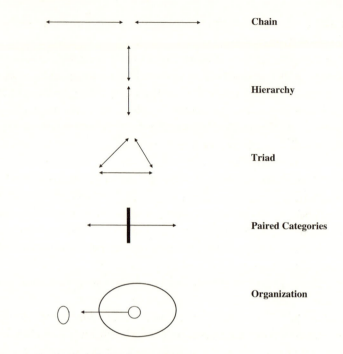

Figure 5-1. Basic Social Configurations

I regard these network configurations as social inventions: perhaps developed incrementally by trial and error, no doubt reinvented independently many times, but when recognized more or less deliberately installed as means of coordinating social life. Humans invented chains, hierarchies, triads, organizations, and categorical pairs as distinctive forms of social relations.

I may be wrong: An alternative line of thought, well represented by Fredrik Barth, regards all existing social structures not as fundamental elements of social life but as variable by-products of generative principles (Barth 1981: 1–118). For Barth, the social structures we identify as kin groups, community networks, and the like resemble instantaneous distributions of vehicles on a stretch of superhighway: coherent, exhibiting recurrent regularities, but not entities in themselves since their structure derives entirely from the actions and interactions of individual drivers.

If Barth's view is correct, my elementary forms could be recurrently emergent outcomes of more elementary social ties. Triads, for example, could emerge simply because stable pairs tend to recruit third parties jointly. Hierarchies could, in principle, simply generalize patterns of asymmetrical interaction. If methodological individualists could specify and validate single-actor decision rules constituting sufficient conditions for the creation of chains, hierarchies, triads, paired categories, and organizations, they would make strong claims for their favored reductionism. Fortunately, it matters little for present purposes whether we are dealing with inventions or emergents; once they are in place people employ them for a wide variety of relational work.

Configurations multiply beyond their elementary forms: chains proliferate into long chains, two-step hierarchies into ten-step hierarchies, triads into dense networks of interconnection, categorical pairs proliferate into triplets, and so on; anyone who works in a civil service, for example, becomes familiar not just with the relation between her rank and adjacent ranks but with a whole ladder consisting of asymmetrical connections.

Configurations also compound with each other; many hierarchies, as we shall see abundantly, incorporate categorical pairs, as when physicians are Caucasian males and nurses who work for them are Filipinas. An imaginary social structure compounding the elements appears in Figure 5-2, which connects hierarchies ABD and ABF, triads BDF and BEF, chain DFG, and categorical pair CD, then through command position A relates the entire organization— the bounded network—to external site X. In this imaginary case, site A enjoys the right to establish binding contracts between the whole and outside actors. A serves simultaneously as a boss and a broker.

Whether or not these five network elements turn out to be the elementary particles of social life, they recur very widely, doing characteristically different forms of social work. Their recurrence poses a triple analytic challenge: to detect those characteristic differences among structures, to identify their causal regularities, and to investigate conditions for the structures' concatenation.

First, characteristic differences exist among the structures. Chains, hierarchies, triads, organizations, and categorical pairs each have their own distinctive operating patterns and consequences. Mark Granovetter's distinction (1985, 1995) of strong ties (those defined by substantial emotion, obligation, range, and durability) from weak ties (more fleeting, neutral, narrow, and discretionary) contrasts two of the basic structures; the distinction gains its importance from the general association of strong ties with small, dense network clumps containing many triads (three-party clusters), of weak ties with long single-stranded chains. On the average, strong ties sustain solidarity, trust, and commitment while circulating a good deal of redundant information. Weak ties break more easily, but also transmit distant information more efficiently.

Granovetter's famous application concerns job finding, where weak ties play an exceptional role because they connect job seekers with a much wider range

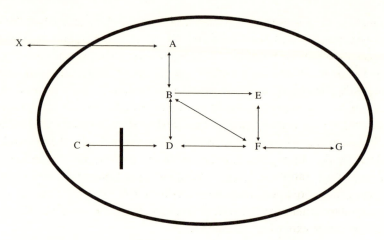

Figure 5-2. Combined Configurations in an Imaginary Social Structure

of opportunities, on average, than do strong ones. Although subsequent research has shown that medium-weak ties, with their modicum of commitment, provide better-quality information than very weak ties, the broad distinction between effects of strong and weak ties has held up well to empirical
scrutiny (Erickson 1996; see also Anderson 1974; Campbell, Marsden, and
Hurlbert 1986; Campbell and Rosenfeld 1986; Corcoran, Datcher, and Duncan
1980; De Schweinitz 1932; Holzer 1987; Laumann 1973; Lin 1982; Lin and
Dumin 1986; Marsden and Hurlbert 1988; Montgomery 1994; Murray, Rankin,
and Magill 1981; Simon and Warner 1992). Weak ties occupy important places
in all sorts of large-scale coordination. Without weak ties, for example, most
people would acquire very little information about current politics, medical
innovations, or investment opportunities.

Second, each of the configurations has its own causal regularities that demand individual attention. In triads, for example, where B and C have a distinctive relation (e.g., are close friends), stability seems to require that relations
AB and AC be similar (e.g., subordination, rivalry, or friendship rather than
subordination in one case and friendship in the other). If two relations (AB
and AC) are similar, solidary, and symmetrical, furthermore, the third (BC)
tends to assume the same form. No doubt such properties help account for the
significance of triads in social structures that promote trust in the face of uncertainty and risk. Behind these apparent regularities lie both mutual learning
and responses to the heightened transaction costs of inconsistency.

Third, we must investigate conditions for concatenation of the elementary structures: which ones fit together effectively under what circumstances, whether the presence of one sort of structure promotes the formation of the other, how many of a given kind an organization can contain without starting to collapse. As evidence concerning diminishing returns from large spans of control suggests, for example, very extensive hierarchies seem to negate their coordination advantages with rising transaction costs, and to invite subversion, shirking, or rebellion as well. No doubt other structural constraints limit the number of categorical pairs any organization of a given size can maintain, as well as viable combinations of categorical pairs with hierarchies. Categorical boundaries requiring mutual avoidance of parties on either side of the boundary except for ritualized encounters, for instance, most likely wreak havoc if installed in the upper reaches of extensive hierarchies.

Such a description of configurations, to be sure, freezes them into ice sculptures when in real life they more greatly resemble recurrent patterns seen in a waterfall. It summarizes different tendencies that we observers might notice in fast-moving transactions among social sites. In fact, the ties in question shift among configurations, as when actors in a chain invoke or abolish a categorical distinction among themselves (friendly neighbors, for example, forget about or suddenly react to racial barriers that lie between them) and members of a hierarchy temporarily behave as a fairly equal triad (lieutenant, sergeant, and private, for example, defend each other against the enemy's fire). Any generalizations we make about these configurations necessarily take the form "**Insofar as ties among sites form triads . . .**"

Recall a crucial point about social processes, including those that produce durable inequality. Designed, prescribed, and inherited social structures never work quite as their participants imagine they should or will. People make incessant mistakes, interactions produce unanticipated consequences, and in many circumstances if everyone actually followed the ostensible rules either organizational disaster or an utter standstill would occur. A master cabinetmaker once came to install in my home a set of handsome bookcases he had built in his shop. With the shelves and hardware, his assistant brought in a large sack. I looked in the sack, and saw several score small, thin wooden wedges. The conversation continued:

"What are those?"

"Shims."

"What for?"

"Well, it's clear you're not a cabinetmaker. We use shims because there's no such thing as a straight wall or a straight piece of wood. Shims straighten up the connections. Otherwise there'd be gaps all up and down the backs of the bookcases, and they might fall off the wall."

In human interaction, people constantly avert disasters and standstills by inserting social shims in the form of self-corrections, reassurances, clarifications, compensatory actions, and mutual aid. Social processes are worse than bookcases, however: because they keep moving, no social shim stays in place very long. Social structures stick together, more or less, precisely because improvisation never ceases.

Figure 5-3 captures some of the variability involved. It represents two dimensions along which social transactions differ: the degree of common knowledge participants in the transactions deploy, and the extent of scripting already available jointly to the parties for such transactions. Scripts range from such general configurations as triads and paired categories to the specific formulas people adopt to withdraw money from a bank. Just as pianists recognize and perform standard scales but also the intricate figures of a Beethoven sonata, interacting humans run from virtually universal routines to those activated by just one social situation.

Similarly, local knowledge extends from tacit understandings concerning connections among different locations in a city acquired by long-term resi-

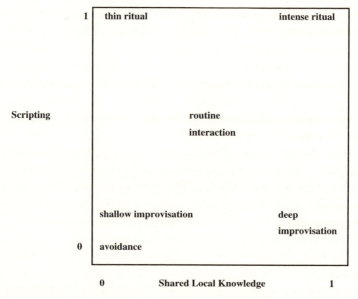

Figure 5-3. Scripting and Local Knowledge in Social Ties

dents to the memory of previous conversations that frames today's lunch between two old friends. Scripts provide models for participation in particular classes of social relations. Shared local knowledge, in its turn, provides means of giving variable contents to those social relations. Among our basic mechanisms, emulation relies chiefly on scripting, while adaptation relies heavily on accumulation of local knowledge.

Sociologists enamored of norms and values have sometimes considered scripts to lie at the center of all durable social processes, with socialization committing newcomers to scripts and sanctions minimizing deviation from them. Such a view involves astonishing confidence in the efficiency and effectiveness of scripting. Because local conditions vary and change incessantly and because social interaction repeatedly involves error, unanticipated consequences, repair, and readjustment, no organization whose members followed scripts to the best of their ability could actually survive; experienced bureaucrats and artisans, for example, know they can block any effective action in their organizations by following official rules meticulously. Scripts alone promote uniformity; knowledge alone flexibility; their combination, flexibility within established limits.

With little scripting and local knowledge available, actors either avoid each other or follow **shallow improvisations** such as the maneuvers pedestrians on a crowded sidewalk adopt in order to pass each other with a minimum of bumping and blocking. Scripting can be extensive and common knowledge meager, as when a master of ceremonies directs participants to applaud, rise, sit, and exit; let us entitle this circumstance **thin ritual**. Here only weak ties obtain. Thin ritual absorbs high transaction costs for the social results that it accomplishes; most people reserve it for very special occasions, and escape it when they can.

Where common knowledge is extensive and scripting slight, we enter the **deep improvisation** of professional jazz, intense sociability, soccer football, passionate sexual relations, and playful conversation. Extensive common knowledge, strong ties, and frequent improvisation reinforce each other. Participants in deep improvisation often draw on relevant scripts, as when a saxophonist inserts a fragment of the "Star Spangled Banner" in the midst of a frenetic riff or old lovers laughingly enact the rituals of formal courtship. But in such instances the script becomes part of a private joke recast by local knowledge.

Intense ritual occupies the diagram's upper right-hand corner—broad common knowledge plus extensive scripting—on the ground that in rich routines such as weddings, coming-of-age ceremonies, military reviews, and college commencements participants (however reluctantly) are affirming shared identities and mutual commitments by the temporary abandonment of improvisation or (more often) the doubling of public scripting with private improvisation in the form of nudges, winks, grimaces, and *sotto voce* comments. Anyone who imagines that intense ritual always expresses or engenders solidarity, however, should remember this: a funeral that revives old grievances and the impeccable but subtly aggressive performance by veteran dance partners who have grown to detest each other both illustrate the possible cohabitation of intense ritual with hostile interaction.

Routine interaction happens in the midsection, combining some scripting with significant local knowledge. As people carry on their social lives in firms, stores, schools, and neighborhoods, they deploy scripted routines such as greetings, payment procedures, apologies for rule violations, and expressions of personal concern, but they temper such scripts with locally applicable shared knowledge—including the shared knowledge encrusted within the scripts of a common language. Since scripts themselves repeatedly misfire, producing unanticipated consequences and minor disasters, people use local knowledge to repair social interactions as they go. Any representation of social life as consisting of norm following and deviance alone therefore misses the knowledge-using and knowledge-generating improvisation that makes effective social interaction possible.

Similarly, the common idea that workplaces ordinarily contain two competing sets of rules, practices, or social ties (the one "official" or "formal," the other "unofficial" or "informal") misses the point: it contrasts scripts with shared local knowledge, when the two necessarily intertwine (Stinchcombe 1990b). Organizations typically herd social interaction toward the middle ground in the scripting/local knowledge space, providing enough scripts that relations have broadly predictable rhythms and consequences, but enough local knowledge that members can improvise effectively in the face of unexpected threats and opportunities.

Like learning a language, establishment of new social ties often follows a zigzag pattern within the space: beginning with a rigidly followed but narrow script, accumulating local knowledge, improvising by means of that knowledge, making mistakes and discovering unanticipated consequences, correcting those mistakes and fixing the consequences until a precarious *modus vivendi* emerges, moving back to acquire new scripts, then broadening common knowledge until at times the newcomer participates in the thick, common-knowledge-assuming rituals of solidarity. By that time, any participant who follows the script rigidly—speaks with schoolbook grammar, observes every formality, works by rule—actually disrupts local social relations, unless she does so as a recognizable joke or as an understood way of controlling outsiders. Scripting and common knowledge operate dialectically, modifying each other so that each script bends under the weight of local knowledge but also limits the loci that share local knowledge, thus making the knowledge common.

By no means all learning processes complete the arc from shallow improvisation through more extensive scripts to deep improvisation. Staying in an unfamiliar city among speakers of an unfamiliar language, I have often found myself acquiring rudimentary familiarity with map, public transportation, and crucial phrases while working out a simple set of interaction routines for survival through the day, rehearsing the relevant scripts anxiously in anticipation of the next encounter, then getting by on that combination of a meager script with dangerously restricted local knowledge. Similarly, many an immigrant works up just enough involvement with the world outside her immigrant niche to avoid serious trouble when navigating that world. Again, the presence of just one important person who lacks familiarity with local language and practices can drive an entire work group or dinner party into the uncomfortable zone of stilted scripting and cramped improvisation. Because transaction costs absorb considerable resources and entail significant risks, acquisition of scripts and local knowledge generally occurs in discontinuous increments and often stops somewhere near the lower left-hand corner of our diagram.

Both scripts and common knowledge vary from particular to general, from local to ubiquitous. Gender relations involve scripts that transcend any particular organization as well as shared understandings that people transfer unreflectively from one setting to another. One of the great secrets of categorical inequality is the ready availability for organizational work of routines, understandings, and their justifications that organizational participants have acquired in other settings. Yet each durable social setting produces both a) some unique scripts and common knowledge, however trivial, available only to its habitués, b) some local variations on the scripts and common knowledge attached to widely relevant categorical distinctions according to such principles as age, race, ethnicity, class, locality, and gender. Marge Kirk, cement truck driver, summed it up this way:

> It takes a lot of energy just to stand your ground—balancing male egos with your right to survive. I wanted a job, I wanted to be a good truck driver, I wanted to be able to pull my weight as a driver. So years have passed now and somehow I survived. The guys are beginning to see me as a real human, not just a broad with legs and boobs. And the dispatcher has passed to the point of seeing me as a driver, I think. (Schroedel 1985: 156–57)

Marge Kirk, a woman in an overwhelmingly male job, had worked her way by means of incessant improvisation to a unique combination of scripts and local knowledge.

Our five configurations—chains, hierarchies, triads, organizations, and categorical pairs—provide widely available scripts. They rely on common knowledge, for example, shared understandings of how superiors and inferiors signal their relations to each other. They also generate common knowledge as people use them, for example, by relying on third parties in triads to patch up disagreements within any particular pair. Together, familiar scripts and accumulated common knowledge lower transaction costs of whatever activities an organization carries on. They thereby raise relative costs of shifting to some other structure of social ties. Managers of organizations ordinarily adopt the five configurations in various combinations as devices for managing social relations within the diagram's midsection, where some scripting and common knowledge combine.

How the configurations work, indeed, depends importantly on where in the two-dimensional space they fall. When goldsmiths who have common knowledge of their craft work together for the first time, they may use familiar scripts to establish hierarchies of reward and deference, but they can start to produce golden articles without extensive ritual. New cadets in military academies, however, ordinarily lack familiarity with both organizational structure and local lore; their superiors make up for those deficiencies by intensive scripting and drumming in of common knowledge. Only later do superiors let military recruits improvise within the limits set by well-known scripts.

Activating the emulation mechanism, managers of organizations often accomplish their work by importing configurations—particular hierarchies, chains, triads, and categorical pairs—with which new organizational members already have considerable experience and therefore common knowledge. Organizations build in educational and class differences with their established patterns of deference, existing links among people from common ethnic origins, triads defined as "teams" recruited from other organizations, and categorical pairs such as physician/nurse or professional/layman. Such borrowing of categorical pairs, as we shall see in detail, plays a crucial part in durable patterns of inequality.

Structure-borrowing managers gain the advantage of low start-up costs for new chunks of organization. But they also take on meanings, relational routines, and external connections whose features and consequences they cannot always control. Many a store manager has hired a few hard-working immigrants for a particular niche only to discover that part of his store has become a patronage network and he an unwitting patron. Many a new lawyer has learned that she will never make partner in her chosen firm because a hidden but powerful hierarchy separates graduates of elite law schools from the rest.

Each configuration, and each combination of configurations, no doubt conforms to its own regularities. I am pursuing the combination of paired categories with hierarchies on the hypothesis that exploitation, opportunity hoarding, emulation, and adaptation converge to favor such a social arrangement and that its widespread insertion in organizations accounts for a major share of all durable inequality. Regularities peculiar to this pair of configurations include the generation of boundary-maintaining beliefs about differences between actors on either side of the boundary, diversion of some returns from exploitation to boundary maintenance, and many more to come.

A comprehensive transactional sociology requires generalization of this analytic mode. Construction of organizations, for example, entails significant effort: delineation of an exclusive perimeter, creation of at least one effective center of authority within that perimeter, establishment of controls over interactions spanning the perimeter. Ronald Coase spurred a revival of organizational analysis in economics by pointing out that without some significant gains from such bounding and installation of hierarchy the very existence of firms posed an embarrassing theoretical problem for market-oriented economists (Coase 1992). Hierarchies, in Coase's formulation, reduce the transaction costs of complex interactions.

As Coase did not say, monopolization of resources underlies organizations. "All organizations," remarks Göran Ahrne, "seem to be founded around a set of collective resources, and access to these resources motivates people to join organizations and to stay with them" (Ahrne 1996: 112–13; see also Ahrne 1994). Ahrne leaves the impression that all clustered resources generate organizations, but that is not the case. The high seas teem with wonderful resources, but their (literal and figurative) fluidity has repeatedly frustrated human efforts to create bounded, exclusive organizations for exploitation of those resources; current struggles over fishing, which threaten the economies of regions as far apart as Newfoundland and Senegal, stem from the easy entry of industrial fishing vessels into almost all the world's abundant seas (Linard 1996).

Organizers normally pursue the effort of creating a new, fully bounded organization successfully only if they can a) capture valuable resources, b) lower transaction costs and/or increase gains in deployment of those resources by means of bounded networks, and c) form cross-boundary ties to sites providing them with sustaining opportunities and assets that will facilitate the realization of gains from the resources.

In these unusual circumstances the creation of a complete perimeter, rather than the guarded frontier of categorical pairing, yields significant returns for resource holders. For a completely bounded organization to survive, those returns must include a margin for the sheer cost of monitoring and sustaining the boundary. Unlike the production of hierarchies, triads, chains, and even paired categories, no one is likely to create a new organization inadvertently. Most organizations, indeed, come into being modeled directly on other existing organizations—firms, associations, lineages, states, parties, households, churches, and similar well-established exemplars. Such borrowing lowers costs of creating new organizations, but it also reduces the structure's conformity to the tasks at hand. Improvisation and the accumulation of shared local knowledge then produce further adjustments to the local situation.

In such circumstances, direct parallels to the opportunity hoarding, emulation, and adaptation that appear in categorical inequality promote formation of organizations. In fact, another way of thinking about organizations is as extreme forms of categorical inequality: frontier extended into a complete perimeter separating ins from outs, social relations across the perimeter restricted and coordinated, hierarchy concentrating control over social relations in one or a few locations.

In themselves, paired categories do not necessarily feature great inequality. In firms using or selling complex technologies, for example, the line/staff distinction separates command hierarchies from positions providing technical services to members of that hierarchy but frequently affords ample rewards on the staff side. Managers sometimes encourage competition for better performance by fostering categorical distinctions among largely interchangeable units, as when a military commander pits companies A, B, and C against each other in competition for displays of solidarity, zeal, and effectiveness.

Consider brokers who make their livings by mediating between two organizations or populations, equal or not. Such brokers enhance their livelihoods by supporting categorical distinctions that keep cross-boundary transactions passing through them instead of knitting together complementary pairs across the boundary. Ethnic leaders often acquire just such interests in maintaining distinctions between dominant classes and their own constituencies; they become stronger advocates of bilingual education, distinctive cultural institutions, and installation of legal categories than many members of their own constituencies (e.g., Hofmeyr 1987).

Rural landlords likewise often set themselves up as interlocutors for their culturally distinct tenants, becoming defenders of that distinctness as they do so without in the least relinquishing their own membership in the cosmopolitan culture (e.g., Rutten 1994). Wherever powerful parties gain from the segregation and coordination of two networks, equal or not, paired categories provide an effective device for realization of that gain.

Consider some quick examples. Stalin knits together an effective political machine by recruiting ethnically identified regional leaders, training them in Moscow, making them regional party bosses, and giving their ethnic identifications priority within partly autonomous political jurisdictions. When the Soviet center later relaxes its grip, political entrepreneurs within regions mobilize followings around those ethnic identities, others mobilize against them, and ostensibly age-old ethnic conflicts flame into civil war.

Again, the founder of a small manufacturing firm, following models already established in his trade, divides the firm's work into clusters of jobs he sees as distinct in character and qualifications, and then recruits workers for those jobs within well-marked categories. As turnover occurs and the firm expands, established workers pass word of available jobs among friends and relatives only to collaborate with them once they join the workforce, those new workers therefore prove more reliable and effective than others hired off the street, and all concerned come to associate job with category, so much so that owner and workers come to believe in the superior fitness of that category's members for the particular line of work.

Another case in point: Householders in an urban neighborhood build up a precarious system of trust on the basis of common backgrounds and shared relations to third parties, live with persons and property at risk to that system of trust, then react violently when newcomers whom they cannot easily integrate into the same networks threaten to occupy part of the territory. In the process, members of the two groups elaborate compelling stories about each other's perfidy and utter incompatibility.

Members of an immigrant stream, finally, peddle craft goods from their home region on big-city streets; some of them set up businesses as suppliers, manufacturers, or retail merchants; new immigrants find work in the expanding trade; and not only an immigrant niche but an ethnically specific international connection provides exclusive opportunities for the next generation. In all these cases, organizational improvisations lead to durable categorical inequality. In all these cases, but with variable weight, exploitation and opportunity hoarding favor installation of categorical inequality, while emulation and adaptation generalize its influence.

When it comes to the determinants of durable inequality, are these special cases or the general rule? We have good reasons for thinking that categorical inequality in general results from varying intersections of exploitation, opportunity hoarding, emulation, and adaptation. I will go further, claiming that much of the inequality seeming to result from individual or group differences in ability actually stems from the same causes:

1. authoritatively organized categorical differences in current performance (e.g., categorically differentiated cooperation or sabotage by fellow workers, subordinates, and supervisors)
2. authoritatively organized categorical differences in **rewards** for performance (e.g., systematically lower pay for blacks than for whites doing similar work) and/or
3. authoritatively organized differences in acquisition of **capacities** for performance (e.g., categorically segregated and unequal schools)

I also argue that similar social mechanisms generate inequality with respect to a wide range of advantages: wealth, income, esteem, protection, power, and more.

Figure 5-4 summarizes the argument's overall flow: Exploitation and opportunity hoarding drive the installation of boundaries, modified by emulation and adaptation. Installation of boundaries directly causes categorically unequal rewards. Indirectly, as a result of experiences in one setting that carry over to another, installation of boundaries shapes the differential accumulation of capacities and ties, which in turn also affect categorically unequal rewards. We might concretize the scheme, for example, by thinking of access to food, which has differed by gender historically across the world as a result of exploitation and opportunity hoarding, modified by emulation and adaptation, but which in turn has strongly affected the relative capacity of females and males to perform sustaining work (Fogel 2004; Sen 1992).

Nutrition turns out to provide quite a general model for categorical inequality, since in most settings feeding differs with categorical membership, but in many settings cumulative effects of feeding elsewhere help explain categorical differences in performance here. In direct parallel, information and social ties acquired now differ categorically, but previous categorical experience strongly affects information and social ties individuals and groups already have at their disposal, not to mention means they have of acquiring new information and social ties.

Again, categorically differentiated family experience strongly affects children's school performance and teachers' evaluations of that performance, which in turn channel children into categorically differentiated, career-shaping educational streams (Hout and Dohan 1996; Taubman 1991). To the extent that teach-

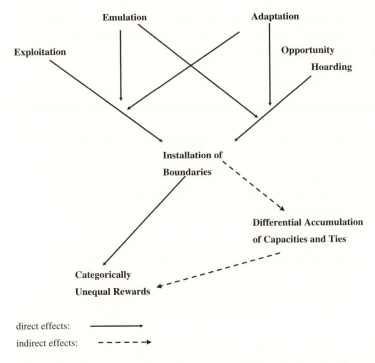

Figure 5-4. Basic Causal Relationships in Categorical Inequality

ers, employers, public officials, and other authorities differentiate their responses to performances in any of these regards categorically, they contribute to durable, authoritatively organized categorical differences. Authorities do, in fact, frequently solve their own organizational problems—how to sort students, whom to hire, what rights to honor—in categorical ways.

Feelings of identity, on one side, and intergroup hostility, on the other, may well accompany, promote, or result from use of categorical differences to solve organizational problems. But the relative prevalence of such attitudes plays a secondary part in inequality's extent and form. Mistaken beliefs reinforce exploitation, opportunity hoarding, emulation, and adaptation, but exercise little independent influence on their initiation. Or so I argue. It follows that reduction or intensification of racist, sexist, or xenophobic attitudes will have relatively little impact on durable inequality in these respects, while the introduction of certain new organizational forms—for example, the installation of different categories, or changed relations between categories and rewards—will have large impacts.

If so, the identification of such organizational forms becomes a significant challenge for social scientists. It also follows that similar organizational problems generate parallel solutions in very different settings, in articulation with very different sets of categories, hence that matches of positions with categories and justifications for such matches vary much more than recurrent structural arrangements—as when similar clusters of jobs acquire contrasting racial, ethnic, or gender identifications in different labor markets. Causal mechanisms resemble each other greatly, while outcomes differ dramatically, thus inviting very different rationalizations or condemnations after the fact. Social scientists dealing with such durable forms of inequality must hack through dense ideological overgrowth to reach structural roots.

Chapter 6

Relational Origins of Inequality

Virtually invisible in the passing crowd of 16th-century English historians, Craig Muldrew stealthily dropped a bomb into analyses of inequality. Muldrew looked closely at uses of credit in commercial transactions, which expanded rapidly after 1540 or so as England engaged more heavily in textile production and continental trade. Legal tender then consisted almost entirely of gold and silver coin. The money supply, however, expanded much more slowly than production of goods and the pace of commerce. Most likely some deflation and some acceleration in monetary circulation occurred as a consequence. But expansion of interpersonal credit—more to the point, of credit among households and the commercial enterprises embedded in those households—far outstripped changes in money as such. Note some crucial effects:

> As credit networks became more complicated, and more obligations broken, it became important before entering into a contract to be able to make judgements about other people's honesty. The more reliable both parties in an agreement were in paying debts, delivering goods or in performing services, the more secure chains of credit became, and the greater the chance of general profit, future material security and general ease of life for all entangled in them. The result of this was that credit in social terms—the reputation for fair and honest dealing of a household and its members—became the currency of lending and borrowing. Credit . . . referred to the amount of trust in society, and as such consisted of a system of judgements about trustworthiness; and the trustworthiness of neighbours came to be stressed as the paramount communal virtue, just as trust in God was stressed as the central religious duty. Since, by the late sixteenth

century, most households relied on the market for the bulk of their income, the establishment of trustworthiness became the most crucial factor needed to gen-erate and maintain wealth. (Muldrew 1998: 148; see also Muldrew 1993)

In the first instance, a household's credit did not depend on its material possessions or its cash on hand. It depended on relations to other households, so much so that people commonly spoke of each other's creditworthiness in terms of their ability to raise money from other people on short notice (Muldrew 1998: 148–72). Muldrew's analysis helps explain why ties of kinship, neighbor-hood, and shared religion remained crucial to risky commercial transactions as an ostensibly rationalizing and depersonalizing market expanded. It also helps explain why in a time of economic expansion members of ascendant commercial classes increasingly condemned proletarians as improvident, bibu-lous, and morally unreliable.

Muldrew's analysis stands Max Weber on his head: where Weber saw the Protestant Reformation as promulgating doctrines of individual responsibility that favored capitalist achievement, Muldrew perceives a transformation of social relations that made a reputation for uprightness crucial to commercial viability. In regions and classes where heterodoxy, mayhem, debauch, and pil-lage had long prevailed, religious, political, familial, sexual, neighborly, and commercial irregularity all came to raise doubts about the creditability of any particular person, household, or social category (see also Wrightson and Levine 1979, 1991).

Muldrew's perception is delightfully subversive; it not only reverses the causal arrow between belief and practice, but also indicates that far from dissolving previously existing social ties, market expansion depended on the creation of far more extensive interpersonal relations. Instead of deriving relations of trust from general culture or contract-enforcing institutions as is currently fashion-able, furthermore, he derives new attitudes and contracting-enforcing institu-tions from alterations in social relations. Despite some concessions to trust as attitude or belief, furthermore, he advances analyses of trust by treating it as a feature of social relations themselves; by implication, trust consists of placing valued resources and outcomes at risk to the malfeasance, mistakes, or failures of (trusted) others. In line with those recent economic historians and analysts of Eastern Europe who have emphasized the significance of trust-sustaining networks for markets and other forms of economic organization, Muldrew insists on the priority of social ties.[1]

---

1. For surveys of trust-sustaining practices, relations, and institutions, see Anthony and Horne 2003; Bates et al. 1998: Besley 1995; Biggart 2001; Biggart and Castanias

Although national governments eventually intervened massively in credit-connected markets by establishing central banks, issuing paper money, and regulating commercial transactions, according to Muldrew, they intervened not in a void but in dynamic networks of connection among households. Indeed, Muldrew argues that credit's expansion eventually produced uncertainties favoring both calls for governmental intervention à la Thomas Hobbes and spread of a more pessimistic, individualistic view of human nature (Muldrew 1998: 315–33; see also Helleiner 2003: 42–46; McGowen 1999).

Meanwhile, local authorities and interacting households fashioned or adapted their own trust-confirming institutions: kinship, common religious affiliation, oath taking, public tokens of indebtedness, earnest payments, courts of settlement, and more. "The phrase 'to pay on the nail,'" reports Muldrew,

> comes from Bristol where there were four bronze pillars erected before the Tolzey—the ancient covered colonnade where merchants conducted their business, and which was connected to the sheriff's court where most debt litigation was initiated. The "nails" are still in existence, and have flat surfaces where downpayments, and payments in cash, would have been made, and the practice of doing so was considered to be symbolic of the trust invested in the agreements. The date of the oldest nail is not known, but the other three were erected as gifts to the city in 1594, 1625 and 1631 to meet the need of increased business. The most interesting fact about the pillars are the inscriptions around the capitals on the religious and social nature of trust, which were comments upon the bargains made over them. One repeated the classical dictum that, "No man lives to himself," and another stated: "The Church of the livinge God is pillar and ground of trewth." (Muldrew 1998: 106–07)

Thus religious beliefs and practices fortified the politics of reputation, but by no means explained the vast changes that were occurring after 1530.

Fundamental alterations of social relations brought new forms, practices, and symbols into everyday prominence. Public oaths, mutual surveillance, and representations of social ties as if they were contracts proliferated. Literature gave expanded attention to credit and contract. "Shakespeare," remarks Muldrew,

2001; Burt and Knez 1995; Castrén and Lonkila 2004; Edwards and Foley 1998; Elster 1999; Elster, Offe, and Preuss 1998; Feige 1998; Gambetta 1993; Gould 1999, 2003; Granovetter 1995b; Guiso, Sapienza, and Zingales 2004; Heimer 1985; Hoffman, Postel-Vinay, and Rosenthal 2000; Landa 1994; Ledeneva 1998, 2004; Levi 1997; Lonkila 1999; Ostrom 1990, 1998; Paxton 1999; Postel-Vinay 1998; Rotberg 1999; Seligman 1997; Shapiro 1987; Solnick 1998; Stark 1995; Tilly 2004d; Warren 1999; Weber and Carter 2003; Woolcock 1998; Wuthnow 2004; Yamagishi and Yamagishi 1994.

94 ▼ Chapter 6

often used this language in metaphors and conceits, as in Sonnet 134 where debt, sureties, bonds, a mortgage and a law suit were all used to describe the relationship between a lover, his former mistress and her new lover. They were also a common feature in drama, with the [*sic*] some of the most obvious examples being Shakespeare's treatment of the ethics of forgiveness and discretion versus the binding force of contract in *The Merchant of Venice*, Philip Massinger's comedy about miserliness and prodigality, *A New Way to Pay Old Debts*, and Webster's tragedy about uncharitable litigation, *The Devil's Law Case*. (Muldrew 1998: 315)

Muldrew backs such general interpretations with systematic analyses covering thousands of 16th-century court cases. His evidence establishes deep, rapid increases both in uses of credit and in disputes about its abuses.

Muldrew makes no claim to explain all changes in English inequality during this period. Nor should he; a more general account would have to integrate massive shifts in demographic structure, migration, agriculture, manufacturing, marketing, and governmental activity (for an informative survey, see Wrightson 1982). The very period Muldrew studies, after all, brought dispossession of English monasteries; establishment of a Protestant state church; protoindustrial expansion; proliferation of international trade, energetic emigration, colonization, and exploration; new laws for control of the poor and regulation of master-servant relations; not to mention rapid growth of the landless population. Any of these processes might plausibly figure in explanations of changing inequality. Yet Muldrew's analysis of credit identifies one important impetus to changing patterns of inequality and implies very different sorts of explanation from prevailing histories of the period. Instead of locating sources of change chiefly in shifting modes of production or in evolving mentalities, Muldrew pivots them on mutations in relations among households (cf. Bearman 1993).

By no means all 16th-century historians would agree. Muldrew's analysis contrasts sharply, for example, with an equally innovative close reading of Gloucestershire's history during the same period. David Rollison intends to show how durable attachments to particular regional cultures created English national culture of the 16th- to 18th-century, including the transfer of the word "country" from the English equivalent of *paese* to the nation's identity. Unlike Muldrew, Rollison presents inequality as largely a cultural matter, a way of seeing and relating different categories of people (Rollison 1992: 248–49). He portrays his anthropological ambitions in this way:

These "thickish descriptions" of the people of one of England's most highly industrialised regions during the transition from feudal-tributary to capitalist

civilization in England are concerned with the nature of the relationship between inherited, or "structural," circumstances and culture, the ways those circumstances are interpreted, represented and communicated. The structure/cul-
ture dichotomy is too crude, for cultures are also structured by abiding idioms,
metaphors and myths which shape the fluid historical surfaces of individual and
collective consciousness. (Rollison 1992: 12)

For Rollison, social and material milieu matters because it shapes human consciousness, which then translates into shared culture. Culture then constrains
perception and action as it supplies the categories—including categories of
class—by which people interpret their experience. Rollison's view comes closer
to the contemporary consensus among historians than does Muldrew's. It also
resonates more directly with today's cultural and social anthropology (Kuper
1999).

Muldrew's observations, if correct, therefore carry implications far outside
16th-century English history. Let me single out just two implications of particular relevance to anthropological theory: first, a fresh view of commercialization and its effects; second, a relational explanation of inequality. The first
bears on the second, which will occupy most of this chapter.

Muldrew's findings significantly challenge common understandings of commercialization and its effects, hence their interest to anthropologists. Whatever
else anthropologists do, they examine causes, correlates, and consequences of
commercialization, on one side, and of incorporation into larger-scale political systems, on the other. The development of anthropology from European
encounters with non-European regions in which Europeans were striving to
establish commercial and political control inevitably placed commercialization on anthropologists' analytical agenda—often, in early formulations, as
the solvent of traditional social structure (Cooper and Stoler 1997; Ferguson
1997; Wolf 1982).

That notion of commercialization as standardizer, stifler, or strangler of
meaningful social life persists into our own time (Guyer 1995; Tilly 1999b;
Zelizer 1994, 1999, 2005c). Muldrew replies that expansion of commercial transactions caused new forms of interpersonal relations, new meanings, and new
social institutions embedding the relations and meanings to arise. Muldrew's
contrary formulation calls anthropologists to reexamine commercialization as
a complex social process having significantly different causes, concomitants,
and consequences from one setting to another.

The same encounter between Europeans and non-Europeans also placed
the intersection of culture and inequality high on the anthropological agenda.
As compared with their cousins in economics or sociology, anthropologists

have paid considerable attention to the ways that cultural variation causes, correlates with, results from, or becomes the instrument of inequality with respect to power, wealth, prestige, and well-being. Such classics as Louis Dumont's *Homo Hierarchicus* placed inequality visibly on the anthropological agenda.

Long before their social scientific cousins, anthropologists recognized that socially constructed cultural differences played significant parts in inequality by class, race, gender, ethnicity, nationality, and other categorical principles. But they continue to divide sharply when it comes to locating culture in the causal processes producing such differentiation. (Let us leap over many a controversy—see Kuper 1999—by defining culture as shared understandings and their representations in language, objects, and practices.) Some analysts of class, gender, race, ethnicity, and national identities, for example, treat such identities as negotiated relations with others (e.g., Brass 1996, 1997; Fitch 1998; Harrison 1995; Karakasidou 1997; Ludden 1996; Ong 1996; Roy 1994; Tambiah 1996, 1997; Brackette Williams 1989; Brett Williams 1991). So doing, they locate culture (or at least that portion of culture implicated in identities) within interpersonal transactions.

Many more analysts of class, gender, race, ethnicity, and national identities, however, center their explanations of identity on culture and/or phenomenology considered as separate from or prior to social interaction (e.g., Appiah and Gates 1995; Blackwood 1998; Daniel 1996; Friedman 1994; Hale 1997; Hart 1996; Nagi 1992; for helpful reviews and critiques, see Cerulo 1997; Cooper 1994; Cornell and Hartmann 1998; Lebovics 1995). Anthropologists who work on categorical differences generally hew closer to Rollison's line than to Muldrew's.

How so? Muldrew's analysis of 16th-century England assigns exceptional importance to processes of social interaction in the interdependent origins of both new cultural forms and new categorical inequalities. He proposes a relational explanation of inequality. Thus Muldrew makes a second claim on anthropologists' attention.

At least the late Eric Wolf would have listened. In the book he published shortly before his death in 1999, Eric Wolf offered anthropological reflections on the interplay between class and culture:

> When first introduced in their present-day senses, these concepts appeared to be wholly incompatible, especially when deployed in political discourse. Yet they do not exclude each other; they occur together and overlap in various ways. Both terms, in fact, claim too much and also too little. They suggest that "classes" or "cultures" represent totalities in their own right—homogeneous, all-em-

bracing entities, each characterized by a common outlook and capable of collective agency.

The advocates of "class" assumed that a common position along a gradient of control over the means of production entails a common interest shared by all members of the class and, hence, common propensities for action. Yet class and classness are better understood in terms of relations that develop historically within a social field. That field subsumes diverse kinds of people, rearranges them, and causes them to respond to new ways of marshaling social labor. One can then speak of the "making" of a class (as did E. P. Thompson in *The Making of the English Working Class*) out of disparate groups of people, who bear diverse cultural heritages and yet must adjust them to the requirements of a social order. Similarly, a class may be "unmade" and its members scattered and reallocated to different groupings and strata. (Wolf 1999: 65)

Thus Wolf advocated a Thompsonian view of class as dynamic social relations. Although I do not suppose that Wolf and Muldrew ever met, they would have had much to talk about. Without employing the term "relational" (which my late friend Wolf would probably have abhorred), both of them favored accounts of inequality in which negotiated social relations figured centrally. This chapter follows in their wake. In explicating and advocating relational analysis, I am advertising a mode of thought that already possesses a substantial anthropological pedigree but has lately fallen out of favor among anthropology's heralds (see, e.g., Barth 1969; Bonneuil 1997; Burawoy and Verdery 1999; Comaroff and Comaroff 1992; Davis 1992; Domínguez 1986; Gal 1987, 1989; Scott 1990; Verdery 1991, 2003).

Since, as Wolf states clearly, the relational account competes with several other approaches to inequality within contemporary anthropology, the advertisement deserves airing. Relational explanations currently occupy a minority position; anthropologists have—wrongly, to my mind—found other positions more attractive. What is at issue? Anthropologists or otherwise, analysts of inequality generally choose among four families of explanation: cultural, functional, coercive, and competitive. In their starkest versions:

- **Cultural** explanations derive inequality from widely held beliefs, values, and practices that promote differential distribution of advantages among social categories. Racism, patriarchy, caste, and similar ideas frequently figure in cultural explanations.
- Functional explanations derive inequality from differential contributions to accomplishment of societal goals, including collective survival. Accounts of the changing prominence of warriors, priests, intellectuals, and merchants often take functional forms.

- Coercive explanations derive inequality from the exercise of power. Views of control over land, military force, or capital as the key to inequality generally give pride of place to coercion.
- **Competitive explanations derive inequality from the passage of individuals or larger social units through sorting processes in which differential attributes and performances lead to differential rewards. One pertinent version of meritocracy is the idea that markets reward the most able and industrious, regardless of origin or connection.**

Let us linger a bit over the fourth family: competitive explanations of inequality. Although cultural, functional, and coercive explanations continue to prevail in anthropology, during recent decades competitive models have come to predominate in history and other social sciences. These days any social scientist who tries to explain, criticize, or influence major social inequalities, past or present, is likely to rely on the same basic model of how inequality comes about. The model features sorting of unequally endowed individuals into unequal positions, one by one. In its simplest versions, it contains just four elements:

1. a set of positions—jobs, public offices, dwellings, prestige categories, and so on
2. unequal distribution of the rewards attached to those positions
3. a sorting mechanism that channels people to different positions
4. individuals who vary in characteristics the sorting mechanism detects

Thus individuals arrive at the scanner, undergo evaluation, get sent to an appropriate position, and therefore receive unequal rewards. For example, Chinese intellectuals of unequal wit, learning, and family background study for imperial examinations, a few of them actually pass, those few move on into the imperial bureaucracy, while failed candidates find careers as scribes, servitors of county governments, or other occupations requiring literacy and cultivation. Similarly, today's American educational systems track youngsters from different social origins into socially segregated schools, which then provide differentiated skills and credentials that mark the youngsters' suitability for contrasting forms of employment. Or so says one simple version of the model.

In mildly complicated versions of the model, elements, positions, sorting mechanisms, and individual differences interact. For example, the number and characteristics of persons who present themselves for sorting (the "labor supply" in some versions) affect the distribution and character of positions ("jobs" in those same versions; for reviews and critiques, see Granovetter and Tilly 1988; Grusky 2001; Grusky and Sørensen 1998; Hanagan 1994; Steinberg 1999; Steinmetz 1993; Tilly and Tilly 1998; Wright 1997).

Both critics and defenders of existing inequalities commonly adopt the same basic explanatory model. Critics typically attack the sorting mechanism as unfair, inefficient, or destructive. They say that assigning people to advantageous or disadvantageous positions on the basis of race, gender, age, nationality, or physical attractiveness produces injustice, misuse of valuable talents, or damage to individual and society. Yet they insist that a sorting mechanism is producing these nefarious effects.

Defenders of the existing system, in contrast, typically stress differences among individuals—differences in energy, knowledge, skill, intelligence, strength, or (more rarely) acceptability to people who already occupy positions connected with those that newcomers might fill. They say that people differ significantly in their capacities to fill various positions, and that efficiency, justice, or even divine will prescribes matching of position to capacity and vice versa. Yet they, too, insist that a sorting mechanism produces the matching in question.

Some kinds of inequality do result from well-organized sorting of competing candidates. The Chinese imperial examination system does appear to have performed a very effective triage (Wong 1997). Competitors for Senate seats, positions on football teams, and places in symphony orchestras do undergo scanning by sorting mechanisms—tryouts, auditions, and elections—in which only candidates with certain characteristics end up in coveted positions. Critics then typically declare that the screening is unfair, inefficient, or destructive. Defenders typically reply that self-selected candidates differ so much in ability that the screening produces a superior outcome to its likely alternatives, such as assignment by seniority or random selection.

Advocates of such standard competitive models have applied them chiefly to income and wealth differences in market economies, especially capitalist market economies. In principle, however, nothing forbids their application to differences in power, reputation, sexual access, health, or other capabilities, as well as to other sorts of economies. To the extent that anthropologists enter general discussions of inequality, they have no choice but to confront the predominance of competitive models in today's analyses.

Concrete explanations of particular inequalities, to be sure, often combine two different accounts of inequality, for example, by arguing that culture determines which attributes competitive sorting processes reward. Nevertheless, the four types of explanation lead in substantially different directions. It is difficult to reconcile functional and coercive accounts of inequality, just as it takes considerable agility to link cultural with competitive explanations.

The line of thought exemplified by Muldrew and Wolf, however, points us in a fifth direction: toward **relational** explanations of inequality. In a relational view, inequality emerges from asymmetrical social interactions in which advantages accumulate on one side or the other, fortified by construction of social categories that justify and sustain unequal advantage. As a rough analogy, consider a conversation involving initially equal partners in the course of which (through wit, guile, knowledge, or loudness) one conversationalist gradually gains the upper hand. We can extend the analogy to many forms of social interaction, brief or prolonged, as well as to interactions among groups or categories of persons.

In addition to adopting a conversational view of inequality-generating processes, relational analysts take a further step entailing serious theoretical consequences. Many theorists of inequality assume, implicitly or explicitly, that they are accounting for relative positions of individuals or groups within an abstract, continuous space—a hierarchy of prestige, a continuum of power, a pyramid of wealth, or something of the sort. In such a view, explanations of inequality and its changes concern either a) movement of social units within the space, for example, lifetime occupational mobility and the rise and fall of particular lineages, or b) alterations of that space's general shape, for example, lengthening of hierarchies and increasing salience of educational differences. Cultural accounts characteristically base such abstract spaces on value systems, functional accounts on societal needs, coercive accounts on conquest, and competitive accounts on efficiency.

The relational story differs significantly. It treats inequality as a feature of transactions among social positions. For the neat multidimensional space of conventional treatments, it substitutes a dynamic tangle of incomplete, clumped, and changing connections. From a relational perspective, inequality appears everywhere, but it rarely crystallizes into neat, continuous hierarchies somehow arraying whole populations into strata. A relational analysis leads to the conclusion that any such hierarchies (which do, indeed, occasionally take shape in bureaucracies, armies, nobilities, and similar honorifically differentiated structures) rest on extensive social effort, only emerge under unusual historical conditions, and undergo incessant pressure for modification. Categories, in such a view, do not consist of mental constructs but of socially negotiated boundaries and changing relations across those boundaries. Most large-scale systems of inequality involve incompletely connected, inconsistent, contested, changing, yet powerful differences among clusters and categories of persons.

Think back to Muldrew. Muldrew's analysis challenges any picture of any single English hierarchy based on culture, function, coercion, or competition. In 16th-century England, households that could not manage credible reputations lost their ability to engage in extensive commercial transactions with other households, and thereby skidded to ruin. Without credit, they failed. In a world that was disappearing, location within patron-client chains defined the opportunities and constraints of most households. In the very different world that was emerging, categorical differences between the reputable and the disreputable, the creditworthy and the worthless, the middling and lower classes, began to govern relations among households. Muldrew's account places cumulative effects of asymmetrical social relations at the heart of his explanation. As in Muldrew's case, relational accounts of inequality commonly make concessions to cultural, functional, coercive, or competitive mechanisms, but center their explanations on cumulative and long-term effects of asymmetrical social interaction.

Muldrew's relational analysis of inequality stands out for its originality and ample historical documentation, but it does not stand alone. Historical anthropologist Don Kalb's analysis of changing class relations in North Brabant, the Netherlands, between 1850 and 1950 boldly takes on recent dismissals of class in studies of Western European industrialization. He sets himself deliberately against interpretations of class as essentially cultural—as consisting of individually carried understandings and their representations in objects and practices. His view of class allots plenty of space to culture, but in the guise of a collective and continuously negotiated feature of interaction.

Drawing considerable inspiration from E. P. Thompson, Kalb shows that a conception of class as a set of dynamic relations rather than as an attribute of individuals helps explain the distinctive politics of shoemakers and electrical workers in the region around Eindhoven. As Kalb puts it:

> My case studies of class formation in subregions of industrializing Brabant tend to illustrate that an anthropological interest in popular culture, discourse, and everyday life can, and indeed should, be wedded to a class-oriented analysis of the sources, operation, and mechanisms of social power and social process. This is so not only because power, change, and inequality are central aspects of social life that ought not be missed by any serious analyst of human affairs (that is, unless he or she accepts political irrelevance), but more importantly because class-oriented analysis can reveal crucial ambiguities, contradictions, divisions, limits, obstacles, and dynamics of culture that cannot be uncovered in other ways. In short, by consciously elaborating an approach based on a materialist idea of class with the intention to study social power and social process, I claim

a more penetrating methodology for explaining and understanding culture. (Kalb 1997: 2)

Like Muldrew, Kalb grounds his analysis in extensive study of personal documents and firm records. Studying the recent past, however, he has the additional advantages of newspaper coverage and his own extensive life history interviews with survivors of the processes he is documenting. To Muldrew's anthropological sensibility Kalb adds anthropological observation of people and places.

Kalb's analysis is the more challenging because it incorporates some coercion and pays considerable attention to culture, but resolutely rejects both functional and competitive accounts of inequality. Kalb centers his explanation on continuously negotiated social relations. His investigation thereby provides a promising model for further anthropological work.

Elsewhere in anthropology, archaeologists have often adopted implicitly relational explanations of inequality. Timothy Earle's synthesis of a long line of investigation concerning the emergence of chiefs, for example, explicitly bases its explanations of emergent political inequality on access of power-accumulating persons to four different sources: military might, ideology, the economy, or other sorts of social relations such as kinship. All four identify the introduction of certain types of incentives into interpersonal ties. Military might introduces coercion into relations with others; ideology introduces belief; economic activity introduces material rewards; while kinship and similar ties, in Earle's view, provide only weak bases for political inequality, apparently because solidarity, mutual knowledge, and collective pressure inhibit differentiation (Earle 1997: 4–9).

Earle then follows this reasoning through analyses of Denmark during the Neolithic and Bronze Ages, the high Peruvian Andes from A.D. 500 to 1534, and the Hawaiian Islands from 800 to 1824. He ultimately gives pride of place to economic networks:

> The strategic uses of each power source depend on historical circumstances and immediate political objectives. The selection of one strategy over alternatives involves comparing the effectiveness and costs of implementation and the length of time that each must be sustained. In the cases considered, *the primary determinant appears to have been the nature of the developing political economy.* The operationalization of one power strategy versus another rested on the ability to intensify and control aspects of the political economy and to use the mobilized surplus to develop central power sources. (Earle 1997: 193–94; italics in original; for related views, see Midlarsky 1999)

Political economy, in Earle's analysis, refers to relations of power involving productive resources. In prehistoric Denmark, for example, chiefs built their power initially by wresting surpluses from local herding economies, but fortified it by means of an ideology identifying superior lineages materialized in conspicuous burial mounds and ceremonial objects acquired through elite trade in prestige goods. While not self-consciously relational, Earle's explanation of increasing political inequality—in the form of emerging chiefdoms—clearly depends on the dynamics of asymmetrical social ties.

I am claiming, then, that well-executed relational accounts of inequality offer an explanatory purchase greater than that of cultural, functional, coercive, or competitive accounts. What might we recognize as a valid explanation of inequality? Let us leave aside the frequent claim that no explanation of social processes is actually possible, because social life is inherently chaotic, because human agency always baffles determinism, or because linguistic, cultural, and/or phenomenological barriers block any effort to identify causes of human behavior.

As we saw in chapter 3, those portions of social science and history that deliberately seek explanations of social phenomena generally choose among three styles of explanation (Bunge 1997, 1998: Elster 1989; Hedström and Swedberg 1998: Little 1991, 1998; Pickel 2004a, 2004b). The first expects social life to exhibit empirical regularities that at their highest level take the form of laws; explanation then consists of subsuming particular cases under broadly validated empirical generalizations or even universal laws. The second accounts for particular features of social life by specifying their connections with putative larger entities: societies, cultures, mentalities, capitalist systems, and the like. Explanation then consists of locating elements within systems. The third regards social units as self-directing, whether driven by emotions, motives, interests, rational choices, genes, or something else. Explanation then consists of reconstructing the state of the social unit—for example, an individual's beliefs at a given point in time and space—and plausibly relating its actions to that state.

A fourth view, however, deserves attention. It claims that explanation consists of identifying in particular social phenomena reliable causal mechanisms and processes of general scope. Causal mechanisms are events that alter relations among some set of elements. Processes are frequent (but not universal) combinations and sequences of causal mechanisms. Social mechanisms are sometimes cognitive, involving changes in perception, consciousness, or intention. They are sometimes relational, involving shifts in connections among social units. They are also sometimes environmental, involving alterations in the surroundings of social units. Explanation then consists of locating robust cognitive, relational, and environmental mechanisms within observed episodes.

In practice, no explanation in this mode can ever be complete. But, I claim, it can be far more adequate than subsuming whole episodes under empirical generalizations, searching for locations of units within larger systems, or reconstructing the social unit's state before and during the initiation of some action. We have, in fact, seen Craig Muldrew, Don Kalb, and Timothy Earle stressing relational mechanisms as they explained significant concrete changes of inequality. Without having signed on to the full explanatory program I am recommending here, they generally exemplify the fourth view of explanation.

Leaving Muldrew, Kalb, and Earle aside, let me sketch an approach to explaining inequality that includes environmental and cognitive mechanisms, but centers on relational mechanisms. My analysis features four relational mechanisms: exploitation, opportunity hoarding, emulation, and adaptation (see Tilly 1998a for an extended exposition). Stated schematically, the argument runs:

- inequality is a relation between persons or sets of persons in which interaction generates greater advantages for one than for another (e.g., a warlord receives tribute from many local chiefs, who receive intermittent protection from exactions by rival warlords)
- inequality results from unequal control over value-producing resources (e.g., in an agrarian economy, some lineages settle on fertile land, others on infertile land)
- paired and unequal categories, consisting of asymmetrical relations across a socially recognized (and usually incomplete) boundary between interpersonal networks, recur in a wide variety of situations (e.g., divisions between mounted warriors and ordinary foot soldiers, between officers and enlisted personnel, between aristocrats and plebeians, form in a surprising range of military organizations)
- the usual effect of such arrangements of paired categories is unequal exclusion of each network from resources controlled by the other (e.g., Sarwa serfs supply skins, meat, and honey to their Tshidi masters, but do not share in the booty of Tshidi hunts)
- an inequality-generating mechanism we may call *exploitation* occurs when persons who control a resource a) enlist the effort of others in production of value by means of that resource but b) exclude the others from the full value added by their effort (e.g., South African gold mines long depended heavily on black labor, but paid black miners barely enough to survive)

- another inequality-generating mechanism we may call *opportunity hoarding* consists of confining use of a value-producing resource to members of an in-group (e.g., through long political struggle American physicians acquired exclusive rights to prescribe a wide variety of drugs, while allocating to American pharmacists exclusive rights to dispense those drugs)
- both exploitation and opportunity hoarding generally incorporate paired and unequal categories at boundaries between greater and lesser beneficiaries of value added by effort committed to controlled resources (e.g., 19th-century English textile mills distinguished sharply between men's work and women's work, with women's work almost universally receiving lesser rewards for similar effort)
- neither exploitation nor opportunity hoarding requires self-conscious efforts to subordinate excluded parties or explicitly formulated beliefs in the inferiority of excluded parties (e.g., recruiting political allies from among former schoolmates inscribes into political divisions whatever divisions by class, gender, ethnicity, or language previously distinguished schools)
- emulation (transfer of existing organizational forms, representations, and practices from one setting to another) generally lowers transaction costs of exploitation and opportunity hoarding when the transferred forms, representations, and practices install paired, unequal categories at the boundaries between greater and lesser benefits (e.g., managers of new hotels adopt essentially the same division of labor by gender, education, ethnicity, and age as old hotels, thus naturalizing the recruitment of cleaners from among poor immigrants and desk clerks from relatively educated immigrants or members of the second generation)
- adaptation (invention of procedures that ease day-to-day interaction, and elaboration of valued social ties around existing divisions) usually stabilizes categorical inequality (e.g., students may well hate their schools, but they entwine friendship, courtship, rivalry, and daily schedules around school routines, thus depending upon and reinforcing whatever distinctions are built into those routines)
- local categorical distinctions are not necessarily unequal, but when they are, their maintenance relies on beliefs and practices that defend and naturalize them (e.g., chemists and their laboratory technicians actually share a great deal of knowledge, but their titles, credentials, powers, privileges, and career trajectories differentiate them)
- local categorical distinctions gain strength and operate at lower cost when matched with widely available paired, unequal categories (e.g., California

lettuce growers long found it advantageous to recruit field hands entirely from among expendable noncitizen Mexican immigrants)

- when many and/or very influential organizations adopt the same categorical distinctions, those distinctions become more pervasive and decisive in social life outside those organizations (e.g., on and around army bases, the military rank system marks housing, entertainment facilities, and public sociability for members of military households as well as for soldiers themselves)
- experience within categorically differentiated settings gives participants systematically different and unequal preparation for performance in new settings (e.g., teachers who treat their pupils differently according to race, gender, and ethnicity predispose those pupils toward different relations with authorities elsewhere and later)
- most of what observers ordinarily interpret as inequality-creating individual differences are actually consequences of categorical organization (e.g., in Singapore native speakers of English, Chinese, and Malay experience such different environments from birth that few of them ever cross boundaries among the schools and careers that separate the three categories)
- for these reasons, inequalities by race, gender, ethnicity, class, age, citizenship, educational level, and other apparently contradictory principles of differentiation form through similar social processes and are to an important degree organizationally interchangeable (e.g., religious, ethnic, linguistic, and racial nationalisms take remarkably similar forms and generate remarkably similar justifications wherever they occur)
- mistaken beliefs about categorical differences play little part in the generation of inequality, indeed tend to emerge after the fact as justifications of inequality and to change as a consequence of shifts in the forms of exploitation or opportunity hoarding as well as in the parties involved (e.g., where populations have long coexisted and frequently intermarried, it takes substantial organizational effort to align people against each other across such boundaries as Hutu-Tutsi or Serb-Croat, but that organizational effort usually generates or fortifies hostile beliefs)
- changing unwarranted beliefs about categorical differences has little impact on degrees and directions of inequality, while organizational change altering exploitation and/or opportunity hoarding has a large impact (e.g., within factories whose departments recruit workers from different migrant streams, stories about the capacities and propensities of different groups of immigrants for various kinds of work take shape rapidly, then fortify the division of labor)

This account of inequality incorporates some elements of conventional cultural, coercive, and competitive accounts. It also takes a weakly functional line—not strongly functional because it does not trace inequality to the service it renders for society at large, but weakly functional because it asserts that viable relations of exploitation and opportunity hoarding generate consequences that in turn sustain those relations. Nevertheless, its principal causes and effects occur within dynamic social relations. It is a strongly relational account.

Here is the sort of causal story this account of inequality implies. Broad similarities exist between inequality-generating processes and conversation: parties interact repeatedly, transferring resources in both directions, bargaining out provisional agreements and contingently shared definitions of what they are doing (see Tilly 1998b). That interaction responds in part to available scripts, but interaction modifies the scripts themselves and only works at all because participants improvise incessantly. Nevertheless, available scripts crucially include paired, unequal categories. Controllers of valuable resources who are pursuing exploitation or opportunity hoarding commonly invent or borrow categorical pairs, installing them at dividing lines between greater and lesser beneficiaries from products of those resources.

In this broad sense, inequality by gender, race, ethnicity, class, religion, citizenship, lineage, and many other categorical principles follows common causal patterns. Explanation of inequality and its changes must therefore concentrate on identifying combinations and sequences of causal mechanisms—notably exploitation, opportunity hoarding, emulation, and adaptation—within episodes of social interaction.

My own concrete studies of inequality (e.g., Tilly 1982, 1984, 1998c) have applied this sort of reasoning chiefly to modern European historical experience and contemporary North America. As the analyses of Muldrew, Wolf, and Earle demonstrate, however, similar mechanisms and processes arise far outside the contemporary West. Every anthropologist who is trying to make sense of changing inequality in postsocialist or postcolonial polities has an opportunity to investigate relational processes of the Muldrew variety. Most likely, exploitation, opportunity hoarding, emulation, and adaptation are producing significant shares of the changes such anthropologists are observing. As compared with more familiar cultural, functional, coercive, and competitive models of inequality, relational models deserve anthropological attention.

Chapter 7

Changing Forms of Inequality

T HESE DAYS ANYONE WHO TRIES TO EXPLAIN, CRITICIZE, OR INFLUENCE major social inequalities in capitalist countries is likely to rely on the same basic model of how inequality comes about. The model features sorting of unequally endowed individuals into unequal positions, one by one. In its simplest versions, as the previous chapter explained, it contains just four elements: a set of *positions*—jobs, public offices, dwellings, prestige categories, and so on; a set of *unequal rewards* attached to those positions; a *sorting mechanism* that channels people to different positions; and *individuals* who vary in characteristics the sorting mechanism detects.

The model calls up a vivid scenario: individuals arrive at the scanner, undergo evaluation, get shunted to an appropriate position, then collect that position's rewards. In more elaborate versions of the scenario, these elements interact; for example, the number and characteristics of persons who present themselves for sorting (the "labor supply" in some versions) affect the distribution and character of positions ("jobs" in those same versions).

Some kinds of inequality do result from such sorting systems. Competitors for positions on football teams, ballet corps, and parliamentary seats undergo scanning by sorting mechanisms—tryouts, auditions, and elections—in which only candidates with certain characteristics end up in coveted positions. Critics then typically declare that the screening is unfair, inefficient, or destructive. Defenders typically reply that a) possible candidates differ greatly in ability, b) the ability of people who occupy high-reward positions strongly affects the relevant organization's overall performance, hence c) the screening produces a superior outcome to its likely alternatives, such as patronage, quotas by social category, assignment by seniority, or random selection.

Proposals to alter such unequal systems understandably concern changes in one or more of the four elements: revamp positions so that opportunities available to the candidates change in some desirable direction; equalize rewards to occupants of comparably worthy positions; fix the sorting mechanism; transform the preparation of possible candidates for selection. Critics of gender inequality in employment have, for example, made all four kinds of proposals: recast jobs so that they give masculine bodies no advantage; establish comparable worth, hence similar rewards, for otherwise similar but predominantly male and predominantly female jobs; monitor hiring so that it is gender blind; give women adequate training so they are well prepared to fill previously all-male jobs (see, e.g., England 1992; Reskin, McBrier, and Kmec 1999).

Sorting systems do not evolve naturally. Like competitive markets and athletic leagues, they rest on extensive social structure, and easily deviate from their ideal forms when participants collude or the underlying institutional structure changes. Competitive electoral systems, for example, depend on extensive institutional underpinnings: widespread schooling; easy travel to polling places; relatively free communications media; barriers to flagrant patronage, coercion, and vote buying. During the second half of the 20th century, a majority of the world's independent countries maintained or installed competitive elections of some sort. Many of them, however, moved from democratic to undemocratic rule despite continuing to stage elections; Argentina, Bolivia, Brazil, Chile, Congo, Ecuador, Ghana, Greece, Grenada, Guatemala, Honduras, Indonesia, Myanmar, Nigeria, Pakistan, Panama, Peru, the Philippines, Sierra Leone, South Korea, Sri Lanka, Sudan, Suriname, Thailand, Turkey, Uganda, and Uruguay all passed through at least one shift from democracy to nondemocracy between 1950 and 1990 (Przeworski, Alvarez, Cheibub, and Limongi 2000: 59–69).

In those many reversions from democratic to undemocratic regimes, incoming oligarchs typically left the apparatus of competitive elections in place, but subverted elections' organizational infrastructure by manipulating media, harassing dissidents, restricting freedom of assembly, and feeding governmental resources to favored candidates. With those changes of institutional underpinnings, previously democratic sorting mechanisms produce undemocratic outcomes. Even well-developed and familiar sorting systems, in short, depend on extensive, supportive social conditions.

Most inequality-generating processes do not, in any case, conform to the sorting model. Even where competitive sorting occurs, individual differences in sorted attributes result from organized social processes that do not themselves conform to the sorting model. In what social surroundings people grow up, for example, deeply and collectively affects their adult characteristics. Resulting differences do not vary continuously, but bunch categorically—by gender, nationality, ethnicity, race, religion, and so on. Closely observed, furthermore, assignment of persons to positions commonly does not result from individual-by-individual scrutiny of all possible candidates but from categorical assignments and mutual recruitment within categories. Indeed, organizations often sustain inequality by building categories directly into their structures: women's jobs, religious ghettos, property qualifications for office, ethnic or linguistic criteria for membership in associations.

Categories matter. To the extent that routine social life endows them with readily available names, markers, intergroup practices, and internal connections, categories facilitate unequal treatment by both members and outsiders. To incorporate an existing category into an organization also incorporates the shared understandings, practices, and interpersonal relations attached to that category. Categories thus transfer shared understandings, practices, and interpersonal relations from setting to setting, making old routines easy to reproduce in new settings.

Categories consist of negotiated collective boundaries within interpersonal networks. Let us consider a "cluster" of persons to consist of individuals who are more closely connected with each other than with others around them. To the extent that all persons or clusters of persons adjacent to a boundary on one side apply names, practices, and understandings that differentiate them from all persons or clusters of persons on the immediate other side of the same boundary, a pair of categories—us and them—exists. Thus mutually acquainted high school students identify each other collectively as grinds and jocks, without ever making complete rosters of all the school's grinds and jocks. So long as the we-they boundary operates locally, such categories easily accommodate heterogeneity in actual attributes (gender, skin color, academic performance, athletic skill, and more) of category members.

At the limit, paired categories need not be mutual; police may, for example, create a category of suspects whose members are unconnected and unaware of being suspects. The FBI's domestic antisubversive program of the 1960s and thereafter created whole categories of suspects, most of whom did not know they had fallen under surveillance (Davenport 2002). The categories that matter most for durable inequality, however, involve both mutual awareness and connectedness: we know who they are, they know who we are, on each side of that line people interact with each other, and across the line we interact with them—but differently.

Categories emerge and change as a result of four processes: encounter, imposition, negotiation, and transfer:

- When previously unconnected clusters of persons *encounter* each other, members of each cluster react to the encounter by creating names, practices, and understandings that mark the points of contact between them. When connected new populations move into old neighborhoods, newcomers and old settlers commonly label each other even if they did not previously have categories for the larger populations to which the two clusters belong.
- Sometimes powerful individuals or clusters *impose* categorical definitions that did not previously apply to others. In January 2002, American authorities created a whole new category—"unlawful combatant"—to contain the captives they transported from Afghanistan to makeshift prisons in Guantánamo, Cuba. The American government specifically denied that the captives qualified as prisoners of war (that is, as members of a different available category entailing different rights and obligations) under the Geneva Convention (BBC 2002).
- More frequently, sets of interacting persons or clusters *negotiate* boundaries having distinctive names, practices, and understandings. American street gangs often assume distinctive names, but also work out relations with different segments of the surrounding population, including members of nearby gangs (Schneider 1999).
- Most often, people *transfer* boundaries, names, practices, and understandings from other settings to the one at hand. During the 1990s, when New York's Korean merchants set up a new delicatessen, they regularly and knowingly hired Mexican immigrants to clean up and tend the flowers, thus establishing a clear distinction between those who ran cash registers and those who worked for the cash handlers. Once the unequal model stood visibly in place, new storekeepers frequently adopted it. The recently arrived Mexican immigrant by the flowers on the sidewalk became a standard Manhattan neighborhood scene.

Categories always produce difference, but they do not necessarily produce inequality. Adjacent peasant communities, for example, always erect boundaries involving names, practices, and understandings. Those boundaries set significant limits to cultivation, grazing, foraging, cooperation, and sometimes sexual relations, but adjacent villages frequently maintain rough equality with each other. Categories produce durable inequality, however, when repeated transactions across the boundary both a) regularly yield net advantages to those on one side and b) reproduce the boundary.

How can that happen? Here is the crucial scenario: members of a clique on one side of a categorical boundary seize control of a value-producing resource of limited availability and allocate a large share of the value produced to themselves, devoting some of the value to reproducing the boundary. The scenario has two variants: exploitation and opportunity hoarding. In *exploitation,* the clique enlists value-producing effort from people on the opposite side of the boundary, but allocates to those others less than the value added by their effort. For example, mine owners hire hewers to send coal up from underground but by no means pay those hewers the full value their effort adds to the mine's production. They use some of the return to create clothing styles, offices, signs, symbols, and guards that reinforce the boundary between management and workers. (Hence many a struggle among hewers, managers, and surface workers.)

In *opportunity hoarding,* the clique excludes people on the opposite side of the boundary from use of the value-producing resource, captures the returns, and devotes some of the returns to reproducing the boundary. For instance, people in the diamond trade organize ethnically recruited circuits for acquisition, cutting, polishing, distribution, and sale of different types of gems, excluding others from their sections of the trade. Some of the monopoly's return goes into reinforcing ethnic ties, thus making new recruits to the trade available.

Two additional mechanisms play significant parts in the maintenance of exploitation and opportunity hoarding: emulation and adaptation. Emulation consists of transferring boundaries, names, practices, understandings, and social ties—in short, categories—from other settings. People setting up a new high-tech firm introduce a division of labor (including distinctions by gender, ethnicity, and age) greatly resembling those of other firms in the industry, and even recruit blocks of people from those other firms to fill similar positions. Compared to inventing and installing new names, practice, understandings, and social ties, emulation greatly reduces the start-up cost of new, internally unequal organizations.

Adaptation consists of all parties' establishment of rewarding social routines that depend on the maintenance of existing categories and/or relations across the categorical boundary. Military conscripts who would rather be elsewhere nevertheless organize rackets, communication systems, friendships, and routines for dealing with officers. Those routines engage them and organize their lives from day to day. Adaptation gives even those who suffer from exploitation and opportunity hoarding short-term incentives for collaboration with existing social arrangements.

Over the long run of human history, a wide variety of value-producing resources have sometimes served as bases of categorical inequality generation. Relevant resources are in short supply, subject to sequestration, widely valued, and capable of producing further value in combination with other resources and/or coordinated effort. At times, for example, control of water, precious gems, exotic spices, salt, and means of transportation have all served exploitation or opportunity hoarding. On the whole, however, the most extensive historical systems of inequality have depended on control of one or more of these value-producing resources:

- coercive means, including weapons, jails, and organized specialists in violence
- labor, especially skilled and/or effectively coordinated labor
- animals, especially domesticated food- and/or work-producing animals
- land, including natural resources located in and upon it
- commitment-maintaining institutions such as religious sects, kinship systems, and trade diasporas
- machines, especially machines that convert raw materials; produce goods or services; and transport persons, goods, services, or information
- financial capital—transferable and fungible means of acquiring property rights
- information, especially information that facilitates profitable, safe, or coordinated action
- media that disseminate such information
- scientific-technical knowledge, especially knowledge that facilitates intervention—for good or evil—in human well-being

All of these resources lend themselves to production of benefits for some recipients by means of coordinated effort. When they are in short supply and relatively easy to circumscribe, they lend themselves to exploitation and opportunity hoarding, hence to the generation of inequality.

Until recent centuries, the early items on the list—coercive means, labor, animals, land, and commitment-maintaining institutions—predominated in the world's production of categorical inequality. Even today, they probably account for the bulk of the world's inequality at the local and regional scales. Between the 18th century and the recent past, however, control over machines gained ever-increasing prominence as a base of exploitation and opportunity hoarding. During the last half century, furthermore, differences built on financial capital, information, media, and scientific-technical knowledge have figured increasingly in the production of inequality, especially at the international level.

Of course, these value-producing resources operate in combination. Once settled agriculture began to prevail in Eurasia 5,000 or so years ago, those who controlled land and animals on a large scale usually also controlled coercive means and acted to contain, to displace, or to co-opt those who deployed coercive means locally. In recent decades, the combination of financial capital and scientific-technical knowledge has gained unparalleled potency in the production of inequality between those who control the combination and those who do not.

To explain and predict the future of categorical inequality across the world, it follows that we must specify changes in a) cliques that control value-producing resources, b) prevailing combinations of resources, c) categories incorporated into relations of exploitation and opportunity hoarding, d) extent of conjunction between exploitation and opportunity hoarding, e) relative prominence of exploitation and opportunity hoarding, f) causes of a–e. Proper specification of changes in all these items will produce explanations and predictions of change in the worldwide distribution of well-being. Over the 21st century, for example, the organization of exploitation and opportunity hoarding in the production, distribution, and consumption of health care will fundamentally affect worldwide differentials in sickness and life expectancy.

In conjunction with old standbys coercion, land, and labor, during the 21st century control of financial capital and scientific-technical knowledge will also shape the fate of democracy. Democracy depends on barriers against the direct entry of unequal categories into public politics. Any substantial weakening of those barriers and any large increase in categorical inequality itself both threaten democracy. They do so by providing beneficiaries of inequality with incentives and means to subvert or opt out of equal rights, equal obligations, equal consultation, and equal protection. A clear understanding of how inequality works provides a first step toward mitigating its harmful effects.

Chapter 8

Unequal Knowledge

I~N ONE OF HIS RICH, PROFOUND STORIES, JORGE LUIS BORGES DESCRIBED~ the infinite library of Babel, which contained every text ever written in any of the world's languages, indeed every sequence of words and thoughts a human mind could possibly conceive. Borges recorded a myth about the Man of the Book, an unknown librarian who had found the book that was "the perfect compendium *of all the rest*" and who thereby had acquired the powers of a god (Borges 1962: 85).

Borges balanced that glimpse of a knowledge monopoly against another vital vision: that of a library, and therefore a world of infinite knowledge, available to everyone. "When it was proclaimed," wrote Borges,

> that the Library comprised all books, the first impression was one of extravagant joy. All men felt themselves lords of a secret, intact treasure. There was no personal or universal problem whose eloquent solution did not exist—in some hexagon. The universe was justified, the universe suddenly expanded to the limitless dimensions of hope. At that time there was much talk of the Vindications: books of apology and prophecy, which vindicated for all time the actions of every man in the world and established a store of prodigious arcana for the future. (Borges 1962: 83)

Borges spoke of Babel's Library, but he spoke with the wisdom acquired as longtime director of Argentina's national library. In Borges's fable, we glimpse the mingling of prediction with vindication—with the hoped-for discovery that past and present have meaning, that we have discerned the meaning, that there was some good reason for the way we behaved. We also glimpse the scholar's wish to find that niche within the library, that hexagon, containing precisely the formula to link past, present, and future. Still we must remember Borges's warning: the library is endless, whereas we are finite. I promise you no more than a guided tour of one section within a vast palace of uncertainties concerning the future of social inequality at a world scale.

Inspired by Borges's speculations, I want to raise four questions that inevitably concern the future of higher education as well as relations among higher education, governments, nongovernmental institutions, and profit-seeking firms. The questions all pivot on knowledge whose consequences affect human well-being: control over production of that knowledge, control over its distribution, and access to that knowledge by people whose well-being it will or could affect. Here are the questions:

1. To what extent and how does unequal access to knowledge generate or sustain larger inequalities in human well-being and suffering?
2. To what extent and how does unequal *control* over the production and distribution of knowledge generate or sustain those inequalities?
3. What is the future likely to bring in regard to unequal production, distribution, and access, including their consequences for human well-being and suffering?
4. What issues for national and international public policy do the answers to the first three questions raise?

I will certainly not provide comprehensive, persuasive answers to the four questions, but at least I will try to show how and why they matter. To shift perspective just a bit, I will start the tour from Canada instead of my customary United States.

Let us concentrate on categorical inequality: those forms of unequal advantage in which whole sets of people on one side of a boundary or the other fare differently. Categorical inequalities include those that divide women from men, Francophones from Anglophones, members of different religious faiths from each other, citizens of different states, and so on. Although most of the same principles apply to individual differences, in our world categorical differences in well-being and suffering overshadow individual variation within categories. Thus most citizens of Canada live much more comfortable lives than do all but the most fortunate citizens of Sierra Leone, Myanmar, or Guatemala.

Categories always produce difference, but they do not necessarily produce inequality. Adjacent peasant communities, for example, always erect boundaries involving names, practices, and understandings. Those boundaries set significant limits to cultivation, grazing, foraging, cooperation, and sometimes sexual relations, but adjacent villages frequently maintain rough equality with each other. Categories produce durable inequality, however, when repeated transactions across the boundary both a) regularly yield net advantages to those on one side and b) reproduce the boundary.

How can that happen? Here is the crucial scenario: members of a clique on one side of a categorical boundary seize control of a value-producing resource of limited availability and allocate a large share of the value produced to themselves, devoting some of the value to reproducing the boundary (Tilly 1998c). Over the long run of human history, a wide variety of resources have sometimes served as bases for generation of categorical inequality. Relevant resources are in short supply, subject to sequestration, widely valued, and capable of producing further value in combination with other resources and/or coordinated effort. At times, for example, control of water, precious gems, exotic spices, salt, and means of transportation have all served the production of inequality.

On the whole, however, the most extensive historical systems of inequality have depended on control of one or more of the resources listed in the previous chapter: coercive means, including weapons, jails, and organized specialists in violence; labor, especially skilled and/or effectively coordinated labor; animals, especially domesticated food- and/or work-producing animals; land, including natural resources located in and upon it; commitment-maintaining institutions such as religious sects, kinship systems, and trade diasporas; machines, especially machines that convert raw materials, produce goods or services, and transport persons, goods, services, or information; financial capital—transferable and fungible means of acquiring property rights; information, especially information that facilitates profitable, safe, or coordinated action; scientific-technical knowledge, especially knowledge that facilitates intervention—for good or evil—in human well-being; media that disseminate information and scientific-technical knowledge. All of these resources lend themselves to production of benefits for some recipients by means of coordinated effort. When they are in short supply and relatively easy to circumscribe, they lend themselves to hoarding, hence to the generation of inequality.

Until recent centuries, the early items on the list—coercive means, labor, animals, land, and commitment-maintaining institutions—predominated in the world's production of categorical inequality. Even today, they probably account for the bulk of the world's inequality at the local and regional scales. Between the 18th century and the recent past, however, control over machines gained ever-increasing prominence as a base of inequality.

Still, four newly prominent bundles of value-producing resources show signs of displacing control over machines from its world dominance of the last few centuries. The first is financial capital—by no means a new element in the world economy, but one whose volume and volatility now lend enormous power to those who control it. Small, well-connected networks of financiers can batter whole national economies by shifting their investments from site to site.

The second is information—as old as the world, but newly prominent with the spectacular expansion of electronic communication. Despite the Internet's promiscuity, information is even easier to hoard than money, machines, and land; all it takes is dedicated circuits and secure memories. Administrative and commercial records, personal files, results of research, and much more reside in databases whose scale dwarfs anything imaginable only a few decades ago.

The third, science, is looming larger by the day. In the form of pharmaceutical development, genetic engineering, biomechanical computing, microelectronics, medical diagnostics, telecommunication, geophysical mapping, and astrophysical exploration, scientific innovation produces possibilities of control, hence of inequality, exceeding all its predecessors.

The fourth type of value-producing resource, media for storage and transmission of capital, information, and scientific-technical knowledge, wields a partly independent influence on inequality. The huge amounts of capital recently invested in publishing, mass media, and electronic communication suggest as much.

Financial capital, information, scientific-technical expertise, and media all currently remain under control of small networks of persons, compared to the world population as a whole. Think about the ranking of the world's major hubs of technological innovation that *Wired* magazine published in 2000. The ranking gave highest place to Silicon Valley, USA. Next in line came Boston, Stockholm, Israel as a whole, Raleigh-Durham-Chapel Hill, London, Helsinki, Austin, San Francisco, Taipei, Bangalore, New York, Albuquerque, and in fourteenth place Montréal, just before Seattle (UNDP 2001: 45). Most readers of this book live in those high-tech precincts, but the great bulk of the world's population does not. Relative to the whole globe, financial capital, information, scientific-technical expertise, and media that store or disseminate all of them huddle together in a small number of privileged enclaves.

Each has expanded with extensive systems of hoarding, which yield increasing advantages to those who live within those systems. Their future impact on inequality will still depend on two other factors: their integration with categorical differences, and their relation to concentrated means of coercion. Although all three have incorporated existing distinctions by gender, age, race, ethnicity, and religion to some degree, so far the largest gap fostered by these emerging bases of inequality separates people with qualifying technical educations from everyone else: MBAs, JDs, computer science degrees, PhDs, and the like. Of course, each arena has its heroic tales of people who succeeded without certification: college dropouts who made billions as investors or Internet entrepreneurs, and so on. Not since the Chinese mandarinate, nevertheless, have specially educated people played so prominent a part in world affairs, and received rewards so definitively separating them from their neighbors. Educators will have to balance between two long-cherished dreams: on one side, forming an intellectual meritocracy that recruits regardless of gender, race, ethnicity, nationality, or religion; on the other, spreading the benefits of knowledge equally through whole populations.

The second unknown is connection between these competing bases of inequality and organized concentrations of coercion. Through most of human history coercive means remained relatively fragmented, dispersed among communities, warlords, thugs, bandits, pirates, mercenaries, feudal retainers, religious organizations, and private armies despite the occasional formation of an empire. Over the last few centuries, humanity performed the surprising feat of placing its major concentrations of coercive means under the control of national governments. The cost was increasingly bloody international warfare. But it brought the benefit of reduction in domestic mayhem—more so, I might add, in other Western countries than in my own United States.

In our own time, that trend seems to be reversing. Civil war, guerrilla war, genocide, politicide, gunrunning, and even mercenary activity have been rising irregularly since World War II (Creveld 1991; Gurr 1993, 2000; Kaldor 1999; Tilly 2003). Despite often being incited by outside states or by paramilitary shadows of existing states, on the whole these homicidal activities are escaping the system of state control over concentrated coercion that grew up between 1750 and 1950 or so. These changes, too, result in part from the unequal distribution of scientific-technical knowledge, broadly defined: the rich world floods the poorer parts of the world with precision-built weapons, but not with the institutions to control them. To the degree that international flows of drugs, arms, oil, gas, military expertise, and precious stones come under the influence of those who already dominate financial capital, information banks, scientific-technical knowledge, and media for their storage or transmission, whole new forms of inequality could form, with disastrous consequences for humanity as a whole.

During the last half century, then, differences built on financial capital, information, scientific-technical knowledge, and media have figured increasingly in the production of inequality, especially at the international level. During the next century, they will almost certainly become even more prominent as bases of categorical inequality both locally and internationally. In recent decades, the combination of financial capital and scientific-technical knowledge has gained unparalleled potency in the production of inequality between those who control the combination and those who do not. In a plea to scientists themselves for action against scientific-technical inequality, United Nations Secretary-General Kofi Annan pointed out that:

> Ninety-five percent of the new science in the world is created in the countries comprising only one-fifth of the world's population. And much of that science—in the realm of health, for example—neglects the problems that afflict most of the world's people.
>
> This unbalanced distribution of scientific activity generates serious problems not only for the scientific community in the developing countries, but for development itself. It accelerates the disparity between advanced and developing countries, creating social and economic difficulties at both national and international levels. The idea of two worlds of science is anathema to the scientific spirit. It will require the commitment of scientists and scientific institutions throughout the world to change that portrait to bring the benefits of science to all. (Annan 2003: 1,485)

We should obviously broaden any survey of unequal scientific-technical knowledge into two closely related bases of inequality: first, information stores and, second, media that distribute both general information and scientific-technical knowledge. We should also recognize that some portions of knowledge produced outside the natural and applied sciences qualify as scientific or technical in the sense that they result from systematic empirical inquiry, accumulate and improve through a process of internal testing and critique, form coherent bodies of falsifiable theory, generate techniques for effective intervention in the world, and yield relatively reliable expectations concerning the likely consequences of such interventions. Archaeology, paleontology, demography, agriculture, clinical medicine, epidemiology, and linguistics, for example, all contain patches of knowledge that qualify as scientific-technical in this sense.

Unequal access to knowledge and unequal control over its production or distribution matter in the 21st-century world not only because of knowledge's intrinsic value but also because its unequal distribution causes other sorts of inequality. Knowledge gives political, financial, and existential advantages to its holders. Returns from knowledge allow its holders to reproduce the institutions and relations that sustain their advantages. In such areas as public health, food supply, environmental quality, and lethal combat, applications of knowledge strongly affect who survives and who lives comfortably.

Knowledge-based inequality prevails in the contemporary world. Consider the obvious case of health care (Deaton 2003). Health care compounds natural science with other forms of knowledge, since it entails training and assignment of health care professionals, distribution systems for drugs and other health-related materials, not to mention extensive knowledge on the part of health care recipients as well as their families or friends. Take an elementary statistic. The United Nations Development Program reports that recently Canada had 229 physicians per 100,000 people, not so high as Norway (413) or Belgium (395), but still one of the world's highest proportions. The proportion fell to less than a twentieth of the Canadian level—11 or fewer physicians per 100,000 thousand people—in Ghana, Lesotho, Comoros, Cameroon, Togo, Nepal, Haiti, Madagascar, Sudan, Tanzania, Congo-Kinshasa, Zambia, Ivory Coast, Senegal, Angola, Benin, Eritrea, and Gambia (UNDP 2001: 158–61).

Although many Canadians can no doubt tell tales of ills they suffered as a result of faulty medical treatment, over the world as a whole the absence of physicians correlates very strongly with high infant mortality, little access to essential drugs, low immunization rates for children, high frequencies of malnutrition, and many deaths from HIV/AIDS. It also correlates with other knowledge-related deficits, such as illiteracy, low school enrollments, and small national investments in scientific research. Of course, national poverty levels help explain the absence of adequate health care, but that is the point: in the contemporary world, access to the knowledge and care embedded in science-based medicine depends on income and wealth, not on need or just deserts.

We could make a similar case for food supply and distribution. Biotechnology and agronomy thrive not in the hungry countries, but in the well-fed ones. They depend heavily on scientific-technical research. Adequate food distribution, in any case, requires not only strong agricultural technology but also extensive organizational effort and protection of potential consumers from human predators. Some relatively poor countries are coping. As compared with Canada's 1999 GDP per capita of US$26,251 in purchasing-power equivalents, China had only about a seventh of that per capita income: $3,617. Yet, on that low income, China managed to have only about 10 percent of its children less than five years old significantly underweight. At similar income levels, 24 percent of Guatemala's youngsters, 28 percent of the Philippines' youngsters, and a full 34 percent of Sri Lanka's youngsters fell below desirable weight levels for their ages (UNDP 2001: 141–51). In the three unhappy countries, inadequate knowledge, defective infrastructure, and civil war interacted to inhibit food supply and distribution.

In China, for all the top-down tyranny we can rightly deplore, since the disastrous famines of the early Communist regime careful crop management based on scientific research but implemented through social technology has produced a remarkable food supply for the country, which has a quarter of the world's population. Between the 1960s and the late 1990s, for example, China went from a relatively minor site of potato production to becoming the world's largest producer of potatoes, turning out almost 50 million metric tons for a sixth of the global potato supply (Lang 2001: 32). Benefiting from scientific agronomy, China more or less deliberately turned from rice toward high-efficiency potatoes.

Or consider mass communications. At the start of the 21st century about 500 million people in the world had Internet access, as compared with fewer than 20 million as recently as 1995 (UNDP 2001: 32). The number is growing fast. Yet the same number means that something like 93 percent of the world's population *lacked* Internet access. At least for the moment, no one who lacks computer knowledge or access can log on to the powerful communication network. With the cheapest Pentium III computers selling for at least US$500, the five-sixths of the world's population living in countries boasting per capita incomes of $4,000 or less per year will wait a very long time for Internet access. Despite the raging success of cellular telephones, the situation does not differ so much for other communications media; in today's Africa, to take the extreme example, newspaper circulation equals 1 percent of the population, fewer than four television sets are operating per 100 people, and only one radio exists for every six people (World Bank 2002: 191).

We could also identify other science- and technology-based interventions in human well-being: some enhance human life and others destroy it, but the benefits and costs distribute with dramatic inequality. High environmental quality, good transportation, high-tech products, and even life-enhancing education concentrate enormously in rich corners of a poor world. Environmental degradation, predatory exploitation of natural resources, lethal combat, military rule, homicide, and polluted water supplies inflict the world's poorer neighborhoods disproportionately. Not all of these, to be sure, result directly and exclusively from the presence or absence of knowledge as such. But all of them spring at least in part from the unequal availability of life-enhancing scientific-technical knowledge, including knowledge of public administration and social processes.

Inhabitants of higher learning's institutions occupy an ambivalent position with respect to unequal control and access. Our institutions specialize in the production, transformation, and diffusion of knowledge. That includes social knowledge of the sort exemplified by censuses and opinion polls, both proud products of social scientific effort. Certainly researchers, professors, students, and even administrators develop an interest in the pursuit and dissemination of knowledge, if only because it justifies their callings and gives them claims to public attention.

On the other side, formidable incentives to practice knowledge hoarding prevail in every academic institution. First comes the understandable preference of specialists to communicate mainly with other specialists within their own communities; physicists, linguists, and economists gain a considerable portion of their satisfaction and self-esteem from communication with other physicists, linguists, and economists. Second, to the extent that a discipline yields results for which a monetary demand exists, producers within that discipline gain, at least in the short run, from channeling dissemination of those results by means of such devices as patents, trademarks, licenses, and closed professional associations; sharp contemporary debates on intellectual property center on how much protection commercially valuable results should receive.

Participants in higher learning also face the problem of reproducing their institutions and, more generally, the conditions that support their chosen work. Every great institution of higher learning ploughs back some of its returns from hoarding knowledge into support of new research. When I taught at the University of Toronto during the 1960s, income from licenses for the insulin whose mechanism Frederick Banting, Charles Best, and their collaborators at the U of T had discovered forty-odd years earlier was still paying for substantial internal research grants. In recent years Columbia University, where I now teach, has been collecting on the order of $160 million per year in revenue from patents and licenses and has been devoting a significant share of that revenue to internal support of research.

Without that sort of outside income, both institutions would have fewer resources for support of new research by their students, faculty, and staff. Yet, of course, the revenue in question means that some persons and organizations that could benefit from the knowledge generated at Toronto and Columbia can't afford to acquire it. The choice becomes even more complicated when outside funds come from organizations—governments, nonprofits, or profit-seeking firms—that have a proprietary interest in the knowledge produced, and therefore are likely both to place restrictions on dissemination of that knowledge and to give greater rewards to institutions or individuals that forward their proprietary interest. We are here, I suppose, to discuss the dilemmas for higher education posed by just such arrangements.

Let me insist: the dilemmas are not chimeras. Each step that universities take to reward and reproduce research capacity in the short run involves some hoarding of knowledge, hence some exclusion of people outside those universities from having control over and benefiting from the accumulation of knowledge. A morally defensible principle might run something like this: research bearing on human welfare should visibly benefit the human populations from which it draws evidence in no more than the medium run, and a significant proportion of the returns that sponsors and researchers gain from the work should flow into application and diffusion of the acquired knowledge to benefit other populations that lack the means of acquiring the knowledge on their own. Even this modest principle would require major changes in the ways that researchers, universities, governments, nonprofit organizations, and profit-seeking firms redistribute knowledge and the means of producing it.

To any such hopeful proposal, cynics and conservatives will raise the objections that Albert Hirschman made famous with the three watchwords perversity, futility, and jeopardy. "According to the perversity thesis," wrote Hirschman,

> any purposive action to improve some feature of the political, social, or economic order only serves to exacerbate the condition one wishes to remedy. The *futility* thesis holds that attempts at social transformation will be unavailing, that they will simply fail to "make a dent." Finally, the *jeopardy* thesis argues that the cost of the proposed change or reform is too high as it endangers some previous, precious accomplishment. (Hirschman 1991: 7)

Perversity says that any attempt to generalize control or access in the domain of scientific-technical knowledge will actually destroy incentives to create new knowledge; drug companies often propose that defense of high prices and restrictive licenses. Another perversity argument warns that the placing of knowledge in malicious or incompetent hands will produce damage rather than benefit; from the late 19th century onward, North America's physicians successfully organized the dispensation of medical care on the basis of that exclusive counter-principle.

Futility, in its turn, declares that most of the world has no capacity to absorb either the knowledge or the potential benefits of high-tech science, hence that we must simply wait for education, democratization, or civilization to do their long-term work before intervening; objections to massive HIV/AIDS prevention have sometimes taken that form. For university people, jeopardy strikes closest to home, for it calls attention both to the high cost of spreading crucial knowledge across the world and the utility of reproducing the persons and institutions that contribute to accumulation of knowledge.

I fear that those who warn of perversity, futility, and jeopardy will carry the day. They have the short-term interests of their own institutions and countries at heart. They appeal to the nationalisms of our day. They point out rightly that we beneficiaries of unequal knowledge have plenty to lose in the short run if massive reorganization occurs in control over the production, diffusion, and application of scientific-technical knowledge. Today's purveyors and beneficiaries of unequal knowledge will not easily sacrifice their advantages. The price, however, will be continued inequality and unnecessary damage to human well-being.

Let me justify these gloomy speculations by reminding you that Borges was a far worse pessimist than I. Toward the end of the fable with which we began, he remarked:

> Perhaps I am deceived by old age and fear, but I suspect that the human species—the unique human species—is on the road to extinction, while the Library will last on forever: illuminated, solitary, infinite, perfectly immovable, filled with precious volumes, useless, incorruptible, secret. (Borges 1962: 87)

There Borges and I part company. In fact, we humans built the library, and we can change it. We can take one step toward a superior future by careful reasoning about processes that generate inequality, wherever and whenever they occur.

Part IV

Boundaries

Chapter 9

Social Boundary Mechanisms

In Buenos Aires, each October Bolivian immigrants of the Charrúa barrio stage the Fiesta of Our Lady of Copacabana, which attracts many native Argentines to its displays of Bolivian dance, crafts, costume, and cuisine. The gala festival gives usually downtrodden *bolivianos* a vital, visually attractive setting in which to assert their distinctiveness, and even their superiority. An announcement of the 1996 fiesta in the local paper included these words:

> We Bolivians are landholders, while you Argentines—especially you porteños—are not landholders, but emigrants who came to occupy a territory. You are all descendants of foreigners; your ethnic group and your ancestors were European. Instead we own our own land, the land called Bolivia, as descendants of Aymaras and Quechuas. It is therefore important that we preserve our identity, since we own a specific territory, since our ancestors tilled that soil and the land is ours. People from Jujuy own their own land because the Incas formerly extended all the way to Tucumán. For these reasons it is important for us to maintain our identity because we are lords of that land, we are lords of all South America, we are the natives, we are not from Europe, we are not immigrants. (Grimson 1999: 71–72)

Once you know that "porteños" means residents of Buenos Aires (a seaport region), that Argentina's Jujuy province abuts the Argentine-Bolivian border, and that the city of Tucumán dominates an Argentine province almost four hundred miles south of the border, you begin to detect an audacious claim of authenticity, difference, and collective rights. Bolivian immigrants to Buenos

Aires vary in the extent to which they stress indigenous origins, Catholic purity, or Bolivian nationality as their distinctive property. But at least on festive occasions they draw a clear boundary between themselves and their Argentine neighbors.

Few people think the Inca Empire will revive and restore indigenous Bolivians to their ancestors' political glory. Yet the claims of Buenos Aires' Bolivian publicists draw on a discourse that elsewhere has figured recurrently in conquest, civil war, ethnic cleansing, international diplomacy, and demands for autonomy: we form a coherent, distinctive people, we were here first, and therefore we have prior rights to the territory. Most such claims fail, but they sometimes prevail, especially when backed by substantial armed force. More surprisingly, many populations that could in principle make such claims do so only intermittently, or never. Furthermore, through much of the year Bolivians who at their fiesta insist on a separate national identity deploy multiple other identities: worker, barrio dweller, woman, customer, even (vis-à-vis nonmigrant relatives in Bolivia) porteño. Neither prevailing identities nor distinctions between categories remain constant. On the contrary, they remain incessantly in play.

One aspect of these familiar circumstances deserves close attention: formation, transformation, activation, and suppression of social boundaries. Together, these alterations present the problem of explaining social boundary change. To be sure, the experience of *porteños bolivianos* involves far more than boundary change; it includes within-boundary transactions such as mutual aid, sociability, and the sending of remittances to relatives in the Andes. It also involves cross-boundary transactions such as the exploitation and denigration suffered by immigrants who are characteristically small in stature, Indian in physiognomy, hesitant in their accented Spanish, and unfamiliar with big-city ways.

We might think of everything about those within-boundary and cross-boundary transactions as peculiar to the recent history of Buenos Aires. Yet the boundary that separates *bolivianos* from *porteños argentinos* displays features readily recognizable across the world. People everywhere organize a significant part of their social interaction around the formation, transformation, activation, and suppression of social boundaries. It happens at the small scale of interpersonal dialogue, at the medium scale of rivalry within organizations, and at the large scale of genocide. Us-them boundaries matter.

Social boundary change sets a number of puzzling questions:

• Why and how do boundaries that at one point matter little or not at all for social life rapidly become salient bases of interaction, so much so that people who live peaceably with difference one month start killing across their boundary the next?

- Why and how does the opposite happen: that seemingly unbridgeable boundaries rapidly become irrelevant, or at least less salient?
- How do divisions between us and them change, such that yesterday's enemies become today's friends, at the same time as other previously less salient sets of people become enemies?
- Why does such a close relation exist between who "we" say we are and which others we identify as "not us"? How does that relation between their identity and ours work?
- How and why do such boundaries come to separate specific social sites from each other while usually remaining irrelevant to relations among a great many other social sites?

I will not try to answer these pressing questions individually but show that a limited number of crucial causal mechanisms appear in adequate answers to all of them. Some of those mechanisms, among other effects, cause boundaries to change. Others consist of boundary change and therefore account for the effects of boundary change.

This chapter provides a preliminary inventory of robust mechanisms a) *precipitating* boundary change, b) *consisting of* boundary change, and thus producing consequences of boundary change. The inventory remains quite preliminary; despite extensive analysis of identities, nationalism, cross-boundary conversation, and related phenomena, no one has systematically catalogued, much less verified, the crucial mechanisms of boundary change.[1] The brief exposition that follows illustrates each candidate mechanism, but by no means provides exhaustive evidence of its uniformity across settings. Nor does it say much about how the mechanisms concatenate and interact.

Let us begin with a definition: what are social boundaries? Social boundaries interrupt, divide, circumscribe, or segregate distributions of population or activity within social fields (Abbott 1995). Such fields certainly include spatial distributions of population or activity, but they also include temporal sequences

---

1. For relevant critiques, syntheses, and symposia as well as exemplary empirical studies, see Ballinger 2003; Boris and Janssens 1999; Brubaker and Cooper 2000; Burguière and Grew 2001; Cerulo 1997; Epstein 1992; Fishman 1999; Friedman 1994; Gal 1989; Jenkins 1994; Joseph 1999; Karakasidou 1995; Kastoryano 2002; Kertzer and Arel 2002; Kogut 1997; Lamont 2001; Landa 1994; Malkki 1995; Mamdani 1996, 2001a; Marx 1998; Monroe, Hankin, and Bukovchik Van Vechten 2000; Niezen 2003; Ron 2003; Sahlins 1989; Sanders 2002; Squatriti 2002; Thorne 1993; Wendt 1994; White 2002; Zelizer 1994, 2005a, 2005b; Zerubavel 1991.

and webs of interpersonal connections. We might therefore define a social boundary minimally as:

> any contiguous zone of contrasting density, rapid transition, or separation between internally connected clusters of population and/or activity.

Thus a thinly populated area between two relatively dense settlements, a regular temporal interruption in some sort of social interaction, or the sparse interpersonal ties between two cliques could all qualify in principle as social boundaries. To emphasize the "social," however, it helps to stipulate some organized human response to the zone in question. Let us concentrate on circumstances in which at least some actors on each side of such a boundary reify it by naming it, attempting to control it, attaching distinctive practices to it, or otherwise creating a shared representation. In this sense, as Lamont and Molnár (2002) argue, a symbolic boundary becomes a necessary component of a social boundary. Thus the definition above narrows to *any contiguous zone of contrasting density, rapid transition, or separation between internally connected clusters of population and/or activity for which human participants create shared representations.*

In the operation of a social boundary, we expect to find:

1. distinctive relations between sites on one side
2. distinctive relations between sites on the other side
3. distinctive relations across the zone between those two
4. on each side, shared representations of the zone itself

Thus the boundary between porteños and bolivianos includes some minimum of relations among porteños, of relations among bolivianos, of relations between porteños and bolivianos, of representations concerning porteño-boliviano differences by porteños, and finally of representations concerning porteño-boliviano differences by bolivianos. For present purposes, the actual contents of the four elements do not matter. It makes no difference to my argument whether relations across the boundary are intense or intermittent, friendly or hostile, formal or informal. What matters is that the relevant social process exhibits all features simultaneously: distinctive relations on each side of a separating zone, distinctive relations across the zone, and shared representations of the zone.

Boundary change consists of formation, transformation, activation, and suppression of such four-part complexes. Boundary change figures importantly in a wide variety of phenomena, including the activation or deactivation of political identities, economic exploitation, categorical discrimination, democratization, and the alterations of uncertainty that promote or inhibit the outbreak of collective violence (McAdam, Tarrow, and Tilly 2001; Tilly 1998a, 2002, 2003). I argue that similar or identical causal mechanisms operate across a very wide range of boundary changes.

Consistent with Mario Bunge's program of mechanistic explanation (Bunge 1997), I also argue that identification of relevant causal mechanisms will produce superior explanations of boundary-involving social phenomena than could any likely invocation of general dispositions in humans or their social structures; of functions performed by boundaries within social systems; or of covering laws in the form "All boundaries _____." This chapter, however, makes no effort to prove that sweeping claim. It suffices here to show that the inventoried mechanisms promise to help explain a wide variety of boundary changes and their consequences.

To avoid confusion concerning the proposed line of explanation, we must distinguish carefully between two clusters of mechanisms: 1) those that precipitate boundary change, and 2) those that constitute boundary change and produce its direct effects. Figure 9-1 schematizes the distinctions and the argument's flow. Mechanisms *precipitating* boundary change singly or in combination include encounter, imposition, borrowing, conversation, and incentive shift. Mechanisms *constituting* boundary change include inscription, erasure, activation, deactivation, site transfer, and relocation. The two classes of mechanisms jointly produce some effects that on careless inspection appear to result from boundary changes alone, for instance, the initiation of ethnic cleansing as a consequence of imposition and activation; even if it occurs more or less simultaneously, the authoritative imposition of a boundary (a precipitant of boundary change) remains causally prior to activation of that boundary (a constituent of that change), which plays a direct causal role in the initiation of ethnic cleansing.

Although the simultaneous generality and unfamiliarity of boundary change as a concept may make the distinction between precipitating and constitutive mechanisms more difficult to grasp, the basic notion is commonplace: in explaining a coup d'état, for example, analysts commonly distinguish between processes that led up to the plotters' attempt to seize power and processes that activated once they actually engaged in the attempt. Again, we easily see the distinction between the long chain of cause-effect links that produced an automobile's brake failure and the responses of driver and vehicle to the failure that produced a fatal crash. Since we are dealing with continuous processes, the

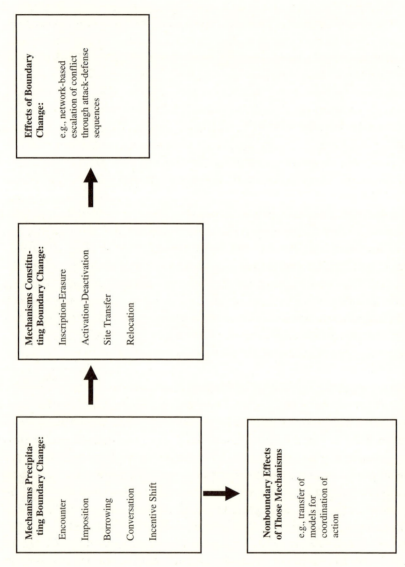

Mechanisms Precipita-
ting Boundary Change:

Encounter

Imposition

Borrowing

Conversation

Incentive Shift

Mechanisms Constitu-
ting Boundary Change:

Inscription-Erasure

Activation-Deactivation

Site Transfer

Relocation

Effects of Boundary
Change:

e.g., network-based
escalation of conflict
through attack-defense
sequences

Nonboundary Effects
of Those Mechanisms

e.g., transfer of
models for
coordination of
action

Figure 9-1. General Causal Relations in Social Boundary Mechanisms

exact line we draw between precipitating and constitutive mechanisms is of course arbitrary. But the distinction clarifies what we must explain, and how.

Future research will have to examine the interplay of precipitating and constitutive mechanisms with care. I make no claim for the exhaustiveness of the two mechanism lists, but I do claim that varying sets of these mechanisms figure prominently in most or all social boundary changes. Obviously, any such claim calls for careful criticism and empirical verification. This chapter merely sets an agenda for further research and theory.

Mechanisms that Precipitate Boundary Change

For all its everyday employment in natural science, the term "mechanism" rarely appears in social-scientific explanations. Its rarity results, I think, partly from the term's disquieting suggestion that social processes operate like clockwork, but mainly from its uneasy coexistence with predominant strategies of explanation in social science: a) proposal of covering laws for complex structures and processes, b) the special case of covering law accounts featuring the capacity of predictors within mathematical models to exhaust the variance in a "dependent variable" across some set of differing but comparable cases, c) specification of necessary and sufficient conditions for concrete instances of the same complex structures and processes, d) location of structures and processes within larger systems they supposedly serve or express, and/or e) identification of individual or group dispositions just before the point of action as causes of that action.

Without much self-conscious justification, most social scientists recognize one or another of these—especially individual or group dispositions—as genuine explanations. They grow uneasy when someone identifies mechanisms as explanations. Even sympathetic analysts often distinguish between mechanisms as "how" social processes work and dispositions as "why" they work. As a practical matter, however, social scientists often refer to mechanisms as they construct partial explanations of complex structures or processes. Indeed, I have drawn most of the illustrations that follow from analyses by social scientists who themselves ignore or even deny the causal efficacy of mechanisms.

Mechanisms often make anonymous appearances when social scientists identify parallels within classes of complex structures or processes. In the study of contentious politics, for example, analysts frequently invoke the mechanisms of brokerage and coalition formation as well as some of the other mechanisms this chapter catalogs (McAdam, Tarrow, and Tilly 2001). If those mechanisms appear in essentially the same form with the same small-scale consequences across a wide range of circumstances, we can call them "robust."

How will we know them when we see them? We choose a level of observation: individual thoughts, individual actions, social interactions, clusters of interactions, durable social ties, or something else. At that level of observation, we can recognize as robust social mechanisms those events that:

1. involve indistinguishably similar transfers of energy among stipulated social elements
2. produce indistinguishably similar rearrangements of those social elements
3. do so across a wide range of circumstances

The "elements" in question may be persons, but they also include aspects of persons (e.g., their jobs), recurrent actions of persons (e.g., their amusements), transactions among persons (e.g., Internet communications between colleagues), and configurations of interaction among persons (e.g., shifting networks of friendship). For economy's sake, I will call all of these "social sites." Social mechanisms divide roughly into cognitive, environmental, and relational events—those centering on individual or collective perceptions, those centering on interactions between social sites and their physical settings, those centering on connections among social sites. The mechanisms featured in this chapter generally combine cognitive and relational components.

Social mechanisms concatenate into processes displaying recognizable internal similarities but are capable of producing variable overall outcomes depending on initial conditions, sequences, and combinations of mechanisms (Tilly 2001a). We are searching for a) robust mechanisms and processes that produce alterations in boundaries among social sites as well as b) other mechanisms and processes that produce the effects of boundary change. Let us begin with mechanisms that precipitate boundary change: encounter, imposition, borrowing, conversation, and incentive shift.

Encounter. When members of two previously separate or only indirectly linked networks enter the same social space and begin interacting, they commonly form a social boundary at their point of contact. To existing distinctive relations within the networks on either side of that point, encounter adds distinctive relations across the zone and shared attribution of meaning from sites on each side. Thus newcomers to a neighborhood whose social backgrounds resemble those of older residents nevertheless find themselves, at least temporarily, on the other side of an insider-outsider boundary (Elias and Scotson 1994). Since members of truly unconnected networks rarely interact, absolutely pure cases of boundary change through encounter hardly ever occur. In combination with other causal mechanisms, nevertheless, encounter plays a significant part in boundary change. As interaction intensifies between clusters of previously unlinked or indirectly linked social sites, boundaries between them become more salient (Javeline 2003; Olzak 1992; Olzak and Uhrig 2001). When interaction declines, conversely, on the average boundaries become less salient.

Imposition. Authorities draw lines where they did not previously exist, for example, distinguishing citizens from noncitizens, landowners from other users of the land, or genuine Christians from insufficiently pious persons. Thus the Soviet state assigns a single titular nationality to each republic and to each person, thereby ensuring that large proportions of the Soviet population belong to minorities within their republics of residence. Later, that opportunistic assignment of nationalities ensures that leaders of Soviet successor states organize their politics around claims to the titular nationality, with the consequence that ethnic Russians outside of post–Soviet Russia face uncomfortable choices among emigration, subordination, and assimilation (Garcelon 2001: 96; Kaiser 1994; Khazanov 1995; Laitin 1998; Martin 2001; Olcott 2002; Suny 1993; Tishkov 1997, 1999, 2004). Imposition frequently produces boundary change as authorities attempt to create new systems of top-down control (Caplan and Torpey 2001; Scott 1998; Scott, Tehranian, and Mathias 2002; Tilly 1999).

Imposition, however, also operates on much smaller scales and for shorter durations. A foreman temporarily divides construction laborers into two squads, one for digging, the other for hauling. A schoolteacher lines up a class in competing teams—A, B, and C—for the day's spelling contest. A parent draws the line between those children who have cleaned their rooms properly (and will thus get their promised rewards) and those who have not (and will thus lose out this time). All these, and many more everyday routines, consist of imposing temporary boundaries. Those who impose such boundaries can, of course, rescind them. I suspect, however, that the mechanism and its reversal produce asymmetrical effects: once an imposed boundary falls into place, it leaves traces of its existence in the relevant social relations and representations even after it loses authoritative backing.

Borrowing. People creating a new organization emulate distinctions already visible in other organizations of the same general class, for example, by instituting a division between hourly wage workers and employees drawing monthly salaries. A great deal of inequality between members of different social categories results from borrowing, as those who create organizations such as schools, firms, and armies follow established models in recruiting categorically by gender, ethnicity, race, or religion to positions that differ significantly in the rewards they afford their occupants and the destinations to which they lead (Cohn 2000; Downs 1995; Levy 1997; McCall 2001; Reskin and Padavic 1994; Tilly 2001b). They are not *inventing* the boundary in question, but installing a familiar sort of boundary in a new location. Borrowing repeatedly produces local boundary change as new forms of organization diffuse. In borrowing, organizers need not intend to produce categorical inequality for massive and durable inequality to result from their intervention.

Conversation. Conversation certainly includes ordinary talk, but it extends to a wider range of similar interactions among social sites. In this broad meaning, conversation occurs wherever exchanges of information modify relations among the parties continuously and bit by bit; relevant information ranges across signals, symbols, actions, reactions, and expressions of emotion as well as words (Tilly 1998b). Conversation has many other effects, but it qualifies as a boundary-causing mechanism when in the course of routine interaction participants incrementally alter relations between social sites by:

- developing distinctive relations within at least two clusters
- establishing distinctive relations across the zone between those clusters
- creating or transforming shared representations of that zone between them

When women first enter male-dominated occupations, the men commonly harass the women and exclude them from their networks, yet day by day women's effective work performance gives them standing—if hardly ever equality!—within the occupation (Eisenberg 1998; Rosenberg, Perlstadt, and Phillips 1993; Schroedel 1985). At the small scale or the large, conversation causes much of incremental boundary change.

Sylvia Fuller shows how similar events altered boundaries at a larger scale in the unlikely setting of rock-climbing enthusiasts. Originally rejected vociferously as unstylish or even unethical, rock climbers who started "hang-dogging" and "rap-bolting"—reconnoitering the site instead of dropping immediately to the ground after a fall, and descending from above to install rock bolts before a climb—carried on a discussion with their critics that redefined the boundary between good and bad practitioners of the art. They did so by arguing correctly that all climbers of difficult sites used some mechanical aids (hence the question was not unaided vs. mechanically assisted ascent) and that the new techniques permitted climbers to brave previously impossible, or at least extremely dangerous, ascents (Fuller 2003: 11). Despite moral condemnation and guerrilla action against their installed bolts, conversation moved hang-doggers and rap-bolters across the boundary into the zone of accepted practice.

Incentive Shift. Participants in boundary processes receive rewards or penalties that affect their pursuit of within-boundary relations, cross-boundary relations, and representations of the boundary zone. They sometimes receive cooperation from others on the same side of a boundary, for instance, while receiving threats from those across the boundary. Changes in boundary-maintaining incentives regularly cause boundary changes. When people are cooperating in dangerous circumstances, for example, signals of fear or defection on the part of collaborators easily cascade into panic, flight, or self-protection. In these circumstances, increases in guarantees that other parties will meet their commitments with regard to onerous or risky bargains such as cooperating in long-distance trade or performing military service augment incentives for participation with same-side partners, while decreases in those guarantees reduce incentives for cooperation (Bearman 1991; Besley 1995; Biggart 2001; Biggart and Castanias 2001; DiMaggio and Louch 1998; Greif 1994; Levi 1997; Tilly 2001c; Van Dyke 2003).

In other versions of incentive shift, guardians of boundaries alter their controls over cross-boundary transactions, making them more or less costly to sites on one or both sides. In East Berlin on 9 November 1989:

> At the end of a long and rambling press conference, Gunter Schabowski, spokesman for the recently defunct Politburo of the East German Social Unity Party (SED), announced in an offhand manner that provisional travel regulations would be in effect until a new law was passed; namely, East Germans could now travel to the West without the usual restrictions on visas. Apparently, neither Schabowski nor the remaining Krenz government had intended to open the Berlin Wall, but East Germans who saw the press conference on television decided to see for themselves. Arriving at the checkpoints, crowds of East Berliners found that the exits were still barred and guarded as they had been for 28 years. Instead of going home to clarify the meaning of Schabowski's strange press conference the next day, they stood their ground shouting, "Open the gate! Open the gate!" to badly outnumbered guards. With television cameras feeding graphic images back to GDR audiences via West German stations, the standoff continued for three hours while the size of the crowds continued to grow.
>
> As taunts and shoving broke out at points of contact, the guards still had no instructions. Finally, at 10:30 P.M., the ranking East German border guards at Bornholmer Strasse and three other crossing points in the center of the city took matters into their own hands and opened the gates. Thirty minutes later, the Interior Minister ratified their decision with an official order. By this time, one of the great celebrations of the century was underway at the Brandenburg Gate as tens of thousands poured through the checkpoints, and Berliners of East and West joined in toasting an historic moment. (Mueller 1999: 698)

The border guards increased incentives for breaching the wall by abandoning the lethal penalties they had previously applied to anyone who crossed without authorization. Any such alteration causes boundary change.

Of course, these mechanisms sometimes occur jointly. Encounter and borrowing work together, for example, when members of two previously separate networks enter the same social space, begin interacting, and immediately adopt templates for their interaction that are available from elsewhere. Encounter and conversation together sometimes produce a cycle: first, creation of a sharp boundary, and then the blurring or redefinition of that boundary as relations across it intensify. What is more, all these mechanisms have more or less equal and opposite counterparts, for example, the segregation that reverses effects of encounters. Blood feuds and violent ethnic conflict often feature surges of encounter, imposition, and borrowing that render boundaries powerfully salient, only to be followed by either complete separation or more routine conversation (Boehm 1987; Gould 1999, 2003; Horowitz 2001; Mamdani 2001b; Petersen 2002; Varshney 2002).

Stepping up the level of magnification, we can always find more microscopic mechanisms within encounter, imposition, borrowing, conversation, and incentive shift. Looking closely at conversation, for instance, we will discover improvisation, turn taking, meaningful hesitation, code switching, and much more (Burke 1993; Fitch 1998; Gal 1987; Gumperz 1982; Sawyer 2001). Identification of robust mechanisms necessarily remains relative to the current level of observation. At that level, robust mechanisms are indistinguishable in their operations and effects across a wide range of circumstances.

Here the relevant level of observation is observable interaction among human social sites rather than, say, individual consciousness or energy flows among continents. For an observer of multiple social sites, then, my argument amounts to saying that each of the crucial mechanisms—encounter, imposition, borrowing, conversation, and incentive shift—produces indistinguishably similar effects on boundaries over a wide range of circumstances. The claim stands, obviously, as a hypothesis for investigation rather than as a postulate or a proven fact.

Mechanisms that Constitute Boundary Change

Encounter, imposition, borrowing, conversation, and incentive shift reliably cause social boundary change, but they do not *constitute* boundary change. Indeed, each of them produces similar effects across a wide range of nonboundary social processes. In other circumstances, for example, the combination of imposition with borrowing reproduces hierarchies or patterns of cooperation without significant activation of social boundaries; effective industrial leaders thus spread established forms of organization from one firm to the next (DiMaggio 2001). Figure 9-1 calls such consequences "nonboundary effects of those mechanisms." Other consequential mechanisms, however, actually occur as part of boundary change and, in combination, produce the effects of boundary change. They include 1) inscription and its reversal, erasure; 2) activation and deactivation; 3) site transfer; 4) relocation. We can review each in turn.

Inscription-Erasure. Remember the elements of a social boundary: distinctive social relations on either side of an intermediate zone, distinctive relations *across* that zone, and, on each side, shared representations of that zone itself. Inscription heightens any and all of these elements; it differentiates social relations on either side more sharply from each other, differentiates relations across the zone more emphatically from those on either side, and/or increases the extensiveness of shared representations on either or both sides. Erasure reverses any or all of these changes.

In Western countries, spatial arrangements of assemblies ordinarily inscribe boundaries between privileged participants and spectators: performers from their audiences, teachers from their pupils, priests from their congregations, sporting teams and referees from the fans. I still remember my shock as Peter Brook's production of Peter Weiss' play *Marat-Sade* ended: after a wrenching performance, the players came out in a row, the audience reestablished its separation from the drama by starting to applaud, but instead of acknowledging their protective perimeter the actors themselves began to applaud grimly, advanced past the stage, then exited through a stunned audience, clapping as they went. They erased the boundary between performers and spectators.

All the causal mechanisms reviewed earlier—encounter, imposition, borrowing, conversation, and incentive shift—can produce inscription or erasure singly and jointly. Imposition and borrowing combine, for example, to convert a patch of lawn into a simulated theater, with its spatial division between players and audience. In an American jury selection room, encounter, conversation, and incentive shift combine to produce fragile but visible divisions into bounded cliques as prospective jurors code each other's ages, genders, educations, occupations, and ethnicities.

Activation-Deactivation. All persons and social sites live in the presence of multiple social boundaries at varying levels of activation or deactivation. For the moment, writing these lines activates the boundary between philosophers of social science and other scholars as it deactivates boundaries involved in my being a teacher, a father, a consumer, and a critic of American foreign policy. Yet some time today I will deactivate the philosopher-other boundary in favor of one or more other divisions. The same mechanism operates at a larger scale than the personal one. Activation of a boundary consists of its becoming more salient as an organizer of social relations on either side of it, of social relations across it, or of shared representations on either side. Deactivation consists of a decline in that boundary's salience.

In his splendid musicological account of jazz performance, Paul Berliner points out the difference that the absence, presence, or composition of an audience make to a group of improvisers. "With the increasing international appeal of jazz," Berliner remarks,

> serious fans abroad also have a special place in the hearts and memories of musicians. "One of the things that can be a pleasure about performing in Europe is that people do the research. They really know who you are, and they want you to play real jazz" (Lou Donaldson). George Duvivier's experience has been similarly gratifying: "In Europe and Japan, audiences are so conscious of what the artist is doing, their applause is always encouraging. They know your name and what you've recorded, and they acknowledge that when you're introduced. Backstage, you can sit for an hour after performances, just signing albums." (Berliner 1994: 457)

Different boundaries activate, however, when the listeners are other jazz musicians, noisy diners, or recording technicians (Berliner 1994: 452–84).

Inscription and activation sometimes operate simultaneously, as do erasure and deactivation. Inscription heightens the social relations and representations that comprise a particular boundary, while activation makes that same boundary more central to the organization of activity in its vicinity. Thus religious zealots often create extensive webs of relations within their faith, guarded relations to nonmembers of the faith, and powerful representations of those nonmembers: *high inscription*. Most of the time, zealots continue to participate in professions, political parties, neighborhood associations, and investments of their capital that involve other us-them boundaries: *low to medium activation*. Yet if a threat to the religious community's survival arises, members begin organizing their activities around the religious boundary alone: *rising activation*. In combination, inscription and activation provide bases for sustained, costly collective action.

Site transfer maintains a boundary, but shifts the exact locations of persons and social sites with respect to differentiated relations on either side of the boundary, cross-boundary relations, and/or representations of the boundary.

Racial passing and religious conversion, for example, present two versions of site transfer in which individual persons or clusters of persons move from one side of a boundary to the other. Rites of passage similarly transfer people across boundaries without erasing those boundaries. Indeed, initiation ceremonies often reinforce the very boundaries across which they transfer individuals. Eric Wolf interpreted the Winter Ceremonials of (American) Northwest Coast peoples in just such a light:

> Among many North American Indian peoples, seekers after sacred power had visions in which they entered into contact with guardian spirits, who bestowed on them both supernaturally charged objects and instructions, and visionary encounters with spirits who endowed their clients with such powers were widespread on the Northwest Coast. The essential plot of the Winter Ceremonial conforms to this pattern in that a spirit kidnaps and consumes the initiand, and in so doing grants him supernatural powers; it then releases him back into normal life as a person transformed by that experience. Unlike the vision in much of North America, however, in the Kwakiutl ceremonial this visionary experience was neither open to all nor specific to the individual visionary. It was confined to sets of people who had acquired the prerogative to enter a sodality that impersonates the supernatural in question, and that prerogative was acted out in a highly standardized and impersonal form, within an organized framework of impersonating performances. (Wolf 1999: 105)

The ceremony Wolf describes clearly transferred persons across the boundary of a privileged sodality while dramatizing the importance of that same boundary. It altered the relation of particular individuals to the boundary.

Not all site transfer, however, consists of individual movement across boundaries. Sylvia Fuller's story about rock climbers shows us conversation (a boundary-precipitating, not a boundary-constituting, mechanism) producing wholesale movement of hang-doggers, rap-bolters, and their practices from the heterodox to the orthodox side of the boundary among experts in that esoteric sport. Ethnic activists often strive for transfer of their entire category from one side to another of a racial or citizenship boundary, and sometimes succeed. In South Africa, leaders of mixed-race populations carried on a gingerly collaboration with apartheid rulers that separated them from the increasingly unified black population and gave them distinctive political rights without rendering them white (Ashforth 1990; Jung 2000; Marks and Trapido 1987; Marx 1991). North American ethnic politics has long featured collective struggles and shifting governmental decisions concerning who qualifies as black, white, Latino, Anglo, Indian, Inuit, or otherwise (Cordero-Guzmán, Smith, and Grosfoguel

2001; Curtis 2001; Domínguez 1986; Omi and Winant 1994; Ong 1996; Pérez Firmat 1994; Peterson 1995).

Relocation combines two or more of the constitutive mechanisms: inscription, erasure, activation, deactivation, and/or site transfer. Within some set of social sites, it alters the major boundaries that are organizing action and interaction. In a simple and frequent scenario, one boundary deactivates while another activates: gender divisions fade while work divisions become more salient. In another, inscription and site transfer conjoin: Bosnian Serb leaders enforce a Serb-Muslim division in previously mixed populations, and families scramble to locate themselves on one side of the line or the other (Bax 2000; Malcolm 1996; Mazower 2000). At the extreme, one boundary replaces another as the organizer of social interaction. Short of that extreme, relocation may end up with interaction oriented to two boundaries, or to none at all.

An unexpected but dramatic case in point comes from soccer violence. Unlike American football, soccer involves little outright violence on the field, most of it accidental and much of it punished as fouls. When soccer matches generate serious damage, spectators and supporters have usually started the trouble. More often than not the violent performers consist of young male fans who have arrived in clusters; fortunately for the death rate, they rarely use weapons more lethal than clubs, broken bottles, and knives (Armstrong 1998; Bromberger 1998, ch. 3; Buford 1991). Deaths become frequent chiefly when police battle unruly fans (Giulianotti, Bonney, and Hepworth 1994).

Leaving aside the fights between rival groups of fans that recurrently take place outside soccer stadiums, soccer violence on the field becomes serious when fans breach the boundary separating spectators from players and referees. That boundary gives way to another separating supporters of one team from supporters of another, easily distinguished by the colors and symbols they wear. Often, however, further relocation occurs as police struggle with all fans on the field regardless of their affiliation, and the previously hostile fans unite to fight back. On a small scale, soccer violence replays the sort of relocation that frequently occurs in the course of wars and revolutions.

Consequences of Boundary Change

As the evocation of wars and revolutions suggests, boundary change produces serious consequences across a wide range of social interaction. It facilitates or inhibits exploitation of one category by another. It likewise facilitates or inhibits mobilization in the forms of social movements or popular rebellions. It

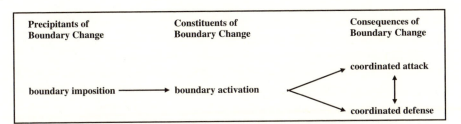

Figure 9-2. An Elementary Causal Sequence Involving Social Boundaries

strongly affects the likelihood, intensity, scale, and form of collective violence (Tilly 2003). Instead of surveying the entire range of boundary change, however, let us trace some of the causal connections we have been examining through three quite different social processes: occupational sex-typing, ethnic cleansing, and immigrant adaptation. In each of them appears a causal sequence of the sort summarized in Figure 9-2.

In this elementary sequence:

- authorities draw lines among social sites where they did not previously exist
- that boundary increases in salience as an organizer of social relations on either side, of social relations across it, and/or of shared representations
- actors on at least one side respond to the boundary's activation by engaging in coordinated attacks on sites across the boundary
- actors on at least one side engage in coordinated defense against those attacks

Figure 9-2 obviously proposes a bare-bones account of the causal connections within these complex processes. Imposition is not a necessary condition of what follows, since encounter, borrowing, conversation, and incentive shift sometimes initiate similar causal sequences. Nor is activation a sufficient condition for the attack-defense portion of the causal story; whether activation generates attacks depends both on initial conditions and on what else happens. I mean simply to identify partial causal parallels among very different social processes. Those parallels result from the operation of identical (or at least very similar) causal mechanisms in widely varying circumstances.

Occupational Sex-Typing. Job assignment by gender accounts for the bulk of male-female wage inequality in capitalist countries. A good deal of sex segregation results not from imposition but from borrowing, as managers set up new offices and firms on existing models, including the assignment of men to higher-paid job categories. But historically the gender composition of certain occupations has sometimes shifted rapidly, either from mixed to single gender or from one gender to the other. (As I suggested earlier, the transition from single-gender to mixed-gender occupations usually occurs more gradually, as a result of conversation combined with incentive shifts.) Although managers initiate and control most such boundary changes, workers on one side or the other of the gender boundary often align themselves with managers in order to pursue their advantage, and sometimes engage in direct struggle across the boundary.

Looking at Great Britain from the 1870s to the 1930s, Samuel Cohn compares the (relatively early) move from male to female clerical workers in the post office with the (quite late) move from male to female clerical workers on the Great Western Railway. The post office originally justified hiring women as telegraph operators on the ground that women would quit to marry relatively young, and therefore never climb the bureaucratic ladder into higher-paid positions. In fact, female post office telegraphers came to like their work, began to enjoy well-paid security, and stayed around to compete for advancement. Women served, furthermore, in two different kinds of offices: within-city and intercity. As Cohn explains:

> Intercity transmission was much more difficult because long cables made connections tenuous; these difficult transmissions required workers to use sensitive and fragile equipment. Furthermore, because of the heavy volume of intercity communication, much of this work was done at night when the utilization rates of the lines were lower. In the original staffing of the telegraph service, men and women worked in within-city and intercity offices and were equally skilled at low-skill and high-skill transmission. Then one day by fiat all the women were moved out of the intercity offices and limited to simple within-city messages. Some men were allowed to stay in within-city galleries, but many were transferred to intercity lines. (Cohn 2000: 92)

In the short run, men protested more than women, since transfers to night shifts brought inconvenience but no increase in pay. Over the longer run, however, the post office began offering promotions selectively to the men of intercity offices on the ground that they were—now!—more skilled. Women who had been operating intercity equipment soon resisted their segregation in lesser-skilled, lower-paid segments of the post office, and many quit in despair or outrage. When even that anticipated response did not thin female ranks sufficiently, the post office imposed a marriage bar: a woman who married lost her job. The authorities also offered substantial dowries to those who left their jobs for marriage. They deliberately promoted turnover in lower-wage female jobs.

Up to this point, the attack-defense portion of our sequence occurred indirectly, with males and females acting chiefly against management. But with the introduction of telephone, telex, and teletype during the years around World War I, the post office moved rapidly toward replacement of male labor by lower-waged female labor, and men began complementing their coordinated appeals to the government and Parliament with verbal—not physical—attacks on women workers. In both the post office and the railways, the conflict exacerbated with the end of World War I. During the war, both industries took on many female clerical workers to replace men who went off to military service, only to generate a struggle over jobs at war's end (Cohn 1985: 152–59). Repeatedly, imposition preceded and helped cause activation, which in turn stimulated attack and defense.

Ethnic Cleansing. Overt violence rarely occurs in occupational sex segregation. Open physical attack, in contrast, identifies ethnic cleansing for what it is. Norman Naimark has written a somber, well-informed account of major European episodes during the 20th century: Armenians and Greeks of Anatolia around World War I, Nazi extermination of Jews, the Soviet Union's forced deportation of Chechen, Ingush, and Crimean Tatars in 1944, expulsion of Germans from Poland and Czechoslovakia at the end of World War II, and Yugoslavia's successive episodes of the 1990s (Naimark 2001; see also Bax 2000; Petersen 2002; Rae 2002). Ethnic cleansing, for Naimark, involves a deliberate program "to remove a people and often all traces of them from a concrete territory" (Naimark 2001: 3). At one extreme of ethnic cleansing lies expulsion, at the other extermination. All of the 20th-century episodes Naimark examines combined some of each.

Imposition played its part in all of Naimark's episodes, for example, in the Nazis' Nuremberg Laws (July 1935) identifying everyone with at least 25 percent Jewish ancestry as a Jew, depriving Jews thus defined of German citizenship, and strictly forbidding marriage of Jews with non-Jews. The Nazis activated the Jewish/non-Jewish boundary in a thousand demeaning and costly ways. Between their arrival in power (1933) and the start of World War II (1939), they exerted strong pressure on Jews to emigrate, leaving their goods behind. Systematic killing of Jews by German forces, however, did not begin until 1941; further activation of the Jewish/non-Jewish boundary then reorganized life—and death—on both sides.

The Nazis' overwhelming military and organizational strength meant that Jews' coordinated defense consisted chiefly not of counterattacks but of mutual aid, mutual concealment, and facilitation of escape for a fortunate few. In the process, Nazi leaders redefined the relevant boundary as separating good Germans not only from Jews but also from Bolsheviks:

> The German attack on Russia was not like the attack on Britain or France, though the Jews were blamed for those conflicts as well. In the Nazi mind, the internationalism of the Bolsheviks blended with the Jewish world conspiracy in a dangerous potion that mortally threatened the German nation and its right to rule Europe. Barbarossa [the Nazi campaign against the Soviet Union] was a crusade to slay the Jewish-Bolshevik demons and remove them from the face of the earth. (Naimark 2001: 75)

Attacks on Jews and on Russians turned increasingly into campaigns of extermination. Although the ratio of expulsion to extermination varied from one20th-century episode of ethnic cleansing to another, in all of them the sequence from imposition to activation to attack and (usually ineffectual) defense applied.

Immigrant Adaptation. With respect to levels of violence, immigrant adaptation generally lies between occupational sex-typing and ethnic cleansing—sometimes generating fierce attacks and counterattacks, but mostly working through competition and conflict on a lesser scale. Yet here, too, one recurrent causal path leads from imposition to activation to attack and defense. A striking case of the imposition-activation-attack-defense causal sequence appears in the experience of African-ancestry West Indian immigrants to the United States. They certainly come from unequal worlds, but ones in which the stark black/white distinction that prevails in the United States dissolves into a much more complex set of boundaries organized around class and ethnicity. "Racism," one New York immigrant told interviewer Vilna Bashi Bobb,

> is not really a priority there [in the West Indies], you know. You don't look at a black and white situation. You more look at an economic situation, you know. It doesn't matter really whether you're black or white or whatever it is. If you don't have the money you don't have the position in society that I'm talking about. If you have the money you have the position. But when I came here I realized that not only is there economics you have to deal with, you have to deal with the color of your skin, so that was kind of a shock to me. (Bashi Bobb 2001: 215)

Caribbean immigrants to New York confront black/white boundaries long since imposed. But the activation of those boundaries varies significantly with their social situation. Migrants who move directly into New York's West Indian enclaves and work in West Indian establishments find themselves insulated from daily black/white distinctions and assimilation into the native-born African American population. Although those first-generation immigrants gradually become aware of American-style racism, Bashi Bobb argues, participation in the immigrant network shields them from its full activation:

> The network acts as a shield in three ways. One, it may limit interaction with whites who may behave in a racist manner. That is, although they are in the primary and secondary labor markets and not in ethnic enclaves, black West Indian immigrants work and live alongside other immigrants like them, because their social space is mainly limited to job and housing niches. Two, these niches bring to the West Indian immigrant population a degree of socioeconomic success relative to their native-born black counterparts, and thus socioeconomic separation from them. Three, the labor-market success that members receive along with access to these labor- and housing-market niches belies the racist stereotypes about the inability of black people to succeed in the United States. (Bashi Boob 2001: 235)

The network also provides a basis for collective resistance to discrimination.

Children of West Indian immigrants, however, lose some of their parents' shielding from the activation of black/white boundaries. They grow up speaking with New York accents, go to New York schools, enter the New York labor market, and often leave whatever remains of the immigrant enclave. They thus become subject to the same sort of attack—mostly day-to-day discrimination, but sometimes assault from nonblack gangs—that African Americans have long experienced. They become African American, and mount their defense against attack in common with other African Americans. The longstanding black/white boundary activates for them. Although each migration stream has its distinctive properties, the sequence of imposition, activation, attack, and defense repeats itself in many immigrant experiences.

The theme should already be familiar from the example of Bolivian immigrants to Buenos Aires. Long before any of the Bolivians observed by Alejandro Grimson arrived in the city, authorities had established a boundary between Argentine citizens and foreigners, not to mention the more specific boundaries separating porteños from others, Argentines from Bolivians, and Creoles from Indians. In Buenos Aires, the arrival of migrants from the Andes activates these boundaries, which in turn leads to the multiple forms of attack that Grimson documents, and generates defensive maneuvers on the part of bolivianos. At least in local festivals where Bolivians gather, those maneuvers include broadcast claims to cultural and historical superiority.

The claims do not prevail, but at least they assert a shared identity and propose an attractive story about the boundary that separates bolivianos from porteños. Grimson sums up:

> Faced with growing social asymmetries and with representations of inequality, immigrants try to broaden their identification as a way of activating networks of mutual aid and solidarity. This does not mean that narrower identities disappear, or stop being used as bases of high-risk relations if not of organizational connections. It means that as the process of moving and settling proceeds in a country they still experience as foreign, migrants seek to generalize their identities and to use their own cultural histories as they do so. (Grimson 1999: 181)

Rather than members of small clusters from particular villages, *porteños bolivianos* become just that: members of categories well defined both by their separation from and by their connection to the social life of Buenos Aires. They become Bolivians. Boundary change transforms their lives. Their experience involves much more than the single-circuit imposition-activation-attack-defense. In one way or another, it includes our full range of causal mechanisms: encounter, imposition, borrowing, conversation, incentive shift, inscription-erasure, activation-deactivation, site transfer, and relocation, not to mention further consequences of those mechanisms. The particular experience of Bolivian migrants to Buenos Aires nicely illustrates the great generality of boundary change as a social process.

Chapter 10

Chain Migration and Opportunity Hoarding

MY FRIENDS WHO MAKE THEIR LIVINGS FROM SURVEY RESEARCH WOULD not have approved. Our rambunctious interview did not conform to professional standards. During the spring of 1988, Pierine Piras, Philippe Videlier, and I sat drinking coffee and nibbling cake in the living room of a modest Mamaroneck, New York, house. Mamaroneck lies on Long Island Sound about twenty miles north of New York City. We were speaking with a man I'll name Franco Bossi, born in Roccasecca, Italy, not far from Rome, ninety-two years earlier.

Given our standard options of English, French, or Italian for the interview's language (none of us had mastered the dialect of Roccasecca), Mr. Bossi had chosen Italian. Mrs. Bossi, in her eighties, and their daughter Rosa, in her sixties, interrupted frequently to contradict, refresh, complete, or refine Mr. Bossi's recollections when they were not urging him to shift from his rusty Italian to his accented, ungrammatical, but fluent English. Mr. Bossi remembered the Mamaroneck of World War I era as very Italian:

> Tutti qui, sto villagio dove stamo me now, tutti Italiani, Italiani, Italiani! La most part era Roccasecca. Tutte le zone . . . Siciliani . . . Calabresi assai, Calabresi assai . . . Napolitani . . . Down in Mamaroneck they use to call a "Guinea Town" because the Italians they calls the "guinea," it's a nickname.

As of the 1910 census, in fact, only about a sixth of Mamaroneck's population was Italian born. In Washingtonville, the section of Mamaroneck away from the water on the wrong side of the railroad tracks, about a third of all households then had Italian-born heads. But teenaged Franco Bossi, recently arrived from Roccasecca with his parents, surely lived in a much more Italian world than that.

Not that his parents had come straight from the old country. "I was not born yet; my father left my mother pregnant," reported Mr. Bossi.

> He went to Brazil. It was a lot of people that say: "Let's go to Brazil! Let's go to Brazil!" A lot of work over there. So my father went there and all the day he picked coffee, bananas, all this stuff, rice, fruits, but the most were in Brazil for coffee. They must have been in the country, but I don't know the name, but that's where they grew coffee. He only stood one year over there. The heat! La calor, ooh! . . . You can't stay there! And the bugs! My father came over here.

He came to the United States around 1898, roughly midway through the first important wave of migration from Roccasecca to Mamaroneck and the rest of Westchester County, which lasted from 1890 or so to World War I. Franco Bossi's father became a construction laborer in Mamaroneck, while Franco himself later found work as a gardener on one of the estates that were springing up along Long Island Sound as the new railroad, then paved motor roads, made Westchester easily accessible to Manhattan. His fellow emigrants and later arrivals concentrated themselves in Westchester's gardening, public works, and connected enterprises, gaining collective advantages by pooling access to jobs and firms.

American restrictions on immigration after World War I greatly slowed the movement of workers from Roccasecca to Mamaroneck and nearby towns. At that point, many more Ciociari (as people from the *paese* including Roccasecca identify themselves) began migrating to France, especially to Lyon's industrial suburbs. But after World War II a new round of migrants took the American road. "My mother and father got married," one fifty-year-old immigrant we can call Anthony Bianco told us,

> and went to France because he had three sisters there, one in Saint-Romain-le-Puy and two in Villeurbanne [both towns in the vicinity of Lyon]. My father stayed three years but then he wasn't happy with life there, it was too hot living next to the glassworks, so he went back to Roccasecca. My brother and I had been born in France—my older brother, who now works for the railroad in Rome. My uncle had a motel in Mamaroneck, and we had gotten married, he was there when we got married and said, "you were born in France, I can sponsor you," so three months later I came here on my French papers.

Anthony Bianco worked for a year as a gardener, then spent nineteen years in construction before becoming a laborer for the county government. His family now has branches in Italy, France, and the United States, each of them concentrated in a few adjacent locations. Other natives of Roccasecca we met in Mamaroneck had lived in Brazil and Argentina. Some had relatives in Toronto, although (in what may be a testimony to either Toronto's hospitality or the United States' immigration controls) we encountered no Roccaseccani who had first emigrated to Toronto only to move on to New York. But a well-established network of kinship and acquaintance links Roccasecca and nearby villages in central Italy, Villeurbanne and adjacent industrial towns in France, São Paulo in Brazil, Buenos Aires in Argentina, Toronto in Canada, and the northern suburbs of New York City.

Fitting fragmentary evidence from Mamaroneck and Lyon into analogies with other migration systems, I conjecture that migration chains connecting Roccasecca with Mamaroneck first took shape in contacts among the village's stonecutters, who went from site to site for construction in Europe, only to return to their farms in the off-season. When contractors started building dams and reservoirs to meet New York City's enormous demands for water late in the 19th century, some of them reached out to Italy for their stonecutters. Most of them brought laborers with them; I speculate, most of them returned to Italy when their jobs were done, but others—both stonecutters and their less skilled helpers—liked the opportunities they saw in the New York area and stayed on. No doubt most of them continued to remit money and bring goods back to Roccasecca, helping their relatives at home, assisting the next round of immigrants, and maintaining their personal claims to membership in the village.

Later migrants moved directly into the construction of roads and railways, or into gardening on the great estates that lined the nearby Atlantic shore. Many more made their bundles and returned to Italy, but again some stayed on, married, settled their families, and bore children who were Americans. By this speculative account, Anthony Bianco arrived in the United States sixty years or so after those who established the Roccasecca-Mamaroneck link, Franco Bossi and his compatriots.

Piras, Videlier, and I undertook the research on migration between Roccasecca and Mamaroneck because it investigated an imperfect but revealing natural experiment in the creation of durable inequality. More precisely, the stream of Italian American migration contributed to the formation of **categorical** inequality in Mamaroneck and vicinity. The production of categorical inequality—the unequal distribution of rewards for effort on either side of a boundary separating sets of persons considered to differ collectively in attributes—occurs by means of four major social mechanisms:

1. **exploitation**: a well-connected set of actors controls a valuable resource, harnesses the efforts of others in the extraction of returns from that resource, and excludes those others from the full value added by their effort
2. **opportunity hoarding**: members of a categorically bounded network acquire access to a resource that is valuable, renewable, subject to monopoly, supportive of network activities, and enhanced by the network's *modus operandi,* then exclude others from use of that resource
3. **emulation**: people in a given setting reproduce organizational models already operating elsewhere, models that incorporate categorical differences in rewards to effort
4. **adaptation**: people in a given setting commit themselves to categorically unequal relations, however unwittingly by a) inventing procedures that ease the effort of day-to-day interaction, and b) elaborating valued social relations around existing divisions

The four mechanisms interact incessantly. In different cultural settings, their various intersections produce very different kinds of inequality: tight hierarchies, hostilities across well-marked boundaries, nearly invisible systems of control, and more. They also account for inequality according to a wide variety of categorical boundaries: citizenship, ethnicity, race, gender, locality, and so on. Here I concentrate on opportunity hoarding, especially as it operates in conjunction with chain migration. Franco Bossi, Anthony Bianco, and their fellow Ciociari built a precarious inequality with their neighbors in Mamaroneck. They did so by hoarding opportunities.

Their opportunity-hoarding strategies differed from those of their close cousins in France. From a thousand-person agricultural village, hundreds of emigrants went to Mamaroneck and vicinity, hundreds more to Villeurbanne's vicinity. In Lyon's suburbs, they generally took factory jobs; their children rapidly became working-class French people with Italian names but little other Italian identification; they moved into a system of sharp class inequality, but did not form a well-defined ethnic community with its own businesses and forms of employment.

In Westchester, Italians whose families also originated in Roccasecca created a distinctive niche. They concentrated heavily in landscape gardening, where the current generation enjoys a near-monopoly of the local business; others cluster in construction, public works, and retail trade. Within family firms, a Catholic parish, and ethnic neighborhoods, they have retained a much stronger identification with Italy and small enterprise. The situation of ethnic Italians in Mamaroneck clearly illustrates the possibility of opportunity hoarding in the absence of major exploitation; Italians gain modest but secure existences by controlling adjacent economic niches and excluding non-Italians from those niches, but in the process they employ little or no non-Italian labor. Moreso than their French cousins, they survive by hoarding opportunities.

Anthony Bianco lived a complicated migration history, but not much more intricate than the average. In any case, his history tells us something far more important than how complicated life is. In Roccasecca, Anthony's family, and most of its neighbors, were peasants. In New York's suburbs, Mr. Bianco's *paesani* have become shopkeepers and landscape gardeners, while others having essentially the same origins have become French industrial workers, Brazilian businessmen or perhaps schoolteachers in Toronto. (My collaborators uncovered a similar range of destinations among closely connected people during their interviews in the region of Lyon.)

Transplanted Italians now bear different kinds of names, speak different languages, wear different clothes, follow different politics, do different kinds of work, have different memories and hopes for the future. What made the difference? In these cases, we're tempted to answer: luck. Ability, determination, and prior wealth or education certainly seem to have mattered little, while the presence of a relative who could provide aid and information mattered a great deal. That presence, however, was not a lucky coincidence, but the pivot of an extensive migration system that brought Roccaseccani to Mamaroneck and nearby towns while carrying their close kinsmen and neighbors to Lyon, São Paulo, Buenos Aires, or Toronto. However much the experience of any particular migrant might seem to depend on chance and individual taste, the experience took shape within stringent limits set by preexisting contacts.

Anyone who studies migration and ethnicity has recognized in my story of Mamaroneck's migrants telltale signs of chain migration and niche formation. A well-defined migration chain fed individuals and families into a set of connected economic niches. Mamaroneck's Italian immigrant niches lack the neatness of those Roger Waldinger and Alejandro Portes have identified in New York, Miami, and Los Angeles, but they likewise display the strong impact of the path by which a given category of people entered the American economy on opportunities open to subsequent members of that category.

In fact, the Mamaroneck story shows us not the perpetuation but the **creation** of a category—Italian Americans—by the migration process itself. It also shows us how subsequent generations use the created category; in a classic case of opportunity hoarding, members of a categorically bounded network retain access to a resource—in this case, a set of employers, clients, and jobs—that is valuable, renewable, subject to monopoly, supportive of network activities, and enhanced by the network's *modus operandi*. Matching the category "Italian American" to the business of landscape gardening sequestered opportunities for poor Italian peasants and their descendants, but also fenced off those opportunities from other people, including the growing number of black residents in Mamaroneck and adjacent Westchester towns. Thus, as compared with Lyon, it reinforced Italian identity as a basis of everyday social relations in Mamaroneck. It sustained dense, bounded networks containing many triads, all three of whose members recognized each other as Italian.

Ciociari who came to Mamaroneck were solving an everyday organizational problem—finding paid work in a strange land—and creating categories more or less inadvertently, but as they did so there took shape a set of social ties in which multiple parties had stakes. Interested parties included kinfolk in Italy and America, fellow Ciociari emigrants, and a variety of local employers. By analogy with other niche builders who tell similar stories today, we can reasonably suppose that they hoarded information about opportunities, shared it chiefly with closely connected others, excluded strangers, maintained contact with their place of origin through letters, remittances, and occasional visits. Thus their interactions with others created durable categorical inequality.

Consider parallels with steelmaking Johnstown, Pennsylvania. In *For Bread with Butter* (1985) and *Insecure Prosperity* (1996), sociologist-historian Ewa Morawska has chronicled the experiences of various East Central European groups and of East European Jews between 1890 and World War II. Americans of Western European origin dominated Johnstown's industry, real estate, and finance. But immigrants from Poland, Ukraine, Byelorussia, Slovakia, Hungary, and adjacent regions constituted the city's rank and file. Typically beginning as general labor, East European Gentiles moved into well-marked niches in manufacturing. Johnstown's Jews, in contrast, immigrated overwhelmingly into retail trade. In both cases, chain migration prevailed. To some extent the two populations recreated their European relations, with frequently multilingual Jews providing merchandise, credit, and literate services for their Slavic and Hungarian neighbors. While both integrating into a system of categorical inequality with American capitalists occupying dominant positions, Jews and Gentiles hoarded opportunities in complementary Johnstown niches.

Similarly, in Ciudad Juárez, Mexico, women find work in low-wage *maquiladoras* chiefly through networks connecting them with women already on the job. When researcher María Patricia Fernández-Kelly looked for work in a *maquiladora* by scanning newspaper advertisements, she followed the exceptional path:

> By using newspapers as a source of information for jobs available, I was departing from the common strategy of potential workers in that environment. As my own research would show, the majority of these workers avail themselves of information by word of mouth. They are part of informal networks which include relatives, friends and an occasional acquaintance in the personnel management sector. Most potential workers believe that a personal recommendation from someone already employed at a maquiladora can ease their difficult path.
>
> This belief is well founded. At many plants, managers prefer to hire applicants by direct recommendation of employees who have proven to be dependable and hard-working. For example, at Electro Componentes de Mexico, the subsidiary of General Electric and one of the most stable maquiladoras in Juárez, it is established policy not to hire "outsiders." Only those who are introduced personally to the manager are considered to fill up vacancies. (Fernández-Kelly 1983: 110)

Members of those same networks—often networks of chain migration from rural regions—also supplied child care, lodging, and social support to women workers. Without enormous effectiveness, networks sustained themselves by hoarding access to low-wage employment in American-owned manufacturing plants.

Mamaroneck Italians' concentration in landscape gardening excludes other potential workers from the business, but it hardly qualifies as exploitation; neither secure control of a productive resource, incorporation of effort by excluded parties, nor appropriation of a substantial surplus marks the position of these modest people. Yet **opportunity hoarding** describes their generally successful strategy. By sequestering technical knowledge, ties to wealthy households and institutions, reputations for good work, and access to capital within an ethnically defined network, they have fashioned a classic immigrant niche. Similarly, Johnstown's Jews lodged themselves in retail trade without creating a system of exploitation.

In neither Mamaroneck, Johnstown, nor Ciudad Juárez, indeed, do we witness the strong complementarity that often develops between exploitation and opportunity hoarding. It occurs when the effort of a favored minority provides a resource-owning elite with means to extract surplus from an essential but otherwise unavailable larger population. In South Africa before 1990, for example, we see extensive complementarity between a) European exploitation

and b) opportunity hoarding by those members of subordinate racial categories—broadly defined as African, Asian, and Coloured—who collaborated with
European rule. Sometimes exploitation and opportunity hoarding coincide
within the same ethnic category; in garment manufacturing across the world,
for example, wealthy immigrants commonly make money by recruiting low-
wage workers from distinctive networks within their own countries of origin
(Light 1984; Portes 1995; Portes and Rumbaut 1990; Waldinger 1986). In
Mamaroneck, Johnstown, and Juárez we observe opportunity hoarding in a
relatively pure, independent form, with crucial resources largely created by efforts of the hoarding community.

What distinguishes opportunity hoarding from other organizations of effort? If members of a network acquire access to a resource that is valuable,
renewable, subject to monopoly, supportive of network activities, and enhanced
by the network's *modus operandi*, network members regularly hoard access to
the resource, creating beliefs and practices that sustain their control. If that
network is categorically bounded, opportunity hoarding thereby contributes
to the creation and maintenance of categorical inequality.

Opportunity hoarding often rests on ethnic categories, members of which
reinforce their control over hoarded resources by means of their power to include or exclude other members with respect to language, kinship, courtship,
marriage, housing, sociability, religion, ceremonial life, credit, and political
patronage. Far-ranging trade diasporas of Gujaratis, Cantonese, Jews, Armenians, Lebanese, and other ethnically homogeneous networks constitute extreme forms of a very general phenomenon.

In all these instances, ethnicity and/or religion supplies the categorical basis
of opportunity hoarding. In other circumstances, however, selective migration
streams single out community of origin or lineage as the salient categorical
principle. Race, gender, schooling, professional training, political affiliation,
and sexual preference all, at times, constitute the networks and categorical distinctions on which opportunity hoarding builds.

How? Opportunity hoarding in general brings together these elements:

1. a distinctive network
2. a set of valuable resources that is renewable, subject to monopoly,
   supportive of network activities, and enhanced by the network's *modus
   operandi*
3. sequestering of those resources by network members
4. creation of beliefs and practices that sustain network control of the resources

Such a network may take a great variety of forms—large or small, hierarchical or egalitarian, organizational or otherwise—but its monopolizing work depends on explicit monitoring and sanctioning procedures that discourage defection, on the presence of many interdependent triads, or both.

We can make a rough distinction between forms of opportunity hoarding that attach their participants directly to an exploiting organization and those that bear only contingent or indirect relations to exploitation. The creation of immigrant niches within manufacturing firms falls emphatically into the first set, regardless of the extent to which the immigrants themselves benefit or suffer from exploitation. A firm or alliance of firms that establishes monopoly or oligopoly over production and sale of a given commodity simultaneously practices exploitation within firm boundaries and opportunity hoarding with respect to all other potential producers and sellers.

More contingent and indirect (albeit powerful) relations of opportunity hoarding to exploitation stem from inheritance within households, kin groups, and ethnic categories. Under capitalism, inequality in regard to inherited wealth generally exceeds inequality in regard to monetary income, since the wealthy customarily draw important returns from their wealth in nonmonetary forms and hoard some portion for transmission to heirs; as income inequality has sharpened in the United States during the last two decades, wealth has become even more unequally distributed (Wolff 1995). Clever lawyers and a favorable tax regime have made it easy for America's wealthy to retain their property from generation to generation (Drew and Johnston 1996). In this case, beliefs in wealth as property, in the inviolability of property rights, and in the priority of interpersonal ties based on birth and marriage all reinforce the centrality of inheritance as a mode of opportunity hoarding.

Other forms of opportunity hoarding lie between immigrant niches and inheritance. Family farms, family-run stores, and other types of small-scale enterprise often operate with little or no directly exploited labor, but nevertheless gain from the "rents" (to take the economist's term) provided by exclusive use of a site, stock, and clientele (Sørensen 1996). Similarly, members of exclusive crafts such as 19th-century glassblowing, printing, and silversmithing characteristically hoard opportunities by maintaining collective control over production and sale of their commodities without employing more than a few exploited helpers and apprentices. All of these arrangements, and more, gain advantages from combining a distinctive network, a set of valuable resources, sequestration of the resources, as well as beliefs and practices sustaining network control of the resources.

Professions, for example, are organizations among practitioners of some common art who control the licensing of all practitioners of that art within their shared territory, exclude unlicensed persons from practicing, and thus secure a monopoly over dispensation of the art's products to nonmembers. Professions typically succeed in establishing their monopolies by enlisting state support for licensing, exclusion, and fee setting in return for a measure of collective responsibility and self-policing. They typically set up their own institutions for recruitment, training, initiation, and discipline of new members. They engage in quintessential opportunity hoarding without necessarily drawing on exploitation as well.

The formation of a licensed profession always involves opportunity hoarding; a network of practitioners who carefully screen new entrants to their ranks enlist state aid in excluding unorthodox, unworthy, unlicensed persons from practicing the same art. Yet professions vary greatly in the extent to which they couple opportunity hoarding with exploitation. Within American health care, for example, physicians who ran hospitals and clinics long combined the two. Nurses, pharmacists, midwives, and members of other such subordinated health professions, in contrast, had to settle mainly for opportunity hoarding.

In capitalist countries dentists, lawyers, and physicians commonly operate very effective monopolies, while professionally organized architects, scientists, social workers, pharmacists, accountants, nurses, midwives, priests, and engineers all have more trouble excluding competitors from their terrains. But all do what they can to maintain categorical barriers between themselves and nonprofessionals. In France, veterinarians were spectacularly successful at adopting the medical model of practice, organization, ideology, and licensing during the 19th century. They followed the classic trajectory of professionalization: establishing schools based on medical science, acquiring recognition from public authorities as experts on such matters as inspection of meat, excluding rivals such as blacksmiths and butchers from their domains, and finally creating a state-backed monopoly of animal medical practice for graduates of their three official schools (Hubscher 1996). Nevertheless, French veterinarians generally operated on too small a scale to make significant gains from exploitation; they acquired their prestige, power, and income from opportunity hoarding.

Organizationally, licensed trades such as hairdressing typically resemble professions; on the ground of protecting public health against dangerous practices, they acquire state protection of a monopoly over services in return for subjection to oversight by a state agency. Often they strengthen that position by establishing their own schools and insisting that licensed practitioners pass through those schools successfully. Take the case of cosmetologists, who in most

American states must acquire licenses to administer beauty treatments, including hair care. In New York State, cosmetologists have come into competition with braiders, who generally learn how to create African-inspired hairstyles from friends and relatives. In order to sell their services legally, New York's braiders must receive cosmetology licenses:

> "If we have to take a minimum of 1,200 curriculum hours and pay up to $10,000 to learn our trade, why shouldn't braiders?" said Barbara G., a black cosmetologist who asked that her full name not be used, expressing concern that her comments might create tension in the mid-town Manhattan salon where she works alongside braiders. (Williams 1997: 4)

Advocates for braiders argue that little of the cosmetology curriculum deals with braiding, that the knowledge involved is distinctive, and that the present arrangement drives braiders into the underground economy. Given the character of opportunity hoarding, New York's braiders will most likely become yet another licensed trade, authorized to operate in a niche just adjacent to those of hairdressers, barbers, and cosmetologists. The interesting question is whether they will then try to exclude others from commercial braiding, and if so whether they will succeed.

Among both professionals and other opportunity hoarders, the valuable resources in question take a wide variety of forms: not only the shared knowledge and access to clients that constitute the major hoarded resources for professions, but also ore deposits among miners, reliable suppliers among import-export merchants, well-cultivated friendships among talent scouts, access to government property and officials among Russian ex-apparatchik entrepreneurs, able graduate students among academic departments. Advantage-giving sequestered knowledge, furthermore, sometimes resides in scripts, local knowledge, and interpersonal ties that members of a network carry over from other experiences, as in the leverage enjoyed by multilingual brokers at the frontiers of distinct but interdependent monolingual populations.

In general, resources that lend themselves well to opportunity hoarding are renewable, subject to monopoly, supportive of network activities, and enhanced by the network's *modus operandi*. These characteristics apply, to be sure, within specifiable limits; a successful opportunity-hoarding drug ring need only control the supply of its narcotics within its own turf, and fight out precise divisions of territory with neighboring rings. A university department that hired all the world's experts in a given specialty might well find outside demand for its expertise declining rather than increasing as a well-behaved monopoly would lead one to expect, since in many academic fields demand depends on having well-placed graduates, clients, and collaborators elsewhere. The value of resources depends on their potential uses outside the circle of hoarders.

Sequestering of resources sometimes takes the form of governmental authorization and licensing favored by organized professions. It often centers on the selective transmission of lore to members of an in-group. But it can also rest chiefly on withholding of crucial information such as the location of a precious commodity; the formula for an elixir, the means of repairing a complex machine; the turns of hand that virtuoso violinists, surgeons, and potters teach each other. Although craft labor markets of printers and glassblowers certainly relied on measures of training and exclusion resembling those of professions, they only operated effectively so long as craft workers themselves knew much more about the manufacturing of the product than their bosses did; beyond that point, bosses generally found less skilled substitutes for stubborn, expensive craftsmen (Jackson 1984; Montgomery 1993; Scott 1974).

Network, valuable resources, and sequestering combine into effective opportunity hoarding when together they yield advantages in relations with actors outside the network. Such advantages do not necessarily depend on or produce categorical inequality. By and large, commercially successful painters hoard access to galleries, critics, and purchasers without drawing sharp lines between themselves and the hoi polloi of painting. Nevertheless, interior categories and their matching with exterior categories lower the cost of hoarding. Within hospitals, the actual work of physicians and nurses overlaps considerably, but the sharp professional line between them reinforces the advantage conferred on physicians by their formal rights to prescribe drugs and courses of treatment. The common doubling of that line with gender, ethnic, and class distinctions lowers its enforcement cost. In such circumstances, opportunity hoarding relies upon, produces, and reproduces categorical inequality.

Intersection between opportunity hoarding within an organization and categorically segregated sources of supply for new recruits to the relevant networks provides a mutually reinforcing system of exceptional power and generality. We discover it recurrently in professional training, residential segregation, aristocratic or caste recruitment of military officers, and a variety of other settings. But in today's capitalist world many of the most dramatic instances take the form of immigrant niches. Hence my concentration here on that very special form of opportunity hoarding.

The admirable literature on immigrant niches and entrepreneurship to which Ivan Light, Roger Waldinger, Alejandro Portes, and their co-workers have made major contributions abounds with evidence concerning the organizational forms and processes involved in opportunity hoarding. Waldinger's study of New York, for example, documents the centrality and persistence of work niches, both job centered and entrepreneurial, to the varied experiences of major ethnic and racial categories since 1940 (Waldinger 1996; see also Model 1985, 1992, 1996; Watkins-Owens 1996). As my own story about Italians in Mamaroneck suggested, even through momentous changes in the overall economy the migration and employment histories of previous generations cast long shadows over the fates of today's category members.

Waldinger makes many of the same observations I have offered on the basis of his and other people's research: ethnic-racial niches form within limits set by the preferences of owners and established workers, but once established easily reproduce themselves because of their reliance on categorically segregated networks for a wide variety of activities on and off the job. Through long struggles, New York's native blacks formed effective niches in different segments of public employment and health care, but in recent decades have repeatedly been beaten into expanding sectors of private-sector and entrepreneurial work by immigrant streams whose members formed niches, supplying compliant, low-wage workers and/or gaining access to ethnically pooled capital. Waldinger also stresses a consequence I have understated so far:

> [F]requent interaction in a highly concentrated niche promotes a sense of group identity. Participation in the niche, one of the salient traits that group members share, helps define who they are. Thus, greater attention is paid to the boundaries that define the niche, and the characteristics of those who can and cannot cross those boundaries. The niche, in other words, identifies an "us" and a "them." (Waldinger 1996: 304)

He might have added: defining the limits of solidarity, trust, and mutual aid as well. To the extent that collaboration within a niche enhances the quality or efficiency of work, and that denial of collaboration accordingly degrades work performance, an effective niche reinforces its survival by delivering superior results to customers and other segments of the same organizations.

Not all niches, however, serve their occupants well. It follows from the very organization of migrant niches that they deliver disadvantages to new entrants under any of four conditions: 1) when the hoarded opportunities in question themselves are declining, 2) when the niche becomes overcrowded relative to the opportunities it commands, 3) when segregation of social life within the niche shuts off its members from superior opportunities outside, 4) when exploitation delivers all of the monopoly gains to entrepreneurs rather than rank-

and-file workers. While some New York garment manufacturers may well be getting rich by exploiting newly arrived Chinese workers, the immigrant workers themselves often live in desperate conditions, outside the reach of minimum-wage laws, protective legislation, and labor organizers.

Recognizing the variable well-being of different migration streams, Waldinger takes a deeply historicist view. He stresses path-dependency, arguing that each category's coping strategies and relations to opportunities at a given time significantly constrain its available strategies and opportunities in the next round. In that regard, he conforms to recent trends in the history and sociology of American immigration (Morawska 1990, 1994; Portes 1995). A historicist view helps make sense of the connections between migration and durable forms of inequality, especially those forms people organize as ethnicity—as structured differences according to imputed national or racial origin. It shows the formation of opportunity hoarding not as an instantaneous rational decision but as a struggle- and error-ridden process sometimes extending over a generation.

For a long time, the standard vision of the immigrant portrayed someone who leaves the old country's security, passes through a period of risk and turmoil, then establishes a definitive equilibrium in the new country. If the immigrant comes to a great city such as New York or Los Angeles, most people find this vision all the easier to accept. Yet actual immigration experiences rarely approximate the classic model; instead we find people moving back and forth over long distances, relying heavily on colleagues, kinsmen, and Landsmänner as they make their ways, maintaining their preexisting personal networks at considerable expense, and generally refusing to become disorganized in the ways that classical theories predict. By now, a whole generation of researchers has documented the dense social ties that commonly accompany long-distance migration and subsequent problem solving.

The old beliefs required active suppression of knowledge that most of us already have. For the histories of our own families, thoughtfully considered, generally contradict all these antitheses of immobility and mobility, order and disorder, contingency and constraint. Our individual and family histories vibrate with movement, with fortuitous connections, with chance meetings, with contingencies having very serious consequences over long periods of time. Yet, seen in perspective, they also embody striking regularities.

Let me illustrate with a personal example. I would not exist—that is, my parents would almost certainly never have met—except for the last-minute decision of my grandfather, a Welsh miner in a time of the mines' decline, **not** to take an available mining job in South Africa but instead to accept the invitation of his brother, a locomotive driver who had emigrated fifteen years earlier, to join him and his family near Chicago and look for work there. (A disputed family tradition says Uncle Chris, the Chicago brother, sent a telegram skillfully mediating between threat and dire prediction: "If you go to South Africa," he is supposed to have cabled, "I'll never speak to you again.")

My grandfather ended up maintaining the machines of an Ovaltine factory in Villa Park, Illinois. His daughters, including my mother, met and married men who lived around Chicago, bore and raised children in the Chicago region. They constructed a tight kinship group consisting chiefly of their family's Chicago branch but ramifying back to Wales and England. Later, I worked summers in the Ovaltine factory to earn money for college . . . and my family often drank Ovaltine.

In one perspective, nothing could be more contingent and individual—a last-minute change of mind about a risky job seals the destiny of an entire family, not to mention their descendants. My grandfather's whim, however, did not cause his brother to leave for Chicago in 1908 or the Rhondda Valley's mines to falter in the 1920s. (Uncle Chris, furthermore, had joined their half brother Sam, who even earlier had migrated to Chicago to work in retail trade.) My grandfather's apparently arbitrary choice took place within strong limits set by previous actions—his and other people's—and had significant effects on all his later choices. Few moments in most lives pose such fateful alternatives as Hugh Stott's 1925 decision to join his brother in Chicago, but much of long-distance migration brings together similar combinations of contingency and constraint.

Although no one involved at the time would have recognized the term, my mother's family was involved in a system of chain migration. We have already encountered the phenomenon among Italian migrants to Mamaroneck. Chain migration is the arrangement in which numerous people leave one well-defined origin serially for another well-defined destination by relying on people from the same origin for aid, information, and encouragement; most chain migrations involve considerable return of migrants to their place of origin.

Many chain migrations begin as **circular** migrations: seasonal, annual, or longer-cycle movement of agricultural workers, craftsmen, or petty merchants from a base to some other well-defined place where temporary work awaits them. Migration from Roccasecca to Mamaroneck probably started with just such circuits of stonecutters. In my mother's family story, the chain was short: from Sam Stott to Chris Stott to Hugh Stott and perhaps a dozen cousins, children, and siblings. Yet it came recognizably from the same sort of process that produces chains spanning multiple generations.

The essence of chain migration was, and is, the existence of continuing contacts between a specific community of origin and a specific community of

destination—Roccasecca and Mamaroneck, a Welsh mining village and Chicago, a Polish *shtetl* and Johnstown. It involves frequent moves of persons between them with help and encouragement from the persons at both ends. Even
including the forced migration of Africans (who arrived literally, but not figu-
ratively, in chains) this sort of continuously connected migration system accounts for the great bulk of the last five centuries' immigration to the Americas. That fact in itself should alert us to the likelihood that what happened to
migrants at one point in time, and how they organized their migration, significantly affected the fate of both their descendants and later migrants.

We could stop there. By now we have plenty of evidence showing that the
presence or absence of prior contacts has a strong effect on the paths and consequences of long-distance migration. In Toronto, Grace Anderson showed
twenty years ago that the initial ties of very similar Portuguese immigrants to
the metropolitan labor market significantly influenced the kinds of jobs with
which they began, which in turn made a large difference to their relative success later on; ability and ambition paled in the light of prior social ties. In New
York, Suzanne Model has shown that among Jews, Italians, and blacks employment by members of the same ethnic category, on the average, contributed
significantly to better jobs and higher incomes (Model 1985).

Model's later work supports those findings with three important qualifications: 1) expanding niches promote such advantages more than fixed or declining niches; 2) as an ethnically segregated migration network saturates a
niche, advantages to latecomers decline or even disappear; 3) niche advantages
depend on the presence of similarly qualified but excluded populations of potential workers. Roger Waldinger's findings generally confirm Model's conclusion. The mutual employment in question grows up especially as a consequence
of collectively organized migration, and constitutes a striking case of opportunity hoarding.

Even in the case of solitary migration, migrants commonly drew information, assistance, and financial aid from network members who had already gone
to America. The frequency of remittances from emigrants to homefolks and of
steamship tickets prepaid by people at the American destination reveals the
extent of that mutual aid. After a New Jersey lecture in which I made the same
point, a second-generation Italian came up to me in indignation, objecting
that "mutual aid" hardly described the situation in which kinsmen in Newark
sent his father a steamship ticket, only to reveal on his arrival in America that
he would have to work off the passage in their bakery at starvation wages; the
day he finished repaying, the father had quit his job, left town, and severed
connections with his rapacious cousins.

Let no one think, then, that the processes I am describing exclude exploitation, conflict, or antipathy. The tying together of people by mutual aid and obligation often breeds rancor as well as respect. Many immigrants gritted their teeth until they had enough money to go back to their communities of origin or rush off to another destination within their networks. Among streams connecting the Mediterranean with North America, typically half or more of the immigrants returned home. The high proportion of Mediterranean migrants who returned after trying their hands in America, or who swung back and forth between the two continents as employment opportunities dictated, superficially a sign of inefficiency in the migration system, actually testifies to the quick, effective flow of information about affairs at both ends of the many chains from the Mediterranean to North America.

In 1906, 435,000 people left Italy for the Americas but a full 158,000 returned, and many "pendulated" between continents for some time (Harney 1984: 74; see also Harney 1985). Although that sort of evidence tells us nothing about how organized or disorganized the migrants were, it contradicts any notion of desperate cutting of ties to the old country. From what else we know about Italian migration, it depended heavily on spectacularly long chains between very specific origins and destinations within the continents. *Padroni,* or labor contractors, who recruited Italian workers for construction or agriculture in distant America, did exist, but they profited from or emerged out of existing migration chains. In any case, they accounted for only a small minority of Italian immigrants.

For decades, American factories did much of their work through subcontracting, farming out the production of major goods to a foreman or independent entrepreneur who actually hired his own labor force and delivered the goods for a price agreed upon in advance. Subcontracting articulates beautifully with chain migration, since the *padrone* has access to an indefinite supply of willing workers over whose fate—and hence whose job performance—she or he can exercise great control. Where an industry's recruitment and supply networks connect with a migration chain and gain exclusive access to the relevant jobs, an ethnically segregated occupational monopoly appears. Since subcontracting is again actually increasing as what David Harvey calls "flexible capital accumulation" extends in capitalist countries, we can reasonably predict an increase in the ethnic segregation of work in cities, like Chicago, where chain migration still prevails (Harvey 1989: 141–72). Again opportunity hoarding thrives.

Ethnic entrepreneurship often forms through a very similar process. When I lived in Toronto during the 1960s, my next-door neighbors were Macedonians.

A steady stream of visitors from Macedonia came through the house next door. One day my neighbor explained, in roughly these terms: "We have short-order restaurants [the day of "fast food" had not yet arrived] and when we need some- one to work in one of them we send back home for a young man. He cleans up and starts cooking as he learns English, then graduates to running the counter. When he's saved up some money and gotten pretty good in English, we try to set him up in his own restaurant. Then he hires newcomers." At that point, as my neighbor didn't say, the new restaurant owner owed plenty of money to his relatives, and had to rely on them for help in recruiting his workforce; these tieships reforged the migration chain. In that way, retail trades often become semimonopolies of one national group or another—Indian newsstands or Korean groceries in New York, Macedonian short-order restaurants or Italian barbershops in Toronto. By means of chain migration, opportunity hoarding contributes to durable inequality.

I have told my story of chain migration and opportunity hoarding chiefly in terms of contemporary North America. Throughout the world, however, simi- lar processes have contributed to inequality for thousands of years. To recog- nize chain migration's prevalence, efficiency, and complementarity to oppor- tunity hoarding requires us neither to condemn it roundly nor to accept its unequal consequences as inevitable. On the contrary: seeing how these perva- sive processes work marks the first step toward effective intervention on behalf of equality. If hoarded niches yield relatively equal rewards, if exits from those niches occur on relatively equal terms, and if barriers exist against conversion of niches into devices for exploitation of others, chain migration and its comple- mentary opportunity hoarding can, over the longer run, actually promote the equalization of opportunity, the mutual aid of migrants, and the productivity of migrant-occupied niches. Instead of seeking to stamp it out, an egalitarian policy should intervene in chain migration to produce just such outcomes.

Chapter 11

Boundaries, Citizenship, and Exclusion

Dᴜʀɪɴɢ ᴛʜᴇ 12ᴛʜ ᴄᴇɴᴛᴜʀʏ, ᴍᴀɴʏ ᴄɪᴛʏ-ʙᴀsᴇᴅ Mᴇᴅɪᴛᴇʀʀᴀɴᴇᴀɴ ᴍᴀɢɴᴀᴛᴇs were consolidating their rule as trade with the Middle East and Asia quickened. Through the work of marriage and inheritance, in 1162 the counts of Barcelona also became kings of Aragon. Within ten years, they had begun new conquests across the Pyrenees. Among other territories, they annexed the small town of Perpignan and its hinterland, Roussillon. Roussillon remained attached, more or less, to Aragonese crowns (and therefore eventually to the Spanish crown) for the next half millennium.

By 1662, nevertheless, France had held title to Roussillon for three years. During the French-Spanish war that had raged intermittently from the 1620s to 1659, French forces had occupied a significant portion of Iberia. In 1640, France had supported major rebellions in Catalonia and Portugal, which only ended with the reintegration of Catalonia into Spanish rule and the permanent independence of Portugal, both in 1659. At the treaty of 1659, however, Louis XIV settled for territorial gains in the Low Countries plus the annexation of Roussillon.

In and around the Pyrenees, "rule" then remained a relative term. Catalan speakers on both sides of the Pyrenees had long produced and merchandised metals, cloth, and salt with little interference from national authorities. But now those Catalans who had fallen under French jurisdiction encountered three salient and inconvenient features of the later 17th-century French state's intervention in the provinces:

- Under a twenty-four-year-old Louis XIV's aggressive rule, every region of the country felt increasing pressure to pay its share of ambitious international wars, expensive internal administration, and debts left from previous borrowing.
- The French-Spanish frontier in the Pyrenees, long a no-man's-land, had begun to matter as a container of income-producing resources, as a marker of French sovereignty, and as a source of customs revenue.
- The king and his agents did not hesitate to visit violence on any ordinary people who dared to resist the royal call for funds.

In addition to pursuing repeated foreign wars, the French army used its force domestically to ensure payment for those wars.

After Cardinal Mazarin's death in 1661, Louis XIV took over France's central administration without a prime minister. But to restore the finances of a country battered by a century of civil and international wars, he relied on tough, resourceful finance minister Jean Baptiste Colbert, 42 years old at Mazarin's death. Colbert in turn managed a small corps of relatives, clients, and officials who owed their survival to his patronage, and who spent much of their remarkable energy scaring up new sources for state revenue (Beik 1985; Dessert 1984; Lynn 1997).

In Roussillon, intendant Macqueron faced the challenges of imposing a government salt monopoly, monitoring taxable trade across the mountains, controlling rebellious mountaineers, and subordinating cities whose consuls clung to their ancient chartered liberties. The intendant worked with a Council of Roussillon cobbled together after the 1659 peace settlement to serve as an intermediary instrument of royal rule. The task at hand: rebuilding the new French province after decades of warfare.

On 4 November 1662, Macqueron wrote from Perpignan to Colbert. Since the government had tied the Roussillon Council's emoluments to revenues from the salt monopoly, he said, its members had an interest in helping impose the new salt administration. "But I think," confided Macqueron,

> that their mediation would be more harmful than profitable, and that it would suffice for them to register and publish the necessary edict or declaration without asking any more of them. They are few in number and almost all aliens in Roussillon, where they have settled since the loss of Barcelona. Furthermore they have fallen out with the Consuls and therefore with the people of Perpignan. Even those who would not oppose the new tax in principle would oppose it simply because the Council had proposed it. (BNMC 112 bis [Bibliothèque Nationale, Paris, Mélanges de Colbert, dossier 112 bis])

Macqueron had to impose French rule in previously Spanish territory, which meant establishing the boundary between French and Spanish, or more precisely between French and not French. On a regional scale, he played his own part in a drama that likewise proceeded at national and international scales. Everywhere Louis XIV was aggressively marking lines between us and them, between French and not French. But in the newly annexed territories the people involved resisted accepting—and especially paying for—the new political arrangements.

All along the Pyrenees, in fact, tax rebellions arose repeatedly for another fifteen years, as Louis XIV and Colbert sought to raise revenue for their expanding state (BNMC 113–72 bis; Nicolas 2002: 56–58; Tilly 1986: 150–51). Despite many a reversal, nevertheless, the commanding king imposed his will on rebellious provinces, including Roussillon. In the process, Louis XIV and his agents sharpened the boundary between French and not French, increased the visibility and costs of exclusion from the French polity, and laid down relations between crown and subjects that eventually became the stuff of French citizenship.

I relish returning to the Old Regime French archives into which I have burrowed repeatedly since the start of my career as an analyst of political processes. But in this chapter let me resist the urge to retrace the construction of French citizenship year by year, province by province, from the 1660s to the present. Instead, let me use French historical experience to illustrate an argument that is currently gaining credence in discussions of boundaries, citizenship, and exclusion. To follow the argument, we must understand citizenship not as a sentiment or a cluster of beliefs but as an organized set of social ties: rights and obligations connecting people who fall under the power of a particular state with agents of that state. In citizenship, those rights and obligations apply broadly to whole categories of persons rather than varying from one individual to the next.

In eight quick points, the argument runs like this:

1. The creation, activation, and transformation of social boundaries— boundary change for short—belong to a crucial, general social process depending on similar mechanisms over a wide variety of circumstances (Tilly 2004a).
2. When a social boundary comes into being, it includes not only a dividing line but also relations on each side of the line, relations *across* the line, and shared stories about those relations.
3. Public politics invariably involves creation, activation, and transformation

of visible us-them boundaries, as well as reversal of those processes: de-struction, deactivation, or restoration of us-them boundaries.

4. Political actors including governments always acquire investments in us-them boundaries and/or programs for their alteration.
5. Every act of political inclusion consists of creating, activating, or trans-forming an us-them boundary, and thus inevitably twins with an act of political exclusion.
6. Indeed, political boundaries often first come into being as defenses of insiders against presumably threatening outsiders.
7. The processes by which political boundaries change define the condi-tions, if any, under which individuals and groups can then cross the boundary in either direction, hence who will next be included and ex-cluded.
8. These principles apply notably to citizenship, a fundamental process of boundary drawing, inclusion, and exclusion across much of the world over the last two centuries.

This brief survey will cover the eight points very unequally, using European historical experience to think through the development of citizenship as a re-organization of boundaries, inclusions, and exclusions. It will use ideas from my earlier work on boundaries and citizenship, but spare you the complexities of that work (Tilly 1995, 1998c, 1999c, 2004a, 2004b). Instead, I will review outstanding books by other scholars to make my points.

Peter Sahlins's insightful historical studies of relations between citizens and the French state help concretize these extremely general arguments. Two of Sahlins's books—one on state identities in the Pyrenees, the other on the natu-ralization of foreigners in France up to 1819—bear directly on boundary change (Sahlins 1989, 2004). Indeed, he called the first book, a doctoral dissertation transmogrified into a delightful monograph, *Boundaries: The Making of France and Spain in the Pyrenees.* In that book, Sahlins makes the case that in Roussillon and the neighboring Cerdanya the treaty of 1659 drew a boundary through a region of common Catalan culture, that the boundary came to organize rela-tions between nominally French and Spanish citizens in unexpected ways, but that it eventually made a significant difference to allegiances, social lives, and connections on either side of the border between the countries.

Catalans of common origin eventually became French or Spanish nationals, but along the way they intermarried extensively, retained a common language for private life, and actually made money from smuggling across the new bor-der so long as the authorities did not police the frontier too effectively. But the boundary eventually separated two rather different forms of political life, two different sorts of relationship between citizens and state. The process of separation itself played a significant part in creating those contrasting forms of political life.

At first, the French-Spanish boundary in the Pyrenees allocated villages and their jurisdictions to one crown or the other without much concern for drawing a precise geographic line. Only at the 1868 Treaty of Bayonne did commissioners draw a territorial boundary and mark it with stones. That marked a shift between two different conceptions of boundaries. As Sahlins puts it:

> The history of the boundary between 1659 and 1868, then, can hardly be summarized as the simple evolution from an empty zone to a precise line, but rather as the complex interplay of two notions of boundary—zonal and linear—and two ideas of sovereignty—jurisdictional and territorial. The two polarities can be found at any given moment in the history of the boundary, although the dominant but hardly unilinear tendency was the collapse of separate jurisdictional frontiers into a single territorial boundary line. The French Revolution gave to the idea of territory a specifically national content, while the early nineteenth-century states politicized the boundary line as the point where national territorial sovereignty found expression. (Sahlins 1989: 7)

We begin to see that conceptions of national boundaries have strong implications for the creation of citizenship, the establishment of categorically defined (rather than particular) rights and obligations connecting subjects of a given state to that state's agents. We also begin to notice that the geographic principle of citizenship—the famous *jus solis*—splits into two rather different subprinciples, one attached to zones, the other attached to precise national boundaries.

In the first geographic subprinciple, which Sahlins calls jurisdictional, a person or group belongs to a social unit such as a fief, a parish, or a duchy; the unit does not necessarily occupy a contiguous territory; the unit may also overlap territorially with other units; and the units, rather than the individuals, belong to the state. Long before 1662, Raymond de Saint-Gilles, count of Toulouse, had also identified himself as "count of Rodez, Gévaudan, Uzès, Nîmes, Agde, Béziers, and Narbonne"—all separate jurisdictions in which he exercised power and from which he drew revenues (Cheyette 2001: 108). The eight places (including Toulouse) in his title did not form anything like a unitary, contiguous administrative unit. Seven bore the names of cities, but one (Gévaudan) referred to a region. Yet in some regards all residents of the eight units were Raymond's subjects.

Collectively, but through the mediation of local rulers, the eight units owed their count regular tribute, military support, and labor service. Occasionally, we catch a historical glimpse of just such a system in operation as we notice that not individuals or households but whole communities owe taxes or quotas of men for military service (Barber 1974; Head 1995). We individualists may find it unsettling to call such an arrangement citizenship, but the arrangement certainly connected people with specific states by means of compelling rights and obligations. France and Spain long operated on just such a subprinciple.

We encounter an irony. In Europe, the word "nation" long designated not all the inhabitants of a politically distinct territory, but a local community of sojourners deprived of full citizenship rights yet enjoying a special corporate status. Among its several definitions of nation, the *Oxford English Dictionary* offers this one:

> In the mediaeval universities, a body of students belonging to a particular district, country, or group of countries, who formed a more or less independent community; still retained in the universities of Glasgow and Aberdeen, in connexion with the election of the Rector.

In universities and towns, such nations often elected their own officials and public representatives, provided for their own security, judged their own members' derelictions and, in time of want, took responsibility for their own food supply. Across Europe, Jews and other religious minorities often figured locally as nations in this sense of the word. They exercised privileges, but lacked full citizenship, even at the local level. The very arrangement gave authorities pretexts and means for expelling whole communities—including religious minorities organized as nations—in times of famine, epidemic, or war (Tilly 1975: 437–40). Long before French revolutionaries hijacked the term, "nation" referred to a jurisdictional form of organization. In that meaning, Catalans still constituted a nation, albeit a threatened nation, in the Roussillon of 1662 (Sahlins 1989: 113–16).

Sahlins calls his second subprinciple *territorial*. It draws a precise geographical perimeter around a specific territory, and assigns citizenship categorically to some or all of the legal occupants of the territory. Such citizenship often creates an array of unequal categories, for example, restricting children, felons, naturalized foreigners, or women to lesser rights and obligations. The territorial principle often displaces the jurisdictional principle in company with the imposition of uniform field administration: division of the territory into equivalent, mutually exclusive administrative units; procedures for taxation, conscription, censuses, and other civic obligations that apply similarly throughout the territory; surveillance and policing on more or less similar principles in all regions; relatively equal access to law and public services from one place to another.

Before the protests begin, let me stress the word *relatively:* in all real cases of territorial citizenship, places differ in their practical access to law and public services as a function of local variation in class, ethnicity, and political connections. Still, on the average such inequalities, compounded and crystallized by previously established charter rights and obligations, make even bigger differences in jurisdictional regimes. As the state of Louis XIV and Colbert moved toward territorial administration, for example, it pioneered the uniform enumeration of local populations that eventually became the census (Bourdelais 2004). Sahlins shows us the French state following a zigzag, even dialectical, course between the 16th and 18th centuries that eventually led from mainly jurisdictional to mainly territorial claims over its citizens.

Catalans of the French Pyrenees were already becoming exceptions in France as a whole by the time France annexed Roussillon and part of Cerdanya. In contrast with Spain, where Catalans maintained exclusive privileges attached to their nationality until the reforms of 1714, in general French 17th-century conquests soon led to incorporation of the newly acquired provinces into the national fiscal, military, and administrative system (Sahlins 1989: 113–23). Defended by the region's internal connectedness and geographic inaccessibility, the jurisdictional arrangements of the high Pyrenees stood out as increasingly exceptional in a unifying, territorializing France. Even there, despite shared culture and language, to be French meant increasingly not to be Spanish, while to be Spanish meant increasingly not to be French. The old distinction between "civic" and "ethnic" forms of citizenship begins to blur. As citizenship gained importance, so did its exclusions. Those exclusions generated and justified myths of ethnicity, of distinctive national cultures and origins, even of *jus sanguinis.* Well before the French Revolution, some elements of 19th-century territorial citizenship were already falling into place.

A second book by Peter Sahlins makes the point even more forcefully. His *Unnaturally French* examines the legal naturalization of foreigners in France from the 17th century to shortly after Napoleon. In feudal law, the *droit d'aubaine* referred narrowly to a monarch's right to seize that portion of a foreigner's property situated within the monarch's territory at the foreigner's death unless the foreigner had native heirs or had received specific legal exemptions. Where resident foreigners held substantial French property (notably in frontier regions), the esoteric royal right affected such questions as whether their direct descendants who resided abroad or collateral descendants living in France had stronger claims to inherit their wealth.

With French state consolidation of the 16th and 17th centuries, however, royal jurists extended the relevant law into a body of exclusions from public offices, religious benefices, and economic activities, as well as into liability for special taxes and judicial disabilities. The Naturalization Tax of 1697—almost forty years into Louis XIV's reign, at a time of intense international war—made those disabilities a significant source of crown revenue as it revoked all previous naturalizations and forced foreigners to pay again.

This money-raising strategy, to be sure, paralleled the marvelous fiscal inventions of the same period that forced men who had bought tax exemptions through ennoblement to pay again for verification of their noble titles and required office holders to grant the crown money either to confirm their titles to the offices or to prevent the creation of new offices that would compete for the same revenues. Still, foreigners remained even more vulnerable than native-born nobles and office holders. These expanding penalties gave resident foreigners increasing incentives to undertake the contingent, expensive, and time-consuming process of naturalization. Naturalization did not make foreigners fully French by popular reputation. But it did remove them from the vulnerable category of tainted and taxable vis-à-vis the monarchy.

More important for present purposes, the augmentation of foreigners' legal disabilities had a strong, unanticipated side effect: it defined rights for the categories of nonforeigners and naturalized foreigners: by negation, nonforeigners and naturalized foreigners became citizens of sorts. During the later 16th-century, citizenship, Sahlins observes:

> became an enlarged, socially inclusive membership category, a juridical condition pertaining to men and women, peasants and nobles, children and adults, servants and masters—and accessible to foreigners by naturalization. (Sahlins 2004: 11)

Eventually, however, domestic legal and political processes undermined the segregation and exploitation of foreigners. During the reign of Louis XIV, individual naturalizations declined in frequency, especially in the many periods of war and economic depression. Just as the Sun King massacred, expelled, or extracted punitive payments from Protestants who did not convert to Catholicism at his revocation of the Edict of Nantes (1685), he generally treated foreigners as an undesirable but exploitable presence.

During the half century between Louis XIV's death (1709) and the middle of the Seven Years War (1759), naturalizations increased remarkably as relative prosperity combined with a shift away from punitive taxation to sale of nationality. Three causes of increase intertwined. Some of the surge in naturalizations after 1715 resulted from the return of children born in the Protestant diaspora to the more tolerant regime of Louis XV. Many others came from territories that Louis XIV had conquered, then lost or gave back in peace settlements.

The largest part of the increase, however, resulted from a genuine alteration of governmental policy toward more liberal granting of naturalization. French jurists, furthermore, successfully opened up a powerful and previously blurred legal distinction. On the one side existed the king's personal right to the droit d'aubaine, which stemmed from the law of nations and therefore belonged to the sovereign. On the other side rose the legal foundations of inheritance and political rights, which belonged to the civil law. Inheritance and political rights thus fell increasingly into the hands of legal officials who spoke for the French nation rather than the grip of the monarch in his own right. In the long run, such a distinction meant that the king might retain rights to specific revenues, but lost the power to decide who were his subjects under what conditions.

Sahlins speaks of the "unfinished revolution of citizenship":

> Unfinished, because when the French Revolution broke out in 1789, the postabsolute model of the citizen had still not acquired a definitive shape. On the one hand, in the public arena, the citizen was increasingly an (adult, male, property-owning) actor in pursuit of the public good, if not a patriot, one willing to be taxed but demanding political representation as its cost. At the same time, the very fact that citizenship was premised on the possession of property, as opposed to the inheritance of property across generations, in and of itself signified the shift of the citizen from the world of nationality law to politics. (Sahlins 2004: 265)

Citizenship began to depend ever more clearly on exclusion, and to correspond ever more closely to public political participation.

As legal enforcement of foreigners' disabilities thus weakened, naturalizations again declined from the 1760s to the Revolution's new citizenship regime of 1789 and thereafter. Regimes of citizenship and naturalization underwent new twists and turns during the Revolution, the Napoleonic regime, and the post-Napoleonic Restoration, up to the outright abolition of the droit d'aubaine in 1819. By that time the growing distinction between civic rights (largely available to foreigners) and political rights (strictly unavailable to unnaturalized foreigners) had transformed the meaning of naturalization. Nonnaturalized foreigners had access to legal protections and many public benefits, but lacked rights of political participation.

Historical intricacies matter less to our inquiry than the general point: French citizenship emerged from efforts to define who was *not* French, but control of its definition shifted away from the crown to lawyers and eventually to representative assemblies largely populated by lawyers. It developed dialectically, constantly defining citizenship in opposition to current definitions of noncitizens and of the liabilities imposed by not being a citizen.

Consider the implications of a third book for our conversation. Although Peter Sahlins has written further excellent and relevant books, we can turn to another analyst who proceeds from a quite different angle: Anthony Marx. Marx's *Faith in Nation* only mentions citizenship in passing, but it centers on a closely related phenomenon: nationalism. In terms that should stir a memory of Peter Sahlins's analyses, Marx defines nationalism as

> a collective sentiment or identity, bounding and binding together those individuals who share a sense of large-scale political solidarity aimed at creating, legitimating, or challenging states. (Marx 2003: 6)

Marx pursues the development of nationalism, thus defined, by analyzing the long-term histories of Spain, France, and England, but harking back to his earlier books' comparisons of South Africa, the United States, and Brazil. Marx argues that such collective sentiments arise through processes of exclusion, directed against those who threaten the nation and/or remain unworthy of inclusion in the nation.

American national identity, Marx claims, formed against the background of African American slavery, the "us" of white America pitted against the "them" of black America. Similarly but much earlier, according to Marx, Spain developed its relatively weak nationalism through opposition to its domestic Jews and Muslims, France acquired a stronger version of nationalism through opposition to domestic Protestants, and English nationalism swelled in opposition to domestic Catholics. The crucial confrontations, furthermore, occurred on the domestic scene rather than in the international arena. As Marx sums up:

> Rulers came to understand that they could not effectively wage war or diplomacy if they were weakened within by civil or religious conflict, could not then recruit troops, be sure that those troops would remain loyal, and avoid challenges from a "third column" tied to external enemies . . . to avoid such difficulties and gain strength, monarchs sought to build national unity and loyalty

through domestic religious exclusion. Activists from below did likewise. (Marx 2003: 79)

Thus popular sentiment and royal will united in opposition to a common enemy.

Personally, I find more persuasive a less psychological, more institutional account of what happened in Spain, France, and England, an account more like that of Peter Sahlins (Tilly 2004b). Nevertheless, I think Marx has put his agile fingers on crucial elements in the formation of both nationalism and citizenship: the drawing and politicization of us-them boundaries, the exclusion of visible others, the foundation of membership on not being something else. In Spain, mobilization against Muslims and Jews, then against their ostensibly Catholic descendants, did indeed help shape prevailing definitions of Spanishness for purposes of nationalism and citizenship. In England, from 1689 to the 19th-century political exclusion of non-Anglicans, and especially of Catholics, deeply affected practices of nationalism and citizenship. It created boundaries that still divide Northern Ireland lethally today. As for France, Marx adds to Peter Sahlins's not Spain and not foreign a third "not" dear to Louis XIV: not Protestant.

As our earlier discussion of French citizenship might suggest, however, Marx's argument runs into a rough patch when it comes to the secularizing French Revolution and the titanic struggles over church and state that roiled France until the early 20th century. Just as we might ask why English nationalism didn't disintegrate when propertied non-Anglican Protestants and then Catholics acquired substantial political rights at the end of the 1820s, we might ask what basis a secular French state offered for exclusive French nationalism and citizenship.

At first, Marx finesses the question. He declares that French revolutionaries substituted royalty and its foreign allies for irreligion as the enemy. He gestures toward France's 19th-century political instability as a consequence of abandoning exclusion. Then he alters the argument subtly. "In rejecting absolutist rule built upon religious exclusion and Catholic passion," he goes on,

France's revolutionaries had assumed that they could have unity and democracy without that glue. To a degree, they were right, though arguably at the cost of the discord over the form of rule that followed. Secular loyalty proved powerful, even as faith reemerged among the populace. That degree of national unity earlier achieved through religious exclusion did persist, notably with France's unity remaining unchallenged, and was then reinforced by extensions of the suffrage. But such unity also proved insufficient to allow for consolidation of democratic authority. France could then project itself as inclusive, with citizenship based on *jus soli*, though in doing so it forgot its earlier exclusionary basis and foreclosed the further use of exclusions to manage diversity or instability. (Marx 2003: 173)

So arguing, Marx actually concedes a point I mentioned in the opening eight-point summary of my argument, but then neglected. The initial process that creates a boundary never continues to operate in the same way indefinitely. The initial process disappears, but the boundary persists. How can that happen? When people put a political boundary in place, they also organize social relations on each side of the boundary, relations across the boundary, and stories about the whole ensemble. In the sense of chapter 5, they adapt. But here they do not simply reinforce inequality; they do political work with the boundary. The work itself alters the relevant boundary, social relations within or across it, and available stories about it. In fact, the boundary often shifts without disappearing, as individuals or groups cross from one side to the other.

To take the obvious example, once the United Kingdom drew the perimeter of full citizenship around well-behaved and propertied adult males on the ground of their greater responsibility for the public weal, the regime opened itself to challenges from other excluded categories of the population, male or female, who had acquired property or could make the case for their own indispensability to the public weal. Working-class Chartists of 1838–1848 said as much: we workers allied with merchants and manufacturers in the push for parliamentary reform that brought the great Reform Act of 1832, but the newly enfranchised merchants and manufacturers closed the door behind them. This bid to move across the boundary explains the otherwise astonishing concentration of a 19th-century workers' movement on purely political reforms: expansion of the suffrage, salaries for members of Parliament, and so on. The People's Charter demanded full citizenship for honest workers—at least if they were male.

One more book clarifies the point. Michael Mann has weighed into the discussions of boundaries and exclusion with a characteristically bulky, reflective, historically informed, and original analysis. Mann's *Dark Side of Democracy* takes Anthony Marx's emphasis on exclusion one step further, into the darkness of ethnic cleansing. Here he replies to common explanations of ethnic cleansing as primitivism, nationalism, statist manipulation, and opportunism. He argues instead that democratization itself, with its frequent coincidence of top-down and (especially) bottom-up patriotism, generates incentives for violent attacks on whole populations identified as belonging to alien ethnic categories. It does so, Mann says, by accentuating claims for popular sovereignty, and increasing the likelihood that people will cast such claims in exclusive ethnic terms; where people committed to distinct ethnic identities make incompatible bids for the same territory—for exclusive sovereignty—they more frequently use force to remove their rivals.

Ethnic cleansing became deadlier and more common in the age of democratization, argues Mann, for two main reasons. First, earlier regimes usually divided on the basis of class rather than of ethnicity. Hence class conflict prevailed, and ethnic majorities (if they existed) lacked the political means to annihilate ethnic minorities. Second, democratic regimes regularly justified their rule by nationalist claims: the state represents the nation. Mann qualifies the argument by pointing out that stably institutionalized democracies less frequently adopt ethnic cleansing than democracies in the making, regimes in which who rules and who has the right to rule remain contested.

In an argument resembling Roger Gould's analysis of intergroup violence (see chapter 2 of this book), Mann offers two scenarios for the transition from intergroup hostility to open violence:

> Actual mass murder required one of two further scenarios. In (a) the less powerful rival was bolstered to fight rather than submit (which does not produce mass murder), believing that help would be forthcoming from coethnics or allies abroad. In (b) a stronger group fears its power is declining in the long run, but can use its present strength to create its own cleansed state without much physical or moral risk to itself. Scenario (a) produces mass murder as an ethnic civil war begins and escalates; (b) produces genocidal preemptive strikes. Yet settler cases are distinct here, since settlers tended to embark on murderous cleansing only when much weaker native populations loom as violent irritants rather than major threats. (Mann 2005: 503)

Mann makes this case in four main ways: 1) by criticizing standard versions of prevalent explanations; 2) by arguing through historical illustrations that ethnic cleansing (properly understood) rarely if ever occurred before the democratic era; 3) by looking closely at the cases of Armenia, the Nazis, Communist regimes, Yugoslavia, and Rwanda; 4) by comparing those cases with the absence of ethnic cleansing (again properly understood) in India and Indonesia. Cumulatively, he provides evidence for a chilling association between nationalist consolidation of regimes and ethnic cleansing. Since that sort of consolidation became much more common in the age of democratization since 1789, Mann's analysis establishes at least an indirect connection between democratization and genocide.

Michael Mann's intervention makes clear that the ancient histories I reviewed earlier still have relevance to the operation of boundaries, citizenship, and exclusion today. Far from expressing a cumulative sense of common properties alone, citizenship still often comes into being through deliberate exclusion. Macedonian nationalists define Albanians out of the polity, and Islamists seek to deny the unfaithful political rights in mainly Muslim countries. Serbian and Israeli governments distinguish sharply between their strategies of policing in their heartlands and at their edges (Ron 2003). Once us-them boundaries form, they take on lives of their own as people on either side attach social relations, stories, and daily practices to them. The combination of boundaries, relations, stories, and practices we call citizenship continues to bind people to particular states by means of rights and obligations, which means that shifts of power to transnational or nonstate institutions threaten existing patterns of citizenship.

Fortunately, if my reading of European history is right, the frequent founding of citizenship by means of forceful, exploitative, often vicious forms of exclusion does not mean that every new version of citizenship must build on us-them ethnicity. Exclusion will continue in the sense that so long as public authorities that deliver benefits exist, the authorities or their constituencies will draw distinctions between those who have rights to those benefits and obligations to back them, on one side, and those who lack the relevant rights and obligations, on the other. Exclusive communities of fate, yes. Exclusive communities of hate, not necessarily.

Part V

Political Boundaries

Chapter 12

Why Worry About Citizenship?

Since the later 18th century, new political regimes have developed the habit of advertising their newness by enacting written constitutions. These days new constitutions address at least three audiences: a population that is supposed to live by its provisions, an international community that must deal with its leaders, and an array of people who will actually run the country. Each of these audiences, furthermore, typically has more than a single ear. Constitutional definitions of citizenship unavoidably speak simultaneously to all three audiences and their diverse internal claques.

The post–Soviet Republic of Kazakstan offers a striking case in point. The republic's 1995 constitution stresses rights and obligations of Kazak citizenship. In a day when a claim to be a coherent indigenous nation forms a crucial part of any bid for internationally recognized sovereignty, how constitution writers answer the question "Who are you?" matters to all three audiences. Savor the preamble's assertive tone:

> We, the people of Kazakstan, united by a common historic fate, creating a state on the indigenous Kazak land, considering ourselves a peaceloving and civil society, dedicated to the ideals of freedom, equality and concord, wishing to take a worthy place in the world community, realizing our high responsibility before present and future generations, proceeding from our sovereign right, accept this Constitution.

The constitution's article 7 specifies that "1. The state language of the Republic of Kazakstan shall be the Kazak language. 2. In state institutions and local self-administrative bodies the Russian language shall be officially used on equal grounds along with the Kazak language. 3. The state shall promote conditions for the study and development of the languages of the people of Kazakstan." One begins to detect that who is Kazak, and who is not, matters intensely in the politics of Kazakstan. As it turns out, who is Kazak also matters to Kazakstan's neighbors.

Small wonder. The constitution's drafters worked against a backdrop of vigorous, often violent contention over national autonomy. The territory people now call Kazakstan centers on the steppe crisscrossed for centuries by caravans between China and Europe. Today's Kazakstan touches the Caspian Sea, Turkmenistan, Uzbekistan, Kyrgyzstan, and China. Across a vast border with the Russian federation it also abuts Siberia, the Urals, and the Volga region. Over most of the last millennium, nomadic Turkic pastoralists have predominated within its territory. But they have endured conquest after conquest.

Conquered by expanding Mongols in the 13th century, the region sustained its own khan from the later 15th century. Forcible integration of the region into the Russian empire during the 18th and 19th centuries, followed by extensive immigration of Russian-speaking farmers from the north, greatly increased Russian cultural and political presence in Kazakstan: "About 1.5 million new colonists from European Russia came to Kazakhstan at the end of the nineteenth century and in the beginning of the twentieth century" (Khazanov 1995: 157). Those changes marginalized the region's nomadic herders and drove many of them into settled agriculture. Self-identified Kazaks took advantage of the Bolshevik Revolution to create an autonomous republic that lasted from 1918 to 1920. Those Kazak nationalists, however, soon succumbed to Soviet military might.

Come to power, Stalin eventually established his characteristic pattern of governing the region through Moscow-oriented Kazaks, and created a full Soviet Republic of Kazakstan in 1936. But Stalin and his successors also built an economic system that made Kazakstan's major industrial and commercial nodes tributaries of centers in Russia and Uzbekistan rather than connecting them with each other. The early 1930s brought forced collectivization of agriculture and fixed settlement of the remaining Kazak nomads. Successive Soviet regimes shipped in technicians, peasants, and political prisoners from Russia, Belorussia, Poland, Ukraine, and the Caucasus as displaced Turkic nomads died out or fled to China. Unsurprisingly, Russian speakers concentrated in and around the Russian-oriented nodes, which meant that ethnic balances varied enormously by region within Kazakstan. Kazaks themselves divided into three large and sometimes hostile clans, or *zhus:* a Great Horde concentrated chiefly in southern Kazakstan, a Middle Horde in the north-central region, and a Lesser Horde, in the west.

Ethnic Kazak Dinmukhamed Kunaev became regional party boss in 1964 and eventually acquired full membership in the Soviet Union's politburo. Kunaev brought a number of Kazaks (especially from his own Great Horde) into his administration. In 1986, however, reformer Mikhail Gorbachev replaced Kunaev with Gennadi Kolbin, an ethnic Russian unconnected with Kazakstan. Students and others thereupon demonstrated against the regime in the capital, Almaty; perhaps two hundred people died in street confrontations and subsequent repression (Olcott 1997: 206). By 1989 Gorbachev had replaced Kolbin with another ethnic Kazak, Nursultan Nazarbaev.

Having ridden the rapids of the Soviet Union's downstream rush, Nazarbaev still rules Kazakstan with a heavy hand. While tolerating (and possibly benefiting from) a great deal of rent seeking by former and present state officials, Nazarbaev has sought to advance a definition of Kazak national identity without alienating either a large domestic Russian minority or the great Russian power to his north. No doubt with an eye to the intermittent civil war in nearby Tajikistan and the volatility of ethnic, linguistic, regional, and religious factions in neighboring Uzbekistan and Kyrgyzstan (Atkin 1997; Fane 1996; Fierman 1997; Huskey 1997; Juraeva and Lubin 1996), Nazarbaev has handled ethnic-linguistic divisions with velvet gloves. The only nationalist group his regime has actively suppressed is the militant Alash Party, which advocates a great state uniting all the Turkic peoples. Meanwhile, the regime resists pressure from outside (especially Russia) for recognition of dual citizenship, and presses its self-identified Russians to declare themselves either foreigners or dedicated citizens of a Kazak state.

For whoever can claim to control the country, the stakes are high. In addition to its share of the Caspian, Kazakstan contains enormous potential wealth in minerals, including estimated oil reserves of 40–178 billion barrels, equivalent to a quarter century of total U.S. oil consumption (Ingwerson 1997: 1). Cocaine, other drugs, and a wide range of valuable contraband flow across the country, with mobsters and officials dividing large profits. Before the economic crises of the 1990s, furthermore, Kazakstan supplied a substantial portion of the Soviet Union's commercial grains. If the state ever establishes an effective system of taxation and investment, it will have abundant revenues to spend, not to mention fortunes to be made in capitalist enterprises (see Feige 1998).

Claimants to that state divide sharply by ethnic category. As of the mid-1990s, demographers enumerated 44 percent of the republic's population as Kazak, 36 percent as Russian, and about 10 percent as "Europeans" of other varieties; the remaining tenth fell into a hundred other nationalities, chiefly Asian in origin (United Nations 1995: I, 6). Although the proportion identified as Kazak was rising through a combination of differential fertility, exits of Russians, in-migration from other parts of Central Asia, and (I speculate) shifts of declared identity on the parts of people with mixed ancestry, the constitution's drafters had to contend with the fact that the country's ostensible nationality accounted for a minority of its population, and that the country's lingua franca was not Kazak, but Russian. Hence great sensitivity to definitions of citizenship.

Referring to subjects of the Kazak state, the constitution refers to the following human entities (and nonentities): The People, citizens, everyone, no one, foreigners, stateless persons, persons, and individuals. It also makes distinctions between minors and full adults, with only full adults (those twenty and over in the case of elections to local assemblies) having the right to vote and hold office. Some rights and obligations apply to everyone, but many of those specified apply to citizens alone. Citizens, according to the constitution, enjoy these rights:

- to change citizenship (a concession to domestic Russians and representatives of Russia who pressed for recognition of dual citizenship)
- not to be extradited except as provided by international treaty
- not to be exiled, and to return freely from abroad
- the state's protection and patronage outside its boundaries
- access to documents, decisions, and other sources of information concerning the citizen's rights and interests
- to form associations (exceptions: a) the military, employees of national security, law-enforcement bodies, and judges must not join parties, trade unions, or actions in support of any political party, b) no associations "directed toward a violent change of the constitutional system, violation of the integrity of the Republic, undermining the security of the state, inciting social, racial, national, religious, class and tribal enmity, as well as formation of unauthorized paramilitary units," c) no political parties, trade unions, or religious parties based in or financed by foreign countries, foreign individuals, or international organizations)
- provision of housing at an affordable price
- ownership of legally acquired property
- minimum wage, pension, social security in old age as well as in case of disease, disability, or loss of breadwinner
- protection of health, including free extensive medical assistance

- free secondary education, plus access to higher education on a competitive basis
- to pay for and receive education in private establishments
- to assemble, hold meetings, rallies and demonstrations, street processions, and pickets peacefully and without arms
- to participate in state affairs directly and through representatives, including collective appeals to public and local self-administrative bodies
- to elect and be elected to public offices (exceptions: a) "citizens judged incapable by a court as well as those held in places of confinement on a court's sentence"), b) "age of a government employee must not exceed sixty years and sixty-five years in exceptional cases," c) restrictions on minimum age, residence, and professional qualifications apply to specific offices)

As compared with these many rights of citizens, the constitution stipulates only a handful of obligations:

- not to violate rights and freedoms of other persons or infringe on the constitutional system and public morals
- to attend secondary school
- to defend the Republic of Kazakstan, and to perform military service "according to the procedure and in the forms established by law"
- to care for the protection of historical and cultural heritage and preserve monuments of history and culture
- to preserve nature and protect natural resources

The constitution applies such weighty obligations as tax payments not to citizens alone but to "everyone." It leaves unmentioned such common obligations of citizenship elsewhere as submitting to censuses, serving on juries, and registering vital events. Nevertheless, it clearly articulates three principles of citizenship that distinguish our own time's prevailing ideas, if not always its practices, from those of almost any previous historical epoch: **first**, citizenship designates not attributes of individuals but a broad categorical relation between the state's agents and a large share of the population falling under the state's jurisdiction; **second**, ethnic categories other than the official national category have no standing with respect to citizenship; **third**, degrees of citizenship exist, at least when it comes to minors, persons aged sixty and over, incarcerated criminals, and court-declared incompetents.

Such principles appear tediously obvious in today's Western world. Yet the existence of citizenship in something like the sense defined by the Kazak constitution sets off our era from all other historical eras. It identifies political institutions that first grew up in Europe and by no means flourish everywhere in the world today. In Kazakstan itself, the current regime repeatedly violates its announced principles of citizenship, notably when it comes to political freedom for voices of opposition. Nevertheless, a constitution's announcement of strong citizenship facilitates the formation of alliances between aggrieved citizens and outside powers.

Within its zone of application, effective citizenship establishes the frame for fierce contention over rights and obligations of different categories within populations subject to a given governmental institution. Given substantial citizenship at a national scale, inequalities by gender, race, national origin, recency of arrival in the territory, employment, income, and welfare become issues of citizenship. In practice, all states compromise citizenship significantly in two ways: 1) by distinguishing among categories and degrees of citizenship that imply different rights, obligations, and relations to authorities; 2) by advertising as general rights and obligations arrangements that actually differ significantly in their applicability to various segments of the state's subject population. This chapter merely draws together the elementary operating principles of citizenship, then reflects on why and how citizenship matters to human welfare.

A little definitional work clarifies essential connections. Let us take *government* to designate any organization that controls the chief concentrated coercive means within some substantial territory, reserving the name *state* for those governments that a) do not fall under the jurisdiction of any other government, and b) receive recognition from other governments in the same situation. Sweden and China qualify as states, while municipalities within their perimeters qualify as governments, but not as states. In principle, citizenship then refers to a relation between 1) governmental agents acting uniquely as such, and 2) whole categories of persons identified uniquely by their connection with the government in question. The relation includes transactions among the parties, of course, but those transactions cluster around mutual rights and obligations. In the case of Kazakstan, we have already seen that those rights and obligations can cover a wide range of social relations.

What are rights and obligations? Imagine X and Y as social actors, including organizations and whole categories of persons. X's rights with respect to Y's include all enforceable claims that X can make on Y, with the crucial feature of enforcement being that authoritative third parties will intervene to promote Y's acceptance of the claims in question. Obligations are nothing but the same enforceable claims seen from Y's perspective. Veterans have rights to pensions in the degree that governmental paymasters have an obligation to pay those pensions, that residents of a state have an obligation to pay taxes in the degree to which fiscal officials have a right to collect those taxes.

Citizenship designates a set of mutually enforceable claims relating categories of persons to agents of governments. Like relations between spouses, between co-authors, between workers and employers, citizenship has the character of a contract: variable in range, never completely specified, always depending on unstated assumptions about context, modified by practice, constrained by collective memory, yet ineluctably involving rights and obligations sufficiently defined that either party is likely to express indignation and take corrective action when the other fails to meet expectations built into the relationship. As observers, we actually witness transactions between governmental agents and members of broadly defined categories, but we abstract from those transactions a cultural bundle: a set of mutual rights and obligations. Precisely insofar as a bundle of rights and obligations actually distinguishes a whole category of the state's subject population defined by their relation to that state rather than by the category's place in the population's general system of inequality, those categorically defined rights and obligations belong to citizenship.

Citizenship resembles the run of contracts in drawing visible lines between insiders and outsiders, yet engaging third parties to respect and even enforce its provisions. It differs from most other contracts in: a) binding whole categories of persons rather than single individuals to each other, b) involving differentiation among levels and degrees of members, and c) directly engaging a government's coercive power. To the extent that governments control substantial resources, including coercive means, these three differentials single out citizenship as a potent form of contract liable to fierce contestation. Military service, eligibility for public office, voting rights, payment of taxes, public education, access to public services, and protection of rent-producing advantages—all frequent items in contracts of citizenship, and all explicitly enumerated in Kazakstan's 1995 constitution—have engaged serious struggle for centuries.

Contracts of citizenship have a history at least as tortuous as that of other major contracts—marital, commercial, or intellectual. For centuries, citizenship bound most Western European people not to organizations like the large, centralized consolidated states of recent experience but to smaller units such as municipalities. Despite emulation and mutual influence from one local polity to another, the small scale produced great variability in conditions of citizenship from place to place (see te Brake 1998 for a convenient orientation).

Between 1750 and 1850 Europe's consolidating states did not so much absorb these earlier forms of citizenship as subordinate or even smash them in favor of relatively uniform categorization and obligation at a national scale.

State consolidation thus thinned citizenship significantly for those who already participated in its rights and obligations at the smaller scale. For them, national citizenship offered a narrower range of rights and obligations than had the burghers' militia service, participation in public ceremonies, supervision of poor relief, moral oversight, and involvement in public finance. For those who had previously lacked substantial local or regional citizenship, however, the establishment of national citizenship brought significant gains in rights at the cost of expanded obligations to national authorities. Much of the widespread Western transition from indirect to direct rule between the 18th and 20th centuries consisted, precisely, of national citizenship's establishing priority over local and regional systems of obligation. Those changes squeezed out autonomous middlemen such as warlords and fief holders, or integrated them directly into national administrative hierarchies.

The distinctive Ottoman path toward direct rule led perilously away from a rather effective system of indirect rule in which separate religious, military, and property-holding segments maintained distinctive compacts with the imperial center. Ironically, the very Western European powers that were aggressively establishing direct rule within their own domestic territories successfully pressed Ottoman authorities to create special statuses for ostensible nationalities, thus hindering the establishment of direct rule and generalized citizenship in the empire. (Those same powers, of course, employed indirect rule widely in their overseas colonies; see Mamdani 1996.) The Ottoman millet system's organizational structure shaped efforts to create citizenship in Ottoman territories. Those efforts generally failed until the empire itself collapsed in military defeat.

Not that any state ever established a single contract of citizenship or an impermeable boundary between citizens and noncitizens. Like Kazakstan, all states differentiate within their citizenries, at a minimum distinguishing between minors and adults, prisoners and free persons, naturalized and native born. Many make finer gradations, for example, by restricting suffrage or military service to adult males, imposing property qualifications for certain rights, or installing a range from temporary residents to probationary applicants for citizenship to full-fledged participants in citizenship's rights and obligations.

Almost all constitutions define a special subset of citizens who are eligible for high public offices. Kazakstan's constitution stipulates that:

A citizen of the Republic shall be eligible for the office of the President of the Republic of Kazakstan if he (*sic*) is by birth not younger than thirty-five and not older than sixty-five, has a perfect command of the state language [i.e., Kazak] and has lived in Kazakstan for not less than fifteen years.

Other stipulations of age and residence restrict citizens' access to other offices, thus creating additional grades within the general category of citizenship.

The European Union is further complicating categories of citizenship by establishing rights that transfer from state to state and by creating some sets of rights connecting whole categories of Europeans not to agents of the states within which they reside but to agents of the union itself. Just as large capitalist firms establish not one uniform contract with all their workers but numerous contracts connecting managers with different categories of workers, states and citizens maintain multiple categories of relationship.

More visibly than in the case of capitalist firms (where a new firm typically borrows a great deal of its organizational structure, including contracts, from existing firms in the same industry), rights and obligations linking citizens to states have formed through struggle. Schematically, we can distinguish between top-down and bottom-up claims. From the top down, state demands for resources and compliance generate bargaining, resistance, and settlements encapsulating both rights and obligations, as when popularly elected parliaments gain power through their role in raising taxes for warfare. From the bottom up, segments of the subject population also acquire rights and obligations by mobilizing to demand state agents' intervention, reorganization, or reallocation of state-controlled resources.

In our own time, we commonly use names like taxation, conscription, and regulation—all of them regularly generating bargaining, resistance, and settlements—for activities falling clearly into the top-down category, reserving names like parties, pressure groups, and social movements for unambiguous members of the bottom-up category. We typically place governmental expenditure, bureaucratic operation, and public services in an intermediate location. Top-down and bottom-up claims often pivot, precisely, on struggles for control over those intermediate locations. Top-down claims regularly generate bottom-up claims, as when military veterans who served reluctantly at the start demand peacetime benefits in recognition of their service, or when dissidents withhold tax payments to back demands for a voice in public expenditure.

Such claims become citizenship rights—enforceable claims—through struggle between governmental agents and categories of the population subject to their governments. Most claim making fails; European workers, for example, made repeated claims for the right to work, none of which ever achieved full realization in any capitalist country's code of citizenship (Hanagan 1999). Women's claims to political participation, in contrast, have enjoyed dramatic success. Because consolidating states essentially conceded popular electoral participation in return for military service and subjection of male-dominated enterprises to war-driven taxation, voting long remained a male prerogative. Eventually, female mobilization and claim making succeeded in opening national polities to women.

The European history of citizenship did not follow a universal pattern. In imperial China, nothing like the bargaining out of specific rights between local groups and national authorities occurred (Wong 1999). No ordinary subject of the Chinese state could call on third parties to enforce his or her categorically defined rights. That legacy of officials bound by virtue but not by enforceable contract carried over into the revolutionary age. Hence recent attempts to define Chinese citizenship proceed against a very different set of assumptions concerning the mutual obligations involved.

We begin to sense why citizenship matters. It encases vital rights and obligations, ones that impinge significantly on life outside the world of constitutional affairs. Effective citizenship imposes strong obligations uniformly on broad categories of political participants and state agents. It thereby mitigates—but by no means eliminates—political effects of inequalities in routine social life. At a national scale effective citizenship is a necessary condition of democracy. The statement holds whether we adopt a substantive definition of democracy (stressing such outcomes as equity and well-being), an institutional definition (stressing such arrangements as contested elections and independent judiciaries), or a political-process definition (stressing relations between a state's agents and people falling under their jurisdiction).

In the political-process definition that strikes me as most useful for explanatory purposes, democracy combines four elements: 1) relatively broad public political participation; 2) relatively equal participation; 3) binding consultation of political participants with respect to state policies, resources, and personnel; and 4) protection of political participants (especially members of minorities) from arbitrary action by state agents. Without effective citizenship, no regime provides sufficient breadth, equality, binding consultation, or protection of participants in public politics to qualify as democratic.

Citizenship is by no means, however, a sufficient condition of democracy. In the West, bargaining over the means of state expansion started generating institutions of citizenship—extensive rights and obligations binding whole categories of their national populations together with state agents—long before broadening, equalization, consultation, or protection reached levels that we might reasonably call democratic. Unlike their tyrannical predecessors, 20th-century authoritarian regimes have commonly created their own versions of citizenship, stronger on obligations than on rights from the citizen's perspective. The building of patron-client relations into citizenship through exchanges of goods for political support actually inhibits democratization (Fox 1994). In Europe as a whole, citizenship began to take democratic forms when conquest, colonization, confrontation, or revolution tore existing webs of privilege. Then those who benefited from undemocratic political arrangements lost the power (sometimes even the incentive) to maintain narrow, unequal political participation, restricted consultation, and arbitrary action by state agents.

By these criteria, independent Kazakstan has established a precarious sort of citizenship, but has remained far from democracy (CSCE [Commission on Security and Cooperation in Europe] 1998: 27–38). The 1995 constitution's announced rights for citizens may look good to the constitution's first audience—various international actors—but they do not much constrain the country's current rulers and provide little protection for their domestic opponents. Elected president without opposition, Nursultan Nazarbaev rules by decree in the absence of a parliament he disbanded—or, more precisely, in the presence of a consultative assembly he created after dismissing the elected parliament. His daughter Dariga Nazarbaeva runs the principal state TV channel, which does not broadcast news of political opposition. His government routinely and massively imprisons political opponents on the basis of forced confessions. Despite constitutional provisions we reviewed earlier, by presidential fiat dissenting political assemblies are largely illegal:

> A March 17, 1995 presidential decree issued while parliament was disbanded remains in force and limits the ability of citizens to participate in unsanctioned demonstrations. Gaining permission for such gatherings is difficult, and authorities have jailed violators. Madel Ismailov, leader of the opposition Working Class Movement, for example, was imprisoned for leading an unsanctioned rally on May 30 [1997] that drew thousands of participants, and many others have been fined. (CSCE 1998: 30)

Single-handedly, President Nazarbaev decided to move the national capital from Almaty to Akmola, a raw mosquito-ridden settlement of 300,000 people in north-central Kazakstan. (Since Akmola means "white tomb," Nazarbaev has since changed the name to Astana, meaning "capital"; Soviet authorities called the place Tselinograd, "city of the virgin lands.") In these and other ways, the regime qualifies as sustaining moderately broad but centrally controlled political participation, unequal and contested citizenship, very limited consultation, and weak protection. The regime operates far from democracy.

In these regards, alas, most of the world's regimes resemble Kazakstan more than they resemble France or Japan. Even more so than in today's well-established parliamentary democracies, citizenship remains contested. Sri Lanka, Nigeria, Ecuador, Indonesia, and Israel all stand witness to the explosive content of controversies about citizenship. Without broad, relatively equal, binding, well-protected citizenship, however, democracy will flourish nowhere. John Markoff rightly points out how much the history of democracy has depended on waves of innovation outside the core of dominant democracies (Markoff 1996b, 1999). Crucial innovations and failures will continue to occur in the efforts of today's poorer undemocratic countries to craft new varieties of citizenship. The future of democratization hangs in the balance.

Chapter 13

Inequality, Democratization, and De-Democratization

CONTRARY TO THE COMFORTING IMAGE OF DEMOCRACY AS A SECURE CAVE into which people can retreat forever from the buffeting of political storms, most regimes that have taken significant steps toward democracy over the last two centuries have later de-democratized at least temporarily. A surprising number of regimes that actually installed functioning democratic institutions then returned to authoritarianism (Arat 1991; Diamond 1999; O'Donnell 1999; Przeworski, Alvarez, Cheibub, and Limongi 1997, 2000). In 20th-century Europe alone, after all, Greece, Italy, Germany, Spain, Portugal, and Vichy France provide visible, violent examples. Over the last half century, Latin America has added Argentina, Bolivia, Brazil, Chile, Ecuador, Guatemala, Honduras, Panama, Peru, and Uruguay to the roster of democratic reversals. Despite the democratic jubilation that greeted the exit of the Soviet Union from state socialism, levels of democracy actually receded after initial rises in Russia, Belarus, and much of central Asia (Freedom House 2002). De-democratization remains a possibility everywhere in the world.

Many analysts from Aristotle onward have thought that inequality threatens democracy, both because democratic politics as such rests on some presumption of equality among participants and because intense inequality encourages its beneficiaries to subvert or opt out of democratic politics. This chapter forwards that intuition by laying out conjectures on interactions between inequality and democratization. It builds on three recent efforts: to provide a general account of categorical inequality and its changes; to provide a general account of democratization and de-democratization; to apply the account of democratization and de-democratization to European experience between 1650 and 2000 (Tilly 2004b).

Durable categorical inequality refers to organized differences in advantages by gender, race, nationality, ethnicity, religion, community, and similar classification systems. It occurs when transactions across a categorical boundary (e.g., male-female) a) regularly yield net advantages to people on one side of the boundary and also b) reproduce the boundary. Although forms and degrees of categorical inequality vary dramatically across times and places, all large human populations have always maintained substantial systems of categorical inequality.

All governments, democratic or otherwise, inevitably intervene in the production of inequality. They do so in three distinct ways: by protecting the advantages of their major supporters; by establishing their own systems of extraction and allocation of resources; by redistributing resources among different segments of their subject populations. Compared with undemocratic governments, broadly speaking, democratic governments offer protection to advantages received by larger shares of their subject populations, create systems of extraction and allocation that respond more fully to popular control, produce more collective benefits, and redistribute resources in favor of vulnerable populations within their constituencies more extensively (Bunce 2001; Goodin, Headey, Muffels, and Dirven 1999; Przeworski, Alvarez, Cheibub, and Limongi 2000).

These very activities, however, involve democratic governments in perpetuating some kinds of categorical inequality. Most obviously, they devote extensive effort to maintaining boundaries—and differences in benefits—between their own citizens and citizens of other countries. But to the extent that they secure property and existing forms of social organization, they also sustain the inequality already built into property and existing forms of social organization. Governmental maintenance of inheritance rights, for example, passes racial and ethnic differences in wealth from one generation to the next (Spilerman 2000).

In order to pinpoint causal connections between inequality and democratization, we must locate democracies with respect to other types of political regime. Political regimes consist of relations a) between governments and political actors under those governments' jurisdiction that interact regularly with those governments and b) among the political actors. All regimes locate somewhere along each of these dimensions:

1. governmental capacity: extent of government agents' control over resources, activities, and populations located routinely within the government's territorial jurisdiction

2. breadth: proportion of the total population constituting or participating directly in political actors that interact regularly with the government
3. equality: the extent to which people who do participate in such political actors have similar access to agents of government
4. consultation: the degree to which political participants exercise binding collective control over governmental agents, resources, and activities
5. protection: the extent of shielding of political participants from arbitrary action by governmental agents

Regimes vary from low to high capacity. They also vary in the extent to which they install *protected consultation,* the combination of breadth, equality, consultation, and protection. Imagine each dimension as varying from 0 (lowest) to 1 (highest). We can call regimes that experience high levels of protected consultation democratic, those that experience low levels of protected consultation undemocratic. In democratic regimes, to be more precise, relations between citizens and agents of government score high on the multiple of breadth, equality, consultation, and protection.

Those distinctions allow us to simplify by adopting the crude classification of figure 13–1. As of the year 2000, *high-capacity undemocratic regimes* included China and Pakistan, *low-capacity undemocratic regimes* Sierra Leone and Haiti,

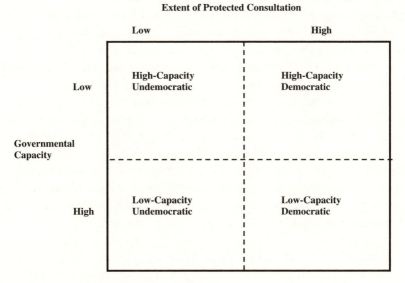

Figure 13-1. A Crude Typology of Regimes

low-capacity democratic regimes Botswana and Jamaica, *high-capacity democratic regimes* Germany and Japan. Obviously, both capacity and protected consultation are matters of degree: no government has ever controlled all the resources, activities, and populations within its territory, and no real regime has ever come close to full breadth, equality, consultation, and protection. The classification clearly leaves some regimes dubious or intermediate: exactly where, for example, should we locate today's India, Israel, Argentina, and South Africa? But figure 13–1 serves reasonably well as a map of the space within which students of democratization and de-democratization are trying to locate trajectories and specify explanations.

Regimes distribute unevenly within the space. Very few low-capacity democratic regimes exist, for two reasons: First, establishment and maintenance of democratic institutions depends on some minimum governmental capacity to provide protection and check egregious challenges to democratic practice. Second, low-capacity democratizing regimes have commonly succumbed to conquests, revolutions, or military takeovers that have in turn produced higher-capacity governments. The more frequent long-run trajectory of democratization runs from low-capacity undemocratic to high-capacity undemocratic to high-capacity democratic government.

My proposed general explanation of increases and decreases in protected consultation features relations among three sites of social interaction: categorical inequality, trust networks, and public politics. Comparison of French, British, and other European experiences between 1650 and 2000 leads me to the working hypothesis that crucial changes in social relations underlying democratization take place in those three sites and their interactions. In the course of democratization, the bulk of a government's subject population acquires binding, protected, relatively equal claims on a government's agents, activities, and resources. In a related process, categorical inequality declines in those areas of social life that either constitute or immediately support participation in public politics.

Networks of trust? A significant shift occurs in the locus of interpersonal networks on which people rely when undertaking risky long-term enterprises such as marriage, long-distance trade, membership in crafts, investment of savings, and time-consuming specialized education; such networks move from evasion of governmental detection and control to partial reliance on government agents and presumption that such agents will meet their long-term commitments. "Partial reliance" need not connect individuals directly to governments; the connections may run through parties, unions, communities, and other organizations that in turn rely on governmental ratification, toleration, support, or protection. People start investing family money in government securities, yield their sons to military service, seek government assistance in enforcement of religious obligations, organize mutual aid through publicly recognized labor unions, and so on.

Reversals de-democratize: when trust networks proliferate insulated from public politics, their proliferation saps state capacity, reduces citizens' incentives to collaborate in democratic processes they find costly in the short run, weakens protections for the bulk of the citizenry, and increases the opportunities of the rich and powerful to intervene selectively in public politics on their own behalf. If, for example, a separatist religious elite forms, its compact size and internal coherence give it the means of pursuing its own interest without supporting the government's more costly collective enterprises.

Only where positive changes in trust network integration, inequality insulation, and internal transformations of public politics all intersect does effective, durable democracy emerge. Reversals in any of the three—for example, organization of public political blocs around major categorical inequalities—promote de-democratization. The explanatory problem, then, is to specify how, why, and when rare democracy-promoting alterations of categorical inequality, trust networks, and public politics coincide.

The solution to that problem lies in specifying processes that promote changes in and among categorical inequality, trust networks, and public politics. Let us group the crucial processes under those headings:

Segregation of public politics from categorical inequality

1. equalization of categories in the subject population at large
2. buffering of public politics from categorical inequality

integration of trust networks into public politics

3. dissolution of insulated trust networks
4. creation of politically connected trust networks

alterations of relations between citizens and governmental agents

5. broadening of political participation
6. equalization of political participation
7. enhancement of collective control over governmental resources and actions
8. inhibition of governmental agents' arbitrary power

We can, of course, break down these broadly specified processes into finer causal mechanisms; the analysis of democratization in chapter 3 did just that. Mechanisms that promote segregation of categorical inequality from public politics (process 2 above), for example, include reduction of privately controlled armed force, formation of politically active coalitions that crosscut categorical inequality, and wholesale increases of political participation, rights, or obligations (e.g., through territorial accessions) that cut across social categories (Tilly 2000a). For present purposes, however, the argument will come across more clearly if we stick with more general processes.

My most general claims follow: First, at least one of the processes under each of the first two headings (categorical inequality and trust networks) and *all* of the processes under the third heading (relations between citizens and governmental agents) must occur for democratization to ensue. Second, reversal of any of the eight processes promotes de-democratization, the decline of protected consultation. The argument as a whole therefore proceeds from specification of necessary conditions for democratization and de-democratization—the three clusters of processes and their reversals—to enumeration of mechanisms that promote or reverse the crucial processes. The point of this chapter is not to spell out the whole analysis, but to close in on the interplay of categorical inequality and public politics. Although I have tried to make them consistent with existing knowledge of inequality, democratization, and de-democratization, the conjectures that follow are not self-evidently true. Some of them are surprising. If true, furthermore, they have strong implications for the future of democracy.

Here are the conjectures:

Without compensating changes in governmental activity, increasing categorical inequality within the subject population decreases breadth, equality, bindingness, and protection of agent-subject relations, and thereby de-democratizes regimes.

Increases in categorical inequality expand the incentives and means of inequality's beneficiaries to subvert or opt out of democratic processes by creating advantageous particular relations to governmental agents, shielding themselves from onerous obligations, intervening directly in governmental disposition of resources, and using their governmental access to extract more advantages from unequal relations with nongovernmental actors.

Similarly, increasing inscription of existing categorical inequalities into public politics decreases the equality, breadth, bindingness, and protection of agent-subject relations, and thereby de-democratizes regimes.

Both organization of major political actors around the boundaries of significant categorical inequalities and enactment of rules for political participation that correspond to such boundaries—especially if excluded parties are those whom existing categorical inequalities already disadvantage in general—undermine protected consultation. In Western political regimes, categorical differences by nobility, religious status, gender, race, and property ownership have supplied the primary bases of inscription in these regards, but elsewhere ethnicity and kinship have figured as well.

Accordingly, diminution of categorical inequalities within the subject population and/or increasing insulation of public politics from existing categorical inequalities, all other things equal, democratizes regimes.

To the extent that all the processes under discussion operate symmetrically, this principle follows logically from the previous two.

Well-being of subjects, on average, increases under democratizing regimes partly because political insulation from inequality is a good in itself and partly because political voice is a good in itself.

On average, people who experience equitable treatment from their governments and/or have direct say in governmental operations gain more satisfaction from politics and display greater willingness to bear burdens for the common good (Frey and Stutzer 2002; Levi and Stoker 2000).

To the degree that democratizing regimes act to reduce categorical inequalities, to insulate public politics from those inequalities, and/or to blunt the effects of those inequalities on basic living conditions such as housing, medical care, and food, they increase the likelihood of their own survival as democratic regimes.

Populist democrats would like this argument to be true, and there are at least fragments of evidence to encourage them (Przeworski, Alvarez, Cheibub, and Limongi 1997).

To the degree that democratizing regimes act to reduce categorical inequalities, to insulate public politics from those inequalities, and/or to blunt the effects of those inequalities on basic living conditions such as housing, medical care, and food, they also increase the overall well-being of their subject populations.

This attractive principle is an article of faith among populist development specialists (see, e.g., UNDP [United Nations Development Program] 2001: 17) but for precisely that reason needs much more careful empirical scrutiny (see also Arat 1991; Fogel 2000; Sen 1992).

Such interventions take two overlapping forms: a) exercise of collective control over value-producing resources and the networks that operate them, b) redistribution of value produced by means of those resources.

Regimes qualify as social democratic to the extent that they engage and co-ordinate both strategies of intervention.

Up to a relatively high point, rising governmental capacity increases the likelihood and impact of beneficent interventions.

Low governmental capacity reduces the efficacy of both regulatory and redistributive efforts. But at very high levels of governmental capacity, runs the reasoning, the opportunity and incentive for governmental agents and other beneficiaries of existing categorical inequality to ally in diverting state power to their own advantage rise irresistibly.

Although in the past controls over coercion, labor, animals, land, commitment-maintaining institutions, and/or machines have played the major part in generating categorical inequality (hence obstacles and threats to democracy), over the next century clique controls over financial capital, information, media, and scientific-technical knowledge will become increasingly significant as causes of categorical inequality, hence as obstacles and threats to democracy.

Already we see considerable signs of shifts in these directions, although their effects on democratization remain to be measured.

Currently democratic regimes that do not exercise new collective controls over financial capital, information, media, and scientific-technical knowledge and/or redistribute value produced by them will therefore risk de-democratization, hence decline in their subject populations' well-being.

This does not mean, to be sure, that regimes can forget about coercion, labor, animals, land, commitment-maintaining institutions, and machines, all of which will continue to figure in the generation of categorical inequality in different parts of the world. But existing barriers to degradation of democratic politics by means of controls over coercion, labor, animals, land, commitment-maintaining institutions, and machines will not suffice to block the effects of financial capital, information, media, and scientific-technical knowledge. Limiting the impact of new inequalities on public politics will constitute one of the 21st century's great challenges for democrats.

If these conjectures are correct, sunny optimism about the durability and inevitable advance of democratization seems utterly misplaced. Just as past democratization has always occurred through struggle, and has frequently suffered reversal, the path ahead contains many an obstacle in the form of new inequalities and their political consequences.

Chapter 14

Political Identities in Changing Polities

Henry VIII was, as you know, a bit of an opportunist. In 1521, at a time when Henry had allied England with the Habsburgs against France and laid claim to the French crown to boot, he wrote a pamphlet against Martin Luther's doctrines. For his efforts, the pope dubbed Henry Defender of the Faith. Churchmen began voicing doubts about that title, however, no later than 1525, when Henry levied a major tax on church property to pay for his wars with Catholic France. As the pope himself delayed in sanctioning Henry's divorce from Catharine of Aragon to marry Anne Boleyn, Henry sacked his papal legate Cardinal Wolsey and, after some maneuvering, declared the English church independent of Rome. The break with the pope brought Henry substantial church revenues. In 1534, Henry rammed through the Act of Supremacy, which made him and his successors heads of an independent English church, while rendering refusal to take an oath of recognition a capital crime of high treason. *Utopia* author and former chancellor Thomas More lost his head for just such a refusal.

By 1536, with the help of Thomas Cromwell, Henry was having Anne Boleyn executed on a trumped-up charge of adultery, beginning dispossession of the monasteries, publishing William Tindale's translation of the Bible, and putting down major rebellions against his religious innovations. By 1539, nevertheless, he was issuing the Six Articles, which defined beliefs and practices greatly resembling those of the Catholic Church except in their substitution of the king for the pope. Through all these gyrations, Henry's men missed no opportunity to seize church revenues or to raise money from church members. After Henry's death in 1547, English believers had to follow twists and turns through reigns of a rather more Protestant Edward VI, a quite Catholic Mary, and a warily Protestant Elizabeth I. The 16th century dragged ordinary English people through a maze of alternating religious and political identities.

In his dense, complex, but ultimately vivid reconstruction of parish life in 16th-century Morebath, Devon, Eamon Duffy has recently demonstrated how deeply the top-down turmoil stirred by Henry VIII and his successors shook local social relations and practices (Duffy 2001). Duffy's chief historical informant, the long-serving vicar Sir Christopher Trychay, did his best to protect his initially Catholic parishioners from the opposite dangers of overeager reform and dogged resistance. But changing definitions of religious and political affiliation, with their accompanying obligations, impoverished the local church, destroyed the rough equality of household involvement in parish affairs that had characterized the early 16th century, and caused recurrent struggles of locals with outsiders who sought to impose or profit from the current realignment.

Henry's 1547 Injunctions, for example, combined an attack on votive lights and sacred images with dissolution of the chantries that had supported memorial masses, the proceeds going to pay for war with Scotland. In sheep-raising Morebath, such a reform simultaneously struck at practices that entwined religion with kinship and forced sale of the church sheep whose wool had provided the major income supporting local devotions.

Most of the time Morebath's people fought their identity battles with weapons of the weak. In 1549, nevertheless, they paid the expenses of sending five local men to a rebel camp near Exeter in what came to be known as the Western Rebellion. More or less simultaneously Edward VI's regime had imposed the Protestant Book of Common Prayer plus new taxes on sheep and cloth to support the expanding wars against France and Scotland. The rebels of 1549 centered their demands on the restoration of religious life more or less as defined toward the end of Henry's reign—largely Catholic beliefs, practices, and identities within a Church of England. The king's forces, backed by foreign mercenaries, slaughtered the rebels. No commoners were going to decide the content of England's religious and political identities as seen from the top down.

Since the destruction of the World Trade Center on September 11, the United States and Europe have been reliving some of the 16th-century's identity struggles. Insistence that rulers know better than citizens where the line between us and them falls, raising of revenue and restriction of liberties in the name of holy war, smiting of enemies and their unwitting or unwilling accomplices with massive military action, and public displays of support for all these measures have a surprisingly 16th-century air about them. But let me suppress the urge to catalog parallels between the Afghan War and the wars of Henry VIII in favor of another, related task: to point out how deeply negotiated political identities affect the work of changing polities.

Rogers Brubaker and Fred Cooper, two students of social processes whose contributions deserve great respect, have recently proposed that we expunge "identity" from our analytic lexicon because the term has acquired too many meanings and too few specifications (Brubaker and Cooper 2000; see also Brubaker and Laitin 1998). I propose instead that we get identity right. We can, I think, escape the search for inner selves about which Brubaker and Cooper rightly complain by recognizing that people regularly negotiate and deploy socially based answers to the questions "Who are you?" "Who are we?" and "Who are they?" Those are identity questions. Their answers are identities—always assertions, always contingent, always negotiable, but also always consequential. Identities are social arrangements.

Identities belong to that potent set of social arrangements in which people construct shared stories about who they are, how they are connected, and what has happened to them. Such stories range from the small-scale production of excuses, explanations, and apologies when something goes wrong to the large-scale production of peace settlements and national histories. Whatever their truth or falsehood by the standards of historical research, such stories play an indispensable part in the sealing of agreements and the coordination of social interaction. Stories and identities intersect when people start deploying shared answers to the questions "Who are you?" "Who are we?" and "Who are they?"

As chapter 1 outlined, identities have four components:

1. a boundary separating me from you or us from them
2. a set of relations within the boundary
3. a set of relations *across* the boundary
4. a set of stories about the boundary and the relations

Thus as of 1536 Henry VIII had forced a boundary between Anglicans and Catholics partially into place; relations within the Anglican and Catholic categories were undergoing rapid renegotiation; relations between Anglicans and Catholics had become matters of negotiation in some places and civil war in others; while many parties including the parson of Morebath had started to fashion, promulgate, and even believe new stories about Anglican-Catholic relations as well as about the boundary separating the two categories.

Identities become *political* identities when governments become parties to them. The religious identities of Morebath parishioners politicized as Henry VIII and his successors began to manipulate and control permissible answers for religiously tinged versions of "Who are you?" "Who are we?" and "Who are they?" The identities of Americans as patriotic or otherwise become even more political as the U.S. government becomes a party to we-they boundaries. Europeans maneuver around similar questions not only in deciding whether to align with U.S. military policy but also in deciding whether Turks are Europeans and whether Muslims in general lie on the opposite side of the we-they boundary.

Many people regard identity claims primarily as a form of self-expression, or even of self-indulgence—what others do when they are too comfortable, too confused, or too distressed for serious politics. I argue, on the contrary, that identity claims and their attendant stories constitute serious political business. Invention of the social movement, for instance, facilitated the staking of claims in the name of previously unrecognized political actors. At various points in U.S. history, social movements helped establish opponents of slavery, and enemies of alcohol, women, African Americans, gays, Vietnam veterans, and indigenous peoples as viable political actors.

As chapter 11 indicated, nationalism provides another example. During the 19th century, nationalist identity claims (whether bottom up or top down) began to make a serious difference to who would hold state power and who would not. Political rights and obligations themselves depend on negotiated claims linking members of established political categories, which means that they, too, involve identity claims. Battling out accepted answers to the questions "Who are you?" "Who are we?" and "Who are they?" with widely accepted stories to back those answers is no self-indulgence; it plays a consequential part in public politics. Available answers to the questions affect the very feasibility of democracy.

More specific agendas emerge for the study of political identities, of stories, of political change, and of their interactions. In each case, we need new work on two classes of problems: generation and constraint.

1. *Generation:* What causes the processes involved to a) begin, b) change? How, for example, did the identity "European" acquire sufficient force that old established states would dissolve national currencies in favor of the euro, and former socialist regimes would reshape themselves in the capitalist image as a step toward admission to the European Union?
2. *Constraint:* Once they are in operation, how do the processes affect social behavior a) on the small scale, b) on the large scale? For example, at what

point and how should we expect participants in European social movements routinely to make claims on behalf of categories that span long-
established national boundaries?

On the whole, my own analyses of these problems have made do with entre-
preneurial-interactive accounts of generation and constraint. Political entrepreneurs in the forms of would-be ethnic leaders and movement organizers
figure prominently in those analyses.

Such political entrepreneurs draw together credible stories from available
cultural materials, similarly create we-they boundaries, activate both stories
and boundaries as a function of current political circumstances, and maneuver
to suppress competing models. Yet interaction among parties to struggle alters
stories, boundaries, and their social reinforcements. In this regard, my account
resembles John Walton's conclusions concerning the narratives of public history:

> Public history is constructed, not, in the main, for the purposes of posterity or
> objectivity, but for the aims of present action (conquest, social reform, building,
> political reorganization, economic transformation). Narratives make claims for
> the virtues of their individual and institutional authors, often as counterpoint to
> rival claimants. They characterize the past in certain ways for the purpose of
> shaping the future. The ability of narratives to effect change depends in the first
> instance on their institutional power; whether they are produced by a powerful
> church, conquering state, fledgling town, or contending voluntary associations.
> (Walton 2001: 294)

Something like that process does often occur. But such an account contains an
excessively instrumental bias. It offers no explanation of the fact that most would-
be political entrepreneurs fail most of the time. Nor does it provide a satisfactory
explanation of day-to-day interactions around political identities, much less why
people sometimes risk their lives in the course of those interactions. Clearly, we
need more subtle and comprehensive explanations of generation and constraint.

In the case of identity stories, we have a few clues concerning generation.
Although no one lives without stories, interacting people create new stories
about their interaction after the fact, as they terminate sequences and seal agreements. The beleaguered 16th-century parson of Morebath mediated between
his parishioners and outside authorities in negotiating new shared accounts of
Christianity and the practices it entailed. Those accounts connected religious
and political identities in a new way, cementing the Anglican Church in place
without entirely transforming day-to-day practices within the village. In that
regard, political stories resemble peace treaties, commencement addresses,

memoirs, annual reports, and labor-management contracts. To be sure, materials for stories come largely from existing cultural repertoires. Visibly viable new stories reassemble familiar elements. Certifying agents such as elders, peers, public authorities, and international organizations monitor stories, and often provide models for their proper construction.

Nationalist stories, for example, bear striking resemblances from one part of the world to another. They speak of shared culture, long-standing tradition, connectedness, common geographic origin, and distinctness from others with whom the claimed nation might be confused. Those common properties do not spring from primordial consciousness, but from a body of nationalist models and practices that have spread through the world since 1789. Still we have no convincing general account of the process by which the specific contents of politically consequential stories—nationalist or otherwise—form and gain credibility. Nor do we have a persuasive account of change in prevailing stories. Similarly, we lack a compelling and comprehensive explanation for generation of the particular boundaries, relations, and stories that constitute political identities.

As for constraint, how do stories and identities produce their effects? In the construction and deployment of politically effective stories, what happens at the small scale of an individual or a pair of individuals, at the large scale of a state or a national movement, and in the interaction between those scales?

Three bad answers readily spring to mind. The first is that stories directly alter individual consciousness in closely similar ways across individuals, before individual consciousness aggregates into collective consciousness. The answer is bad because it provides no account of how exposure to stories interacts with previous learning across individuals who have varied considerably in previous experience. We could, after all, plausibly expect such individuals to adopt different, even contradictory, stories. How does relative uniformity in public storytelling come about? Much less does the aggregation of individual consciousness explain how people who have their doubts about shared stories nevertheless cooperate in their public promulgation.

The second commonly proposed bad answer is that society does it: those stories that serve society as a whole or (more likely) reinforce the interests of dominant groups come to prevail. This second answer is woefully inadequate because it invokes a dubious agent—society as a whole or a unified dominant group—and begs the question of how that agent does its work. Holistic ontologies keep returning to social science in such forms as evolutionary models and world-system analyses. But their vagueness with respect to agency—who does what to whom, why, and how—has greatly diminished their popularity among social scientists at large. That vagueness renders society-does-it answers unhelpful explanations for the prominence of stories and identities in political change.

A third frequent bad answer credits culture, as the repository of collective experience, with the production of constraint. The answer is even worse than the first two because it combines their defects: It begs the question of how culture—that is, shared understandings and their representations in objects and practices—changes as it invokes a dubious agent. Like "society does it," the cultural answer fails to specify how that agent creates its effects in social life. Unquestionably, available culture figures importantly in political storytelling and identity politics. People undoubtedly draw on previously known representations and practices as they struggle with each other. But how? Since struggling people are constantly modifying their definitions of who they are and what they are fighting about, exactly how does culture constrain them?

Let me suggest three possible good answers as possible alternatives to the bad answers. Call them entrepreneurship, creative interaction, and *cultural ecology*. The three would take future work in somewhat different directions, but they would not necessarily yield incompatible results.

Entrepreneurship? We might improve a crude entrepreneurial account by following up analogies with intellectual, artistic, and religious schools. In those fields investigators usually discover strong network effects, polarization effects, and mutual reinforcement of common culture, with brokers both connecting and dividing crucial actors. We can certainly see glimmers of the same effects in the history of identity politics. In British social movement politics, for example, offstage connections among such entrepreneurs as William Cobbett and Francis Place clearly affected which stories and identities became prominent in successive campaigns for parliamentary reform.

Creative interaction appears most visibly in such activities as jazz and soccer. In these cases, participants work within rough agreements on procedures and outcomes; arbiters set limits on performances; individual dexterity, knowledge, and disciplined preparation generally yield superior play, yet the rigid equivalent of military drill destroys the enterprise. Both jazz and soccer, when well executed, proceed through improvised interaction, surprise, incessant error and error correction, alternation between solo and ensemble action, and repeated responses to understandings shared by at least pairs of players. After the fact, participants and spectators create shared stories of what happened, and striking improvisations shape future performances.

We can see creative interaction at work, for example, in the two-century-old process by which solemn processions and presentations of petitions evolved into street demonstrations. If we could explain how human beings bring off such improvisatory adventures, we could be well on our way to accounting for how sets of interacting people store histories in contentious repertoires, conversation, rights and obligations, war and peace, and similar phenomena.

Cultural ecology? Social life consists of transactions among social sites, some of them occupied by individual persons, but most of them occupied by shifting aspects or clusters of persons. None of the sites, goes the reasoning, contains all the culture—all the shared understandings or representations—on which transactions in its vicinity draw. But transactions among sites produce interdependence among extensively connected sites, deposit related cultural material in those sites, transform shared understandings in the process, and thus make large stores of culture available to any particular site through its connections with other sites.

All this may sound mysterious, implausible, and difficult. Yet as a practical matter we often assume a simple version of cultural ecology: challenged by an impending purchase, an intellectual conundrum, or a weighty personal choice, we turn to a wise friend or colleague not necessarily because she will have the right answer, but because she will know whom to ask or where to search. A computer model of cultural ecology would feature distributed intelligence.

A politically sensitive version of cultural ecology would take us into the thick of meaningful, solidarity-sustaining social ties. It would help us learn why ostensibly irrational high-risk activism occurs, and how mobilized people manage the contradictions of small-scale bonding and large-scale confrontation. Thus we might discover that identity politics creates its illusions of unity by means of incessantly negotiated interchange among distinct sites, and then fixes its illusions by means of collectively produced stories. We can see signs of cultural ecology, for example, in James Scott's, Viviana Zelizer's, and Eamon Duffy's documentation of dispersed local knowledge as a counter to uniform top-down templates.

Consider entrepreneurship, creative interaction, and cultural ecology to be three cloudy mirrors held up to narrative and identity processes from different angles. Analysts of stories, identities, and political change face the challenge of clearing the mirrors, or creating better glasses. Improved vision should help us explain how Europeans are creating new identities, acting as if they believed their own shared answers to the question "Who are you?" and creating consequential stories about the past, present, and future of Europe.

Chapter 15

Invention, Diffusion, and Transformation of the Social Movement Repertoire

WRITING AN INTRODUCTION TO THE 1888 ENGLISH EDITION OF THE COMmunist Manifesto, Friedrich Engels recalled the years immediately after the failed revolutions of 1848: "Wherever independent proletarian movements continued to show signs of life, they were ruthlessly hunted down" (Marx and Engels 1958: I, 26). He contrasted that dismal time with the subsequent advance of international working-class solidarity:

> Thus the history of the "Manifesto" reflects, to a great extent, the history of the modern working-class movement; at present it is undoubtedly the most widespread, the most international production of all Socialist literature, the common platform acknowledged by millions of working men from Siberia to California. (Marx and Engels 1958: I, 27)

History did not treat Engels's optimism of 1888 kindly. But his vigorous vision of the previous forty years certainly reflected one of the 19th-century's most sensational examples of political transfer. Although no socialist regimes existed anywhere at the time, socialist creeds, organizations, practices, programs, and statements were moving widely across the Western world, and starting to engage activists outside the West as well.

By no means did 19th-century socialism constitute Europe's first contribution to the spread of political forms among polities. From a broad European base, after all, the Roman Empire established relatively uniform political practices in significant sections of Asia and North Africa. The Catholic Church and then Protestant sects created globe-spanning networks of political diffusion along with their theological messages. During the same era that Engels was describing in 1888, furthermore, political entrepreneurs in Europe and North America were eagerly adopting a new form of popular politics that eventually established itself across the globe, wherever democratization began its uncertain but fateful course.

I mean the social movement, in the historically specific form that originated in northwestern Europe during the later 18th century, became widely available for popular making of claims there and in North America during the 19th century, then underwent combined spread and transformation across all the continents during the 20th and 21st centuries.

As it developed in the West after 1750, the social movement emerged from an innovative, consequential synthesis of three elements:

1. a sustained, organized public effort making collective claims on target authorities; let us call it a *campaign*
2. employment of combinations from among the following forms of political action: creation of special-purpose associations and coalitions; public meetings; solemn processions; vigils; rallies; demonstrations; petition drives; statements to and in public media; pamphleteering; call the variable ensemble of performances the *social movement repertoire*
3. participants' concerted public representations of WUNC: worthiness, unity, numbers, and commitment on the part of themselves and/or their constituencies; call them *WUNC displays*

Unlike a one-time petition, declaration, or mass meeting, a *campaign* extends beyond any single event—although social movements often include petitions, declarations, and mass meetings. Campaigns center on *claims:* claims for the adoption or abolition of public programs, claims for recognition of the claimants' existence, and/or claims for ratification of their standing as specific kinds of political actors such as indigenous peoples or constituted parties. A campaign always links at least three parties: a group of self-designated claimants, some object(s) of claims, and a public of some kind. The claims may target governmental officials, but the "authorities" in question can also include owners of property, religious functionaries, and others whose actions (or failures to act) significantly affect the welfare of many people. Not the solo actions of claimants, object(s), or public, but interactions among the three constitute a social movement.

The social movement *repertoire* overlaps with the repertoires of other political phenomena such as trade union activity and electoral campaigns. During the 20th century, special-purpose associations and crosscutting coalitions in particular began to do an enormous variety of political work across the world well outside social movements. But the integration of most or all of these performances into sustained campaigns marks off social movements from other varieties of politics.

The term WUNC sounds odd, but it represents something quite familiar. WUNC displays can take the form of statements, slogans, or labels that imply worthiness, unity, numbers, and commitment: Citizens United for Justice, Signers of the Pledge, Supporters of the Constitution, and so on. Yet collective self-representations often act them out in idioms that local audiences will recognize, for example:

worthiness: sober demeanor; neat clothing; presence of clergy, dignitaries, and mothers with children

unity: matching badges, headbands, banners, or costumes; marching in ranks; singing and chanting

numbers: headcounts, signatures on petitions, messages from constituents, filling streets

commitment: braving bad weather; visible participation by the old and handicapped; resistance to repression; ostentatious sacrifice, subscription, and/or benefaction

Particular idioms vary enormously from one setting to another, but the general communication of WUNC connects those idioms.

Taken singly, each of these elements drew on and adapted previously existing political practices, for example, sporting of electoral colors; humble petitions to kings; or marches of militias, artisans' guilds, and religious organizations. But the combination of campaign, repertoire, and WUNC displays acquired a generality and staying power none of its predecessors had ever achieved. Together, furthermore, they made a powerful assertion of popular sovereignty: we, the people, have the right to voice on our own initiative; worthy, united, numerous, and committed, we have the capacity to change things.

Many political transfers center on specific programs or practices and involve self-conscious deliberation at the receiving end concerning whether to adopt the item and how: enact constitutional provisions, create health insurance, build model housing, agitate for British-style parliamentary reform, and so on. Invention, diffusion, and transformation of the social movement interacted with these other sorts of political transfers, but generally involved more extensive changes in the political context than did narrower shifts. The social movement's invention, diffusion, and transformation deeply altered the arena of contentious politics—contentious in the sense that social movements involve collective making of claims that, if realized, would conflict with someone else's interests, politics in the sense that governments of one sort or another figure somehow in the claim making, whether as claimants, objects of claims, allies of the objects, or monitors of the contention (McAdam, Tarrow, and Tilly 2001).

Never, so far as I know, did activists ever debate the general question "Should we adopt the social movement model as a whole?" Yet once the social movement crystallized, campaigns, performances, and WUNC displays evolved mainly as a bloc rather than as a mere mail-order catalog of individual political tools. People who started to demonstrate, for example, also typically began forming special-purpose associations and conducting press campaigns.

That evolution *en bloc* identifies important resemblances between social movements and other major political inventions such as electoral systems, newspapers, interest-group organization, and public-opinion polling; despite adaptation and variation from country to country and time to time, the sheer existence of these institutions in one regime has provided significant models for other regimes. To sort out the parallels fully, we would have to untangle three sets of causes:

- parallel changes in political regimes, such as democratization, that produce similar effects more or less independently
- transfers and adaptations of organizational forms, such as legislatures, that then produce similar effects in different settings
- political transfers of specific institutions as such

For the sake of clarity and economy, let us concentrate here on relatively direct transfers from one national regime to another. In this brief chapter, I can only sketch a way of thinking about social movement history that should therefore help in the analysis of political transfer at large. Instead of presenting all the fascinating nuances and qualifications that the history of social movements requires, I will lay out the argument in great raw chunks for greater visibility. Precisely because the social movement combined and adapted previously established political practices, any search for original invention of the social movement necessarily identifies multiple candidates. Activists in the Nordic countries, for example, began using popular associations in religiously based reform campaigns during the later 18th century, and multiplied such campaigns during the 19th (Lundqvist 1977; Öhngren 1974; Seip 1974, 1981; Stenius 1987; Wåhlin 1986). Given its deployment of petitions, pamphlets, and popular associations, one might also tag the Dutch Patriot mobilization of the 1780s as an originator of the social movement (te Brake 1989, 1990; Kossmann 1990; Schama 1977).

France could likewise qualify as a founder. Between 1787 and 1793, French revolutionary activists certainly formed politically oriented associations at a feverish pace, made concerted claims by means of those associations, held public meetings, marched through the streets, adopted slogans and badges, produced pamphlets, and implemented local revolutions through most of the country (Hunt 1978, 1984; Jones 2003; Markoff 1996a; McPhee 1988; Woloch 1970, 1994). My sometime-collaborator Sidney Tarrow has tentatively identified the American Revolution as the matrix from which the full-fledged social movement emerged (Tarrow 1998: 38). So both France and the American colonies might dispute Scandinavian and Dutch claims to priority in the social movement's invention.

Finally, Great Britain's own popular mobilization on behalf of American colonial rights as well as its almost contemporaneous initiation of national campaigns against the slave trade contend strongly for recognition as the crucial starting point for social movements at a national scale (Brewer 1976, 1989; Carrington 2002; Davis 1987; Drescher 1982, 1986; Rudé 1962, 1971; Temperley 1981; Walvin 1980, 1981). Proliferation of candidates on two sides of the North Atlantic recalls R. R. Palmer's famous argument that the democratic revolution arose in substantial areas of the Atlantic region more or less simultaneously during the 18th century (Palmer 1959, 1964).

In that case, the search for separate starting points might turn out to be idle, since the individual manifestations of the social movement would simply represent multiple responses to the spread of the same powerful ideas. Even in that case, however, it would be worthwhile to trace the original appearance and subsequent spread of the social movement's major elements. That tracing would help us explain later episodes in which social movements clearly formed outside their areas of original prevalence. As I read the evidence, in any case, the sheer spread of ideas falls far short of explaining the social movement's diffusion and adaptation (Tilly 2004c).

In order to sort out priority claims as well as to trace the subsequent spread of the social movement, it helps to break the central question into four parts. Observing popular collective action in any particular regime, we can ask separately about resemblance, combination, availability, and spread:

1. *Resemblance*: Does this particular campaign, performance, or WUNC display resemble those that commonly occur in full-fledged social movements?
2. *Combination*: Does this particular campaign combine performances and WUNC displays in a recognizably similar manner to social movements elsewhere?
3. *Availability*: In this setting, is the characteristic combination of campaigns, performances, and WUNC displays now widely available for different issues, claimants, and objects of claims?
4. *Spread*: Did this regime's available combination of campaigns, performances, and WUNC displays provide influential immediate models for social movement activity outside the regime?

If we ask only the resemblance question, we can no doubt trace back social movements for centuries before the 1760s. After all, such characteristic social movement performances as marches and public meetings have long, long genealogies, and such episodes as the Protestant Reformation surely included sustained campaigns. The combination question bites harder, since it pretty much narrows us to the candidates I mentioned earlier: Nordic countries, the Netherlands, France, the American colonies, and Great Britain.

Adding the questions of availability and spread, however, tips the balance toward Great Britain, where from antislavery campaigns during the late Napoleonic Wars onward the characteristic combination of campaign, repertoire, and WUNC displays not only characterized popular politics continuously, but also provided significant models for social movement activity elsewhere. Even in the new United States the social movement complex did not become a readily available and imitable model of public politics until somewhat later, with British-initiated antislavery providing a major stimulus to that political transformation.

A century-by-century comic-book history of the social movement from the 18th century onward would look something like this:

18th century: Multiple elements of the social movement beginning to cohere, for example, in John Wilkes's British expansion of election campaigns and public marches on behalf of free speech and citizens' rights or Samuel Adams's linking of Boston's skilled workers and merchants in campaigns against Great Britain's arbitrary exactions. Consider a characteristic, if minor, example of political transfer: the cap of liberty that eventually figured so widely in late 18th-century and early 19th-century social movements. The Liberty Cap, derived from the headgear that Romans placed on the head of an emancipated slave, had a long iconic history in Great Britain. Borrowed from the Dutch as William of Orange became English King in the Glorious Revolution of 1688–1689, it had represented Dutch liberation from Spain. In Britain, it came to signify liberty in the Wilkite sense (Epstein 1994: 78–80; see also Harden 1995). In fact, during the Wilkite agitation of the 1760s William Hogarth produced a famous, savage drawing of the ugly Wilkes holding a pole topped by a Liberty Cap.

During the *19th century* we find the social movement operating chiefly in relatively democratic Western countries, but the roster now extends at least intermittently to most of northwestern Europe; some southern European countries such as Spain, Italy, and Greece; most of North America; Latin American countries including Argentina and Uruguay; and some hotspots among European colonies such as India. Among the century's social movement transfers we witness the generalization of street demonstrations, May Day, and red or black flags to symbolize insurrection. We also register the formation of intellectual and political exiles who support dissident activity in their home countries, and in the process often export ideas or practices from their host regimes (Anderson 1991; Hanagan 1998, 2002; Keck and Sikkink 2000).

The *20th century*, in this comic-book history, accelerates the pace of innovation and diffusion. Across the world, we observe increasing reliance of social movement activists on access to mass media eventually including not only newspapers but also radio, television, and eventually electronic communication (Granjon 2002; Hocke 2002; Koopmans 2004; Scalmer 2002a, 2002b). In a parallel way, we witness the rise of the professional, durable social movement organization and its entrepreneurs as coordinators of claim making (Keck and Sikkink 1998; Mayer 1997; Meyer and Tarrow 1998). We see student movements proliferating and communicating not only within schools but also on the public streets. Among workers, we notice the invention and diffusion of such models as the factory occupation. At least in the more democratic Western countries, we witness a certain regularization of relations between demonstrators and specialized police forces (Earle, Soule, and McCarthy 2003; Emsley and Weinberger 1991; Fillieule 1997b; Lindenberger 1993, 1995; della Porta 1995; della Porta and Reiter 1998; Robert 1996; Sommier 1993; Tilly 2003: 201–31).

The incipient *21st century* alters the social movement scene once again. Although social movements in recognizable 20th-century style continue to predominate even in a Western Europe under transformation by the European Union (Imig and Tarrow 2001), international coordination of protests against such transnational institutions as the World Trade Organization becomes more extensive and frequent (Anheier and Themudo 2002; Bennett 2004a; Smith 1997, 2002; Tarrow 2002, 2003; Lesley Wood 2004). Despite the fact that the nerve centers of those protests continue to locate in rich northern countries, elsewhere dissident members of elites—notably students and professionals— adopt campaigns, social movement performances, and WUNC displays from time to time as they simultaneously address international media and voice opposition to their own regimes. International transfers include the human chain to advocate debt relief for poor countries and the ubiquitous circle-di-agonal symbol, on the model of a European no-parking sign, calling for the ban of the World Trade Organization.

Instead of taking these great chunks of time, we might also trace the social movement's history by following one or another of its major performances through the two and a half centuries in question. A history of the street dem-onstration, for example, poses important questions for political transfer. Ex-amined closely, the demonstration separates into three partly distinguishable streams: the public meeting in an enclosed space, the assembly in an open pub-lic space, and the disciplined street march. The three sometimes combine, as when participants in a mass meeting march through city streets from their stadium to city hall. Yet each stems from a somewhat different prehistory, with substantial country-to-country variation according to political structure and legal codes.

Broadly speaking, the social movement versions of public meetings adapted the rights of corporate groups such as religious congregations to assemble for their private business, public assemblies extended civic ceremonies such as cel-ebrations and executions to citizen-initiated gatherings, and street marches converted authorized processions (once again, usually of corporate bodies) into initiatives taken by the demonstrators themselves. In individual countries, dif-ferent versions of the demonstration have produced abundant histories (see, e.g., Blackstock 2000; Deneckere 1998; Duyvendak 1994; Farrell 2000; Favre 1990; Fillieule 1997a; Jarman 1997; Munger 1981; Pigenet and Tartakowsky 2003; Robert 1996; Schweitzer and Tilly 1982; Tartakowsky 1997, 1999, 2004). Yet the central models of public meeting, open assembly, and street march have acquired enough similarity that a viewer of television through most of the world can almost instantly recognize a demonstration as it flashes across the screen.

The demonstration's unity in diversity poses an important problem for stu-dents of political transfer. Sidney Tarrow rightly stresses modularity as a dis-tinguishing characteristic of social movement performances (Tarrow 1998: 37–

41). As compared with local shaming ceremonies, institutions of popular justice, and patron-client politics, such performances as the demonstration and the petition drive transferred much more easily across places, regimes, issues, and actors (Tilly 1993b).

Nevertheless, three features of the demonstration and related performances introduce significant particularity into their histories: first, their evolution from distinctive national traditions; second, the negotiation and adaptation that goes into the very process of diffusion; and third, the local culture that informs the actual operation of any transplanted performance (Auyero 2001; Avritzer 2002; Barber 2002; Chabot 2000; Chabot and Duyvendak 2002; Cope 1996; Esherick and Wasserstrom 1990; Faue 2000; Greiff 1997; Jarman 1997; Marston 1989; Mirala 2000; Scalmer 2000, 2002a, 2002b; Andrew Wood 2001). "Modular" performances ordinarily show two faces: one presenting a recognizable visage to the outside world, the other encoding local secrets and symbols. How that happens presents a puzzle of capital importance for students of contentious politics and political transfer.

In this brief introduction to the problem, as promised, I can do no more than sketch a way of thinking about it. Let me suggest that we identify a small bundle of mechanisms as they recur in different combinations with varying aggregate effects across episodes of political transfer. They include tactical innovation, bargaining, negotiated diffusion, brokerage, certification, and local adaptation. Speaking in terms of social movements rather than of political transfer in general, let us consider each one in turn:

Tactical innovation may result in part from prior deliberation on the part of political entrepreneurs, but it always occurs in the course of interaction among claimants, objects of claims, and third parties. It involves modifying known interaction routines, noticing the modification's effects, and incorporating the modified routine into the local claim-making repertoire. Thus we see 19th-century Western European demonstrators substituting written signs containing demands or slogans for the nonverbal symbols and banners that prevailed during the early part of the century.

Bargaining includes proposing terms—and often counter-terms—for some possible interaction, then reaching agreement among parties concerning both the performance of that interaction and the response of the parties to its outcome. In this regard, we regularly discover 20th-century movement organizers working out a meeting place or line of march with local police.

Negotiated diffusion identifies the familiar sequence in which a local group of activists learns of a tactical innovation made elsewhere, deliberates on its adoption, and creates a local variant of the interaction routine. For example, the network called Jubilee 2000 stimulates widespread adoption of the human chain as a way of dramatizing demands for poor countries' debt relief (Pettifor 2001).

Brokerage often figures in negotiated diffusion. In its simplest form, brokerage consists of an intermediary's creating closer connections than previously existed between two or more social sites: persons, groups, places, or something else. Brokers sometimes continue to mediate the connections, and sometimes step away once the connections exist. As a case in point, consider the enormous influence of women's organizations as standardizers of American feminist claim making across the country after 1890 (Clemens 1997).

Certification occurs when some authoritative entity—a ruler, a political leader, a tribunal, a nongovernmental organization, or something else—endorses an action, person, group, stated identity, or claim, thus signaling an increased likelihood that the entity and its allies will act to support the action, person, group, stated identity, or claim. De-certification also occurs when an authoritative entity condemns an action, person, group, stated identity, or claim, thus signaling increased probability of negative response to future appearance of the condemned element. Think about how the U.S. government provided backing to activists during the early phases of the American civil rights movement, not to mention how the government later turned against black nationalists (McAdam 1999, introduction).

Local adaptation happens when in the course of political interaction a tactical innovation adopted from elsewhere modifies, with participants incorporating locally relevant symbols, rituals, persons, and/or social connections. Consider how much the same American civil rights activists modified the practice of nonviolence as they engaged in active, risky making of claims (Chabot 2000; Chabot and Duyvendak 2002).

Let me be clear. I don't claim that tactical innovation, bargaining, negotiated diffusion, brokerage, certification, and local adaptation coexist in every transfer of the social movement from one place to another. Even less do I claim that the ensemble exhausts the roster of mechanisms causing political transfer at large. At a minimum, for example, any comprehensive history of constitutions and their duplications would have to assign a central place to conquest. I do claim, however, that in the history of social movements the six mechanisms have frequently occurred in each other's company, and that their specific combinations and sequences have strongly affected how social movements changed.

If this claim holds up, it sets an important agenda for historical research. Through what agents, channels, and mechanisms did the actual diffusion of the social movement's elements occur? For recent social movements, the question has taken on new interest, as transnational coordination of social movement programs and actions increases (Bandy and Smith 2004; Bennett 2004a, 2004b; Chabot and Duyvendak 2002; Imig and Tarrow 2001; Mertes 2004; Rajagopal 2003; Scalmer 2000, 2002b; Tarrow 2001, 2002, 2003; Tarrow and McAdam 2004). But well-grounded historical analyses remain rare. Understandably, students of social movements past and present customarily locate them firmly in their local or national contexts as they exaggerate the autonomy and originality of those movements.

In one of the more thoughtful reviews of the topic, John Markoff stresses three factors that promote social movements' crossing of national frontiers:

1. replication of structural circumstances from one country to another
2. transmission of a cultural model through available media and by means of easily transferable inventions
3. movements of people—for example, sailors and students—across national frontiers (Markoff 1996b: 29–31).

We should probably add a fourth factor to Markoff's list: deliberate creation of international organizations for the promotion of programs and coordinated actions (Anheier and Themudo 2002; Keck and Sikkink 1998, 2000; Riles 2000; Smith 1997, 2002).

Negotiated diffusion, brokerage, and certification, followed by local adaptation, figure prominently in all factors but the replication of structural circumstances. During the later 20th century, partly in response to the rising prominence of international institutions such as the European Community and the World Bank, the fourth factor—deliberate creation of international organizations—began to play a much larger part in the political transfer of the social movement repertoire. At the same time, that transfer began to transform the repertoire, for example, by establishing international days of protest timed to the staging of international economic forums (Lesley Wood 2004).

What happened earlier? As my earlier cartoons suggest, from the 18th century onward political brokers (e.g., Thomas Paine), international organizations (e.g., antislavery societies), and mass media (e.g., newspapers) all promoted transfer of social movements ideas, programs, and practices from country to country. But how they interacted and changed from then until now remains uncertain for lack of adequate historical work. A rich set of opportunities opens up for historical research on political transfer. For the moment, my sketch of relevant mechanisms raises questions rather than provides answers.

Looking at any particular locality, we can sketch an idealized cycle in which tactical innovation and bargaining occur simultaneously, negotiated diffusion and brokerage overlap, brokerage and certification increase the probability of negotiated diffusion, de-certification decreases that probability, but local adaptation terminates the cycle as a new round of tactical innovation begins. The social movement as a whole emerged through multiple cycles of this kind, but so on a smaller scale did each of its elements: the writing of pamphlets, the petition drive, the street march, the campaign for recognition, the wearing of slogan-bearing badges, and so on down the entire roster.

Of course, the serious work starts there. We must ask whether the idealized cycle actually recurs in sufficiently regular form to justify identifying it as a robust process and seeking to analyze its overall dynamics (Tilly 2001a). We must scrutinize the individual mechanisms to determine not only how uniform they are but also what triggers them, in what circumstances, and exactly how they produce their effects. Unless we eventually develop some power to anticipate which forms of political transfer will and won't occur in specified circumstances, the whole exercise may provide the means of more coherent conversation about the subject, but it won't contribute much to the long-term goal of systematic explanation. Judging from the help these simple ideas offer in unraveling the complex history of social movements, however, they deserve careful attention elsewhere in the realm of political transfers.

References

Abbott, Andrew (1995): "Things of Boundaries," *Social Research* 62: 857–82.

Abell, Peter (2004): "Narrative Explanation: An Alternative to Variable-Centered Explanation?" *Annual Review of Sociology* 30: 287–310.

Ahrne, Göran (1994): *Social Organizations: Interaction Inside, Outside and Between Organizations.* London: Sage.

——— (1996): "Civil Society and Civil Organizations," *Organization* 3: 109–20.

Almeida, Paul D., and Mark Irving Lichbach (2003): "To the Internet, From the Internet: Comparative Media Coverage of Transnational Protests," *Mobilization* 8: 249–72.

Anderson, Benedict (1991): *Imagined Communities: Reflections on the Origin and Spread of Nationalism.* London: VERSO.

Anderson, Grace M. (1974): *Networks of Contact: The Portuguese and Toronto.* Waterloo, Ontario: Wilfrid Laurier University Publications.

Anderson, Richard D., Jr., M. Steven Fish, Stephen E. Hanson, and Philip G. Roeder (2001): *Postcommunism and the Theory of Democracy.* Princeton, N.J.: Princeton University Press.

Anheier, Helmut, and Nuno Themudo (2002): "Organisational Forms of Global Civil Society: Implications of Going Global," in Marlies Glasius, Mary Kaldor, and Helmut Anheier, eds., *Global Civil Society 2002.* Oxford: Oxford University Press.

d'Anjou, Leo (1996): *Social Movements and Cultural Change: The First Abolition Campaign Revisited.* New York: Aldine de Gruyter.

Annan, Kofi (2003): "A Challenge to the World's Scientists," *Science* 299 (7 March), p. 1485.

Anthony, Denise, and Christine Horne (2003): "Gender and Cooperation: Explaining Loan Repayment in Micro-Credit Groups," *Social Psychology Quarterly* 66: 293–302.

Appiah, Kwame Anthony, and Henry Louis Gates Jr., eds. (1995): *Identities.* Chicago: University of Chicago Press.

Arat, Zehra F. (1991): *Democracy and Human Rights in Developing Countries.* Boulder, Colo.: Lynne Rienner.

Armstrong, Gary (1998): *Football Hooligans: Knowing the Score.* Oxford: Berg.

Ashforth, Adam (1990): *The Politics of Official Discourse in Twentieth-Century South Africa.* Oxford: Clarendon Press.

Atkin, Muriel (1997): "Thwarted Democratization in Tajikistan," in Karen Dawisha and Bruce Parrott, eds., *Conflict, Cleavage, and Change in Central Asia and the Caucasus.* Cambridge: Cambridge University Press. Democratization and Authoritarianism in Postcommunist Societies: 4.

Auyero, Javier (2001): "Glocal Riots," *International Sociology* 16: 33–53.

——— (2003): *Contentious Lives: Two Argentine Women, Two Protests, and the Quest for Recognition.* Durham, N.C.: Duke University Press.

Avritzer, Leonardo (2002): *Democracy and the Public Space in Latin America.* Princeton, N.J.: Princeton University Press.

Azar, Edward, and Josph Ben-Dak, eds. (1973): *Theory and Practice of Events Research.* New York: Gordon and Breach.

Ballinger, Pamela (2003): *History in Exile: Memory and Identity at the Borders of the Balkans.* Princeton, N.J.: Princeton University Press.

Bandy, Joe, and Jackie Smith, eds. (2004): *Coalitions Across Borders: Transnational Protest and the Neoliberal Order.* Lanham, Md.: Rowman & Littlefield.

Barber, Benjamin (1974): *The Death of Communal Liberty: The History of Freedom in a Swiss Mountain Canton.* Princeton, N.J.: Princeton University Press.

Barber, Lucy G. (2002): *Marching on Washington: The Forging of an American Political Tradition.* Berkeley: University of California Press.

Barbera, Filippo (2004): *Meccanismi sociali: Elementi di sociologia analitica.* Bologna: Il Mulino.

Bárcena, Iñaki, Pedro Ibarra, and Mario Zubiaga (1995): *Nacionalismo y ecología: Conflicto y institutionalización en el movimiento ecologista vasco.* Madrid: Libros de la Catarata.

Barfield, Thomas J. (1989): *The Perilous Frontier: Nomadic Empires and China.* New York: Blackwell.

Barnes, Jonathan, ed. (1984): *The Complete Works of Aristotle.* 2 vols. Princeton, N.J.: Princeton University Press.

Barth, Fredrik, ed. (1969): *Ethnic Groups and Boundaries: The Social Organization of Culture Difference.* Bergen-Oslo: Universitetsforlaget.

——— (1981): *Process and Form in Social Life. Selected Essays of Fredrik Barth: Volume I.* London: Routledge and Kegan Paul.

Bashi Bobb, Vilna (2001): "Neither Ignorance nor Bliss: Race, Racism, and the West Indian Immigrant Experience," in Héctor R. Cordero-Guzmán, Robert C. Smith, and Ramón Grosfoguel, eds., *Migration, Transnationalization, and Race in a Changing New York.* Philadelphia: Temple University Press.

Bates, Robert H., et al. (1998): *Analytical Narratives.* Princeton, N.J.: Princeton University Press.

Bax, Mart (2000): "Holy Mary and Medjugorje's Rocketeers. The Local Logic of an Ethnic Cleansing Process in Bosnia," *Ethnologia Europaea* 30: 45–58.

BBC (2002): "QandA: What Next For Guantanamo Prisoners?" *BBC News* online, 21 January, front page.

Bearman, Peter S. (1991): "Desertion as Localism: Army Unit Solidarity and Group Norms in the U.S. Civil War," *Social Forces* 70: 321–42.

——— (1993): *Relations into Rhetorics. Local Elite Social Structure in Norfolk, England, 1540–1640.* New Brunswick, N.J.: Rutgers University Press.

Beik, William H. (1985): *Absolutism and Society in Seventeenth-Century France.* Cambridge: Cambridge University Press.

Beissinger, Mark (2002): *Nationalist Mobilization and the Collapse of the Soviet State.* Cambridge: Cambridge University Press.

Bennett, W. Lance (2004a): "Communicating Global Activism," *Information, Communication and Society* 6: 143–68.

——— (2004b): "Social Movements Beyond Borders: Understanding Two Eras of Transnational Activism," in Donatella della Porta and Sidney Tarrow, eds., *Transnational Protest and Global Activism.* Lanham, Md.: Rowman & Littlefield.

Berliner, Paul F. (1994): *Thinking in Jazz: The Infinite Art of Improvisation.* Chicago: University of Chicago Press.

Bermeo, Nancy (2003): *Ordinary People in Extraordinary Times: The Citizenry and the Breakdown of Democracy.* Princeton, N.J.: Princeton University Press.

Besley, Timothy (1995): "Nonmarket Institutions for Credit and Risk Sharing in Low-Income Countries," *Journal of Economic Perspectives* 9: 169–88.

Biggart, Nicole Woolsey (2001): "Banking on Each Other: The Situational Logic of Rotating Savings and Credit Associations," *Advances in Qualitative Organization Research* 3: 129–53.

Biggart, Nicole Woolsey and Richard P. Castanias (2001): "Collateralized Social Relations: The Social in Economic Calculation." *American Journal of Economics and Sociology* 60: 471–500.

Blackstock, Allan (2000): "'The Invincible Mass': Loyal Crowds in Mid Ulster, 1795–96," in Peter Jupp and Eoin Magennis, eds., *Crowds in Ireland c. 1720–1920.* London: Macmillan.

Blackwood, Evelyn (1998): "Tombois in West Sumatra: Constructing Masculinity and Erotic Desire," *Cultural Anthropology* 13: 491–521.

Boehm, Christopher (1987): *Blood Revenge: The Enactment and Management of Conflict in Montenegro and Other Tribal Societies.* Philadelphia: University of Pennsylvania Press. First published by University Press of Kansas, 1984.

Bonneuil, Noël (1997): "Jeux, équilibres et régulation des populations sous contrainte de viabilité. Une lecture de l'oeuvre de l'anthropologue Fredrik Barth," *Population* 52: 947–76.

Borges, Jorge Luis (1962): *Ficciones.* New York: Grove.

Boris, Eileen and Angélique Janssens, eds. (1999): "Complicating Categories: Gender, Class, Race and Ethnicity," *International Review of Social History* 44, supplement 7, entire issue.

Bottomore, Thomas, ed. (1983): *A Dictionary of Marxist Thought.* Cambridge, Mass.: Harvard University Press.

Bourdelais, Patrice (2004): "The French population censuses: Purposes and uses during the 17th, 18th and 19th centuries," *History of the Family* 9: 97–113.

Bowles, Samuel, and Herbert Gintis (1998): "The Evolution of Strong Reciprocity," Working Paper 98–08–073, Santa Fe Institute Economics Research Program.

Brady, Henry E., and David Collier, eds. (2004): *Rethinking Social Inquiry: Diverse Tools, Shared Standards.* Lanham, Md.: Rowman & Littlefield.

te Brake, Wayne (1989): *Regents and Rebels: The Revolutionary World of the 18th Century Dutch City.* Oxford: Blackwell.

——— (1990): "How Much in How Little? Dutch Revolution in Comparative Perspective," *Tijdschrift voor Sociale Geschiedenis* 16: 349–63.

——— (1998): *Shaping History: Ordinary People in European Politics, 1500–1700.* Berkeley: University of California Press.

Brass, Paul R. (1994): *The Politics of India Since Independence.* Cambridge: Cambridge University Press. The New Cambridge History of India, IV-1, 2nd ed.

———, ed. (1996): *Riots and Pogroms.* New York: New York University Press.

——— (1997): *Theft of an Idol: Text and Context in the Representation of Collective Violence.* Princeton, N.J.: Princeton University Press.

Bratton, Michael, and Nicolas van de Walle (1997): *Democratic Experiments in Africa: Regime Transitions in Comparative Perspective.* Cambridge: Cambridge University Press.

Brewer, John (1976): *Party Ideology and Popular Politics at the Accession of George III.* Cambridge: Cambridge University Press.

——— (1989): *The Sinews of Power: War, Money and the English State, 1688–1783.* New York: Knopf.

Broadbent, Jeffrey (1998): *Environmental Politics in Japan: Networks of Power and Protest.* Cambridge: Cambridge University Press.

Brockett, Charles D. (1992): "Measuring Political Violence and Land Inequality in Central America" *American Political Science Review* 86: 169–76.

Bromberger, Christian (1998): *Football, la bagatelle la plus sérieuse du monde.* Paris: Bayard.

Brubaker, Rogers, and Frederick Cooper (2000): "Beyond 'identity,'" *Theory and Society* 29: 1–47.

Brubaker, Rogers, and David D. Laitin (1998): "Ethnic and Nationalist Violence," *Annual Review of Sociology* 24: 423–52.

BU (2004): "Humanistics," Institute for the Advancement of the Social Sciences, Boston University *www.bu.edu/uni/iass/humanistics/index.html,* viewed 7 November 2004.

Buford, Bill (1991): *Among the Thugs.* New York: Vintage.

Bunce, Val (2001): "Democratization and Economic Reform," *Annual Review of Political Science* 4: 43–66.

Bunge, Mario (1997): "Mechanism and Explanation," *Philosophy of the Social Sciences* 27: 410–65.

——— (1998): *Social Science Under Debate: A Philosophical Perspective*. Toronto: University of Toronto Press.

Burawoy, Michael, and Katherine Verdery, eds. (1999): *Uncertain Transition: Ethnographies of Change in the Postsocialist World*. Lanham, Md.: Rowman & Littlefield.

Burguière, André, and Raymond Grew, eds. (2001): *The Construction of Minorities: Cases for Comparison Across Time and Around the World*. Ann Arbor: University of Michigan Press.

Burke, Peter (1993): *The Art of Conversation*. Ithaca, N.Y.: Cornell University Press.

Burt, Ronald S., and Marc Knez (1995): "Kinds of Third-Party Effects on Trust," *Rationality and Society* 7: 255–92.

Campbell, Karen E., Peter V. Marsden, and Jeanne S. Hurlbert (1986): "Social Resources and Socioeconomic Status," *Social Networks* 8: 97–117.

Campbell, Karen, and Rachel Rosenfeld (1986): "Job Search and Job Mobility: Sex and Race Differences," *Research in the Sociology of Work* 3: entire issue.

Caplan, Jane, and John Torpey, eds. (2001): *Documenting Individual Identity: State Practices in the Modern World*. Princeton, N.J.: Princeton University Press.

Carrington, Selwyn H. H. (2002): *The Sugar Industry and the Abolition of the Slave Trade, 1775–1810*. Gainesville: University Press of Florida.

Castrén, Anna-Maija, and Markku Lonkila (2004): "Friendship in Finland and Russia from a Micro Perspective," in Anna-Maija Castrén, Markku Lonkila, and Matti Peltonen, eds., *Between Sociology and History: Essays on Microhistory, Collective Action, and Nation-Building*. Helsinki: SKS/Finnish Literature Society.

Cerulo, Karen A. (1997): "Identity Construction: New Issues, New Directions," *Annual Review of Sociology* 23: 385–409.

Chabot, Sean (2000): "Transnational Diffusion and the African-American Reinvention of the Gandhian Repertoire," *Mobilization* 5: 201–16.

Chabot, Sean, and Jan Willem Duyvendak (2002): "Globalization and Transnational Diffusion Between Social Movements: Reconceptualizing the Dissemination of the Gandhian Repertoire and the 'Coming Out' Routine," *Theory and Society* 31: 697–740.

Cheyette, Fredric L. (2001): *Ermengard of Narbonne and the World of the Troubadours*. Ithaca, N.Y.: Cornell University Press.

Cioffi-Revilla, Claudio (1990): *The Scientific Measurement of International Conflict: Handbook of Datasets on Crises and Wars, 1495–1988 A.D.* Boulder, Colo.: Lynne Rienner.

Clemens, Elisabeth S. (1997): *The People's Lobby: Organizational Innovation and the Rise of Interest Group Politics in the United States, 1890–1925*. Chicago: University of Chicago Press.

Clutton-Brock, T. H., M. J. O'Riain, P. N. M. Brotherton, D. Gaynor, R. Kansky, A. S. Griffin, and M. Manser (1999): "Selfish Sentinels in Cooperative Mammals," *Science* 284: 1640–44.

Coase, Ronald (1992): "The Institutional Structure of Production," *American Economic Review* 82: 713–19.

Cohn, Samuel (1985): *The Process of Occupational Sex-Typing: The Feminization of Clerical Labor in Great Britain*. Philadelphia: Temple University Press.

——— (2000): *Race, Gender, and Discrimination at Work*. Boulder, Colo.: Westview.

Coleman, James S. (1990): *Foundations of Social Theory*. Cambridge, Mass.: Harvard University Press.

Collier, Ruth Berins (1999): *Paths Toward Democracy: The Working Class and Elites in Western Europe and South America*. Cambridge: Cambridge University Press.

Comaroff, John, and Comaroff, Jean (1992): *Ethnography and the Historical Imagination*. Boulder, Colo.: Westview.

Cooper, Frederick (1994): "Conflict and Connection: Rethinking Colonial African History," *American Historical Review* 99: 1516–45.

Cooper, Frederick, and Ann Laura Stoler, eds. (1997): *Tensions of Empire: Colonial Cultures in a Bourgeois World*. Berkeley: University of California Press.

Cope, Meghan (1996): "Weaving the Everyday: Identity, Space, and Power in Lawrence, Massachusetts, 1920–1939," *Urban Geography* 17: 179–204.

Copland, Ian (1998): "The Further Shores of Partition: Ethnic Cleansing in Rajasthan 1947," *Past and Present* 160: 203–39.

Corcoran, Mary, Linda Datcher, and Greg J. Duncan (1980): "Most Workers Find Jobs Through Word of Mouth," *Monthly Labor Review*, August 1980, 33–35.

Cordero-Guzmán, Héctor R., Robert C. Smith, and Ramón Grosfoguel, eds. (2001): *Migration, Transnationalization, and Race in a Changing New York*. Philadelphia: Temple University Press.

Cornell, Stephen, and Douglas Hartmann (1998): *Ethnicity and Race: Making Identities in a Changing World*. Thousand Oaks, Calif.: Pine Forge.

Creveld, Martin van (1991): *The Transformation of War*. New York: Free Press.

CSCE [Commission on Security and Cooperation in Europe] (1998): *Political Reform and Human Rights in Uzbekistan, Kyrgyzstan and Kazakstan*. Washington, D.C.: CSCE.

Curtis, Bruce (2001): *The Politics of Population: State Formation, Statistics, and the Census of Canada, 1840–1875*. Toronto: University of Toronto Press.

Daniel, E. Valentine (1996): *Charred Lullabies: Chapters in an Anthropography of Violence*. Princeton, N.J.: Princeton University Press.

Davenport, Christian (2002): "Understanding Covert Repressive Action," unpublished paper. College Park: University of Maryland.

Davis, John (1992): *Exchange*. Minneapolis: University of Minnesota Press.

Deaton, Angus (2003): "Health, Inequality, and Economic Development," *Journal of Economic Literature* 41: 113–58.

Deneckere, Gita (1998); *Sire, het volk mort: Sociaal protest in België: 1831–1918*. Antwerp: Baarn, Ghent: Amsab.

De Schweinitz, Dorothea (1932): *How Workers Find Jobs: A Study of Four Thousand Hosiery Workers in Philadelphia*. Philadelphia: University of Pennsylvania Press.

Dessert, Daniel (1984): *Argent, pourvoir, et société au Grand Siècle.* Paris: Fayard.

Diamond, Larry (1999): *Developing Democracy: Toward Consolidation.* Baltimore, Md.: Johns Hopkins University Press.

Diani, Mario (1988): *Isole nell'arcipelago: Il movimento ecologista in Italia.* Bologna: Il Mulino.

——— (1995): *Green Networks: A Structural Analysis of the Italian Environmental Movement.* Edinburgh: Edinburgh University Press.

Diani, Mario, and Ron Eyerman, eds. (1992): *Studying Collective Action.* Newbury Park, Calif.: Sage.

DiMaggio, Paul, ed. (2001): *The Twenty-First-Century Firm. Changing Economic Organization in International Perspective.* Princeton, N.J.: Princeton University Press.

DiMaggio, Paul, and Hugh Louch (1998): "Socially Embedded Consumer Transactions: For What Kinds of Purchases Do People Use Networks Most?" *American Sociological Review,* 63: 619–37.

Domínguez, Virginia R. (1986): *White by Definition: Social Classification in Creole Louisiana.* New Brunswick, N.J.: Rutgers University Press.

Downs, Laura Lee (1995): *Manufacturing Inequality. Gender Division in the French and British Metalworking Industries, 1914–1939.* Ithaca, N.Y.: Cornell University Press.

Drescher, Seymour (1982): "Public Opinion and the Destruction of British Colonial Slavery," in James Walvin, ed., *Slavery and British Society, 1776–1946.* Baton Rouge: Louisiana State University Press.

——— (1986): *Capitalism and Antislavery: British Mobilization in Comparative Perspective.* London: Macmillan.

——— (1994): "Whose Abolition? Popular Pressure and the Ending of the British Slave Trade," *Past and Present* 143: 136–66.

Drew, Christopher, and David Cay Johnston (1996): "For Wealthy Americans, Death Is More Certain than Taxes," *New York Times,* December 22, 1996:1, 30–31.

Duffy, Eamon (2001): *The Voices of Morebath: Reformation and Rebellion in an English Village.* New Haven, Conn.: Yale University Press.

Dumont, Louis (1970): *Homo Hierarchicus: An Essay on the Caste System.* Chicago: University of Chicago Press.

Duneier, Mitchell, and Harvey Molotch (1999): "Talking City Trouble: Interactional Vandalism, Social Inequality, and the 'Urban Interaction Problem,'" *American Journal of Sociology* 104: 1263–95.

Duyvendak, Jan Willem (1994): *Le poids du politique: Nouveaux mouvements sociaux en France.* Paris: L'Harmattan.

Earl, Jennifer, Sarah A. Soule, and John D. McCarthy (2003): "Protest under Fire? Explaining the Policing of Protest," *American Sociological Review* 68: 581–606.

Earle, Timothy (1997): *How Chiefs Come to Power: The Political Economy in Prehistory.* Stanford, Calif.: Stanford University Press.

Edwards, Bob, and Michael W. Foley (1998): "Beyond Tocqueville: Civil Society and Social Capital in Comparative Perspective," *American Behavioral Scientist* 42, no. 1, entire issue.

———— (1999): "Is It Time to Disinvest in Social Capital?" *Journal of Public Policy* 19: 141–73.

Eisenberg, Susan (1998): *We'll Call You If We Need You: Experiences of Women Working Construction.* Ithaca, N.Y.: ILR Press.

Elias, Norbert, and John L. Scotson (1994): *The Established and the Outsiders: A Sociological Enquiry into Community Problems.* 2nd ed. London: Sage.

Eliasoph, Nina (1998): *Avoiding Politics: How Americans Produce Apathy in Everyday Life.* Cambridge: Cambridge University Press.

Elster, Jon (1989): *Nuts and Bolts for the Social Sciences.* Cambridge: Cambridge University Press.

———— (1999): *Alchemists of the Mind: Rationality and the Emotions.* Cambridge: Cambridge University Press.

Elster, Jon, Claus Offe, and Ulrich K. Preuss (1998): *Institutional Design in Post-communist Societies. Rebuilding the Ship at Sea.* Cambridge: Cambridge University Press.

Emirbayer, Mustafa (1997): "Manifesto for a Relational Sociology," *American Journal of Sociology* 103: 281–317.

Emirbayer, Mustafa, and Jeff Goodwin (1994): "Network Analysis, Culture, and the Problem of Agency," *American Journal of Sociology* 99: 1411–54.

Emirbayer, Mustafa, and Ann Mische (1998): "What Is Agency?" *American Journal of Sociology* 103: 962–1023.

Emsley, Clive, and Barbara Weinberger, eds. (1991): *Policing in Western Europe: Politics, Professionalism, and Public Order, 1850–1940.* New York: Greenwood.

England, Paula (1992): *Comparable Worth: Theories and Evidence.* New York: Aldine de Gruyter.

Epstein, James A. (1994): Radical Expression. Political Language, Ritual, and Symbol in England, 1790–1850. New York: Oxford University Press.

Erickson, Bonnie H. (1996): "The Structure of Ignorance," keynote address to the International Sunbelt Social Network Conference, Charleston, S.C.

Esherick, Joseph W., and Jeffrey N. Wasserstrom (1990): "Acting Out Democracy: Political Theater in Modern China," *Journal of Asian Studies* 49: 835–65.

Farrell, Sean (2000): *Rituals and Riots: Sectarian Violence and Political Culture in Ulster, 1784–1886.* Lexington: University Press of Kentucky.

Fane, Daria (1996): "Ethnicity and Regionalism in Uzbekistan: Maintaining Stability through Authoritarian Control," in Leokadia Drobizheva, Rose Gottemoeller, Catherine McArdle Kelleher, and Lee Walker, eds., *Ethnic Conflict in the Post-Soviet World: Case Studies and Analysis.* Armonk, N.Y.: M. E. Sharpe.

Faue, Elizabeth, ed. (2000): "The Working Classes and Urban Public Space," special issue of *Social Science History* 24, no. l, entire issue.

Favre, Pierre, ed. (1990): *La Manifestation.* Paris: Presses de la Fondation Nationale des Sciences Politiques.

Favre, Pierre, Olivier Fillieule, and Nonna Mayer (1997): "La fin d'une étrange lacune de la sociologie des mobilisations. L'étude par sondage des manifestants.

Fondements théoriques et solutions techniques," *Revue Française de Science Politique* 47: 3–28.

Feige, Edgar (1998): "Underground Activity and Institutional Change: Productive, Protective, and Predatory Behavior in Transition Economies," in Joan Nelson, Charles Tilly, and Lee Walker, eds., *Transforming Post-Communist Political Economies.* Washington, D.C.: National Academies Press.

Ferguson, James (1997): "Anthropology and Its Evil Twin. 'Development' in the Constitution of a Discipline," in Frederick Cooper and Randall Packard, eds., *International Development and the Social Sciences: Essays on the History and Politics of Knowledge.* Berkeley: University of California Press.

Fernandez, Roberto, and Doug McAdam (1988): "Social Networks and Social Movements: Multiorganizational Fields and Recruitment to Mississippi Freedom Summer," *Sociological Forum* 3: 357–82.

Fernández-Kelly, M. Patricia (1983): *For We Are Sold, I and My People: Women and Industry in Mexico's Frontier.* Albany: State University of New York Press.

Fierman, William (1997): "Political Development in Uzbekistan: Democratization?" in Karen Dawisha and Bruce Parrott, eds., *Conflict, Cleavage, and Change in Central Asia and the Caucasus.* Cambridge: Cambridge University Press. Democratization and Authoritarianism in Postcommunist Societies: 4.

Fillieule, Olivier (1997a): *Stratégies de la rue: Les manifestations en France.* Paris: Presses de la Fondation Nationale des Sciences Politiques.

———— (1997b): "Maintien de l'ordre," special issue of *Cahiers de la Sécurité Intérieure.*

Fishman, Joshua A., ed. (1999): *Handbook of Language and Ethnic Identity.* New York: Oxford University Press.

Fitch, Kristine L. (1998): *Speaking Relationally: Culture, Communication, and Interpersonal Connection.* New York: Guilford.

Fogel, Robert William (2000): *The Fourth Great Awakening and the Future of Egalitarianism.* Chicago: University of Chicago Press.

———— (2004): *The Escape from Hunger and Premature Death, 1700–2100: Europe, America, and the Third World.* Cambridge: Cambridge University Press.

Fox, Jonathan (1994): "The Difficult Transition from Clientelism to Citizenship: Lessons from Mexico," *World Politics* 46: 151–84.

Franzosi, Roberto (1998a): "Narrative Analysis, or Why (and How) Sociologists Should Be Interested in Narrative," *Annual Review of Sociology* 24: 517–54.

———— (1998b): "Narrative as Data: Linguistic and Statistical Tools for the Quantitative Study of Historical Events," *International Review of Social History* 43, Supplement 6: New Methods for Social History, 81–104.

Fredrickson, George M. (1997): *The Comparative Imagination: On the History of Racism, Nationalism, and Social Movements.* Berkeley: University of California Press.

Freedom House (2002): "Freedom in the World 2002: The Democracy Gap," *www.freedomhouse.org/research/survey2002.htm,* 29 March 2002.

Frey, Bruno S., and Alois Stutzer (2002): "What Can Economists Learn from Happiness Research?" *Journal of Economic Literature* 40: 402–35.

Friedman, Jeffrey (2004): "Introduction: What Can Social Science Do?" *Critical Review* 16: 143–45.

Friedman, Jonathan (1994): *Cultural Identity and Global Process.* London: Sage.

Fuller, Sylvia (2003): "Creating and Contesting Boundaries: Exploring the Dynamics of Conflict and Classification," *Sociological Forum* 18: 3–30.

Gal, Susan (1987): "Codeswitching and Consciousness in the European Periphery," *American Ethnologist* 14: 637–53.

——— (1989): "Language and Political Economy," *Annual Review of Anthropology* 18: 345–69.

Gambetta, Diego (1993): *The Sicilian Mafia: The Business of Private Protection.* Cambridge, Mass.: Harvard University Press.

Gamson, William A., Bruce Fireman, and Steven Rytina (1982): *Encounters with Unjust Authority.* Homewood, Ill.: Dorsey.

Garcelon, Marc (2001): "Colonizing the Subject: The Genealogy and Legacy of the Soviet Internal Passport," in Jane Caplan and John Torpey, eds., *Documenting Individual Identity: State Practices in the Modern World.* Princeton, N.J.: Princeton University Press.

Gerner, Deborah J., et al. (1994): "Machine Coding of Event Data Using Regional and International Sources," *International Studies Quarterly* 38: 91–119.

Giugni, Marco G., and Florence Passy (1997): *Histoires de mobilisation politique en Suisse: De la contestation à l'intégration.* Paris: l'Harmattan.

Giulianotti, Richard, Norman Bonney, and Mike Hepworth, eds. (1994): *Football, Violence, and Social Identity.* London: Routledge.

Goldstone, Jack A. (1994): "Is Revolution Individually Rational? Groups and Individuals in Revolutionary Collective Action," *Rationality and Society* 6: 139–66.

Goldstone, Jack A., and Charles Tilly (2001): "Threat (and Opportunity): Popular Action and State Response in the Dynamics of Contentious Action," in Ronald Aminzade et al., eds., *Silence and Voice in Contentious Politics.* Cambridge: Cambridge University Press

Goodin, Robert E., Bruce Headey, Ruud Muffels, and Henk-Jan Dirven (1999): *The Real Worlds of Welfare Capitalism.* Cambridge: Cambridge University Press.

Goodwin, Jeff, James Jasper, Charles Tilly, Francesca Polletta, Sidney Tarrow, David Meyer, and Ruud Koopmans (1999): "Mini-Symposium on Social Movements," *Mobilization* 14: 27–136.

Gould, Roger V. (1999): "Collective Violence and Group Solidarity: Evidence from a Feuding Society," *American Sociological Review* 64: 356–80.

——— (2003): *Collision of Wills: How Ambiguity about Social Rank Breeds Conflict.* Chicago: University of Chicago Press.

———, ed. (2005): *Rational Choice Controversy in Historical Sociology.* Chicago: University of Chicago Press.

Granjon, Fabien (2002): "Les répertoires d'action télémathiques du néo-militantisme," *Le Mouvement Social* 200: 11–32.

Granovetter, Mark (1985): "Economic Action and Social Structure: The Problem of Embeddedness," *American Journal of Sociology* 91: 481–510.

—— (1995a): *Getting a Job: A Study of Contacts and Careers.* 2nd ed. Chicago: University of Chicago Press. First published in 1974.

—— (1995b): "The Economic Sociology of Firms and Entrepreneurs," in Alejandro Portes, ed., *The Economic Sociology of Immigration: Essays on Networks, Ethnicity, and Entrepreneurship.* New York: Russell Sage Foundation.

Granovetter, Mark, and Charles Tilly (1988): "Inequality and Labor Processes," in Neil J. Smelser, ed., *Handbook of Sociology.* Newbury Park, Calif.: Sage.

Greenfeld, Liah (1992): *Nationalism: Five Roads to Modernity.* Cambridge, Mass.: Harvard University Press.

—— (2003): *The Spirit of Capitalism: Nationalism and Economic Growth.* Cambridge, Mass.: Harvard University Press.

Greif, Avner (1994): "Cultural Beliefs and the Organization of Society: A Historical and Theoretical Reflection on Collectivist and Individualist Societies," *Journal of Political Economy* 102: 912–50.

Greiff, Mats (1997): "'Marching Through The Streets Singing and Shouting': Industrial Struggles and Trade Unions Among Female Linen Workers in Belfast and Lurgan, 1872–1910," *Saothar 22. Journal of the Irish Labour History Society,* 29–44.

Grimson, Alejandro (1999): *Relatos de la diferencia y la igualdad: Los bolivianos en Buenos Aires.* Buenos Aires: Editorial Universitaria de Buenos Aires.

Grusky, David B., ed. (2001): *Social Stratification: Class, Race, and Gender in Sociological Perspective.* 2nd ed. Boulder, Colo.: Westview.

Grusky, David B., and Jesper B. Sørensen (1998): "Can Class Analysis Be Salvaged?" *American Journal of Sociology* 103: 1187–1234.

Guiso, Luigi, Paola Sapienza, and Luigi Zingales (2004): "The Role of Social Capital in Financial Development," *American Economic Review* 94: 526–56.

Gumperz, John J. (1982): *Discourse Strategies.* Cambridge: Cambridge University Press.

Gurr, Ted Robert (1993): *Minorities at Risk: A Global View of Ethnopolitical Conflicts.* Washington, D.C.: U.S. Institute of Peace Press.

—— (2000): *Peoples Versus States: Minorities at Risk in the New Century.* Washington, D.C.: U.S. Institute of Peace Press.

Guyer, Jane I., ed. (1995): *Money Matters.* London: Heinemann.

Hale, Charles R. (1997): "Cultural Politics of Identity in Latin America," *Annual Review of Anthropology* 26: 567–90.

Haidt, Jonathan, and Craig Joseph (2004): "Intuitive Ethics: How Innately Prepared Intuitions Generate Culturally Variable Virtues," *Daedalus* Fall 2004: 55–66.

Hanagan, Michael P. (1994): "New Perspectives on Class Formation: Culture, Reproduction, and Agency," *Social Science History* 18: 77–94.

———— (1998): "Irish Transnational Social Movements, Deterritorialized Migrants, and the State System: The Last One Hundred and Forty Years," *Mobilization* 13: 107–26.

———— (1999): "The Right to Work and the Struggle Against Unemployment: Britain, 1884–1914," in Michael Hanagan and Charles Tilly, eds., *Extending Citizenship, Reconfiguring States.* Lanham, Md.: Rowman & Littlefield.

———— (2002): "Irish Transnational Social Movements, Migrants, and the State System," in Jackie Smith and Hank Johnston, eds., *Globalization and Resistance: Transnational Dimensions of Social Movements.* Lanham, Md.: Rowman & Littlefield.

Harden, J. David (1995): "Liberty Caps and Liberty Trees," *Past and Present* 146: 66–102.

Hardin, Russell (1995): *One for All: The Logic of Group Conflict.* Princeton, N.J.: Princeton University Press.

Harney, Robert (1984): *Dalla frontiera alle Little Italies.* Rome: Bonacci.

————, ed. (1985): *Gathering Place: Peoples and Neighborhoods of Toronto, 1834–1945.* Toronto: Multicultural History Society of Ontario.

Hart, Janet (1996): *New Voices in the Nation: Women and the Greek Resistance, 1941–1964.* Ithaca, N.Y.: Cornell University Press.

Harvey, David (1989): *The Condition of Postmodernity: An Enquiry into the Origins of Cultural Change.* Oxford: Blackwell.

Head, Randolph C. (1995): *Early Modern Democracy in the Grisons: Social Order and Political Language in a Swiss Mountain Canton, 1470–1620.* Cambridge: Cambridge University Press.

Hechter, Michael (1987): *Principles of Group Solidarity.* Berkeley: University of California Press.

Hedström, Peter, and Richard Swedberg, eds. (1998): *Social Mechanisms: An Analytical Approach to Social Theory.* Cambridge: Cambridge University Press.

Heimer, Carol A. (1985): *Reactive Risk and Rational Action: Managing Moral Hazard in Insurance Contracts.* Berkeley: University of California Press.

Hirsch, Eric L. (1990): "Sacrifice for the Cause: Group Processes, Recruitment, and Commitment in a Student Social Movement," *American Sociological Review* 55: 243–54.

Hirschman, Albert O. (1991): *The Rhetoric of Reaction: Perversity, Futility, Jeopardy.* Cambridge, Mass.: Harvard University Press.

Hoffman, Philip T., Gilles Postel-Vinay, and Jean-Laurent Rosenthal (2000): *Priceless Markets: The Political Economy of Credit in Paris.* Chicago: University of Chicago Press.

Hofmeyr, Isabel (1987): "Building a Nation from Words: Afrikaans Language, Literature and Ethnic Identity, 1902–1924," in Shula Marks and Stanley Trapido, eds., *The Politics of Race, Class and Nationalism in Twentieth-Century South Africa.* London: Longman.

Holzer, Harry J. (1987): "Informal Job Search and Black Youth Unemployment," *American Economic Review* 77: 446–52.

Horowitz, Donald L. (2001): *The Deadly Ethnic Riot.* Berkeley: University of California Press.

Hout, Michael, and Daniel P. Dohan (1996): "Two Paths to Educational Opportunity: Class and Educational Selection in Sweden and the United States," in Robert Erikson and Jan O. Jonsson, eds., *Can Education Be Equalized? The Swedish Case in Comparative Perspective.* Boulder, Colo.: Westview Press.

Hug, Simon, and Dominique Wisler (1998): "Correcting for Selection Bias in Social Movement Research," *Mobilization* 3: 141–62.

Hunt, Lynn (1978): *Revolution and Urban Politics in Provincial France: Troyes and Reims, 1786–1790.* Stanford, Calif.: Stanford University Press.

——— (1984): *Politics, Culture, and Class in the French Revolution.* Berkeley: University of California Press.

Imig, Doug, and Sidney Tarrow (2001): "Mapping the Europeanization of Contention: Evidence from a Quantitative Data Analysis," in Doug Imig and Sidney Tarrow, eds., *Contentious Europeans: Protest and Politics in an Emerging Polity.* Lanham, Md.: Rowman & Littlefield.

Ingwerson, Marshall (1997): "Into the Steppe of Genghis Khan Ride the Conquerors of a Sea's Oil Bounty," *Christian Science Monitor,* electronic edition, 18 August 1997.

Inkeles, Alex, ed. (1991): *On Measuring Democracy, Its Consequences and Concomitants.* New Brunswick, N.J.: Transaction.

Jackson, Robert Max (1984): *The Formation of Craft Labor Markets.* Orlando, Fla.: Academic Press.

Jarman, Neil (1997): *Material Conflicts: Parades and Visual Displays in Northern Ireland.* Oxford: Berg.

Jasso, Guillermina (1999): "How Much Injustice Is There in the World? Two New Justice Indexes," *American Sociological Review* 1999: 133–68.

Javeline, Debra (2003): *Protest and the Politics of Blame: The Russian Response to Unpaid Wages.* Ann Arbor: University of Michigan Press.

Jenson, Jane (1998): "Social Movement Naming Practices and the Political Opportunity Structure," Working Paper 1998/114, Instituto Juan March de Estudios e Investigaciones, Madrid.

Johnston, Alastair Iain (1995): *Cultural Realism: Strategic Culture and Grand Strategy in Chinese History.* Princeton, N.J.: Princeton University Press.

Jones, Peter (2003): *Liberty and Locality in Revolutionary France: Six Villages Compared, 1760–1820.* Cambridge: Cambridge University Press.

Joseph, May (1999): *Nomadic Identities: The Performance of Citizenship.* Minneapolis: University of Minnesota Press.

Jung, Courtney (2000): *Then I Was Black: South African Political Identities in Transition.* New Haven, Conn.: Yale University Press.

Juraeva, Gavhar, and Nancy Lubin (1996): "Ethnic Conflict in Tajikistan," in Leokadia Drobizheva, Rose Gottemoeller, Catherine McArdle Kelleher, and Lee Walker, eds., *Ethnic Conflict in the Post-Soviet World: Case Studies and Analysis.* Armonk, N.Y.: M. E. Sharpe.

Kaiser, Robert J. (1994): *The Geography of Nationalism in Russia and the USSR.* Princeton, N.J.: Princeton University Press.

Kalb, Don (1997): *Expanding Class: Power and Everyday Politics in Industrial Communities, The Netherlands, 1850–1950.* Durham, N.C.: Duke University Press.

Kaldor, Mary (1999): *New and Old Wars: Organized Violence in a Global Era.* Cambridge, UK: Polity.

Karakasidou, Anastasia N. (1997): *Fields of Wheat, Hills of Blood: Passages to Nationhood in Greek Macedonia, 1870–1990.* Chicago: University of Chicago Press.

Kastoryano, Riva (2002): *Negotiating Identities: States and Immigrants in France and Germany.* Princeton, N.J.: Princeton University Press.

Keck, Margaret, and Kathryn Sikkink (1998): *Activists beyond Borders: Advocacy Networks in International Politics.* Ithaca, N.Y.: Cornell University Press.

——— (2000): "Historical Precursors to Modern Transnational Social Movements and Networks," in John A. Guidry, Michael D. Kennedy, and Mayer N. Zald, eds., *Globalizations and Social Movements: Culture, Power, and the Transnational Public Sphere.* Ann Arbor: University of Michigan Press.

Kertzer, David I., and Dominique Arel, eds. (2002): *Census and Identity: The Politics of Race, Ethnicity, and Language in National Censuses.* Cambridge: Cambridge University Press.

Khawaja, Marwan (1993): "Repression and Popular Collective Action: Evidence from the West Bank," *Sociological Forum* 8: 47–71.

Khazanov, Anatoly M. (1995): *After the USSR: Ethnicity, Nationalism, and Politics in the Commonwealth of Independent States.* Madison: University of Wisconsin Press.

King, Gary, Robert O. Keohane, and Sidney Verba (1994): *Designing Social Inquiry. Scientific Inference in Qualitative Research.* Princeton, N.J.: Princeton University Press.

Kogut, Bruce (1997): "Identity, Procedural Knowledge, and Institutions: Functional and Historical Explanations for Institutional Change," in Frieder Naschold, David Soskice, Bob Hancke, and Ulrich Jürgens, eds., *Ökonomische Leistungsfähigkeit und institutionelle Innovation. Das deutsche Produktions- und Politikregime im internationalen Wettbewerb.* Berlin: Sigma.

Kohli, Atul (2004): *State-Directed Development: Political Power and Industrialization in the Global Periphery.* Cambridge: Cambridge University Press.

Koopmans, Ruud (2004): "Movements and Media: Selection Processes and Evolutionary Dynamics in the Public Sphere," *Theory and Society* 33: 367–91.

Kossmann, E. H. (1990): "Liep de Nederlandse Patriottenbeweging op de Franse vooruit?" in J. Craeybeckx and F. Scheelings, eds., *De Franse Revolutie en Vlaanderen.* Brussels: VUB Press.

Kuper, Adam (1999): *Culture: The Anthropologists' Account.* Chicago: University of Chicago Press.

Lafargue, Jérôme (1996): *Contestations démocratiques en Afrique.* Paris: Karthala and IFRA.

Lagrange, Hugues (1989): "Strikes and the War," in Leopold Haimson and Charles Tilly, eds., *Strikes, Wars, and Revolutions in an International Perspective.* Cambridge: Cambridge University Press.

Laitin, David D. (1998): *Identity in Formation: The Russian-Speaking Populations in the Near Abroad.* Ithaca, N.Y.: Cornell University Press.

——— (1999): "The Cultural Elements of Ethnically Mixed States: Nationality Reformation in the Soviet Successor States," in George Steinmetz, ed., *State/Culture. State Formation after the Cultural Turn.* Ithaca, N.Y.: Cornell University Press.

Lake, David A., and Donald Rothchild (1998): "Spreading Fear: The Genesis of Transnational Ethnic Conflict," in David A. Lake and Donald Rothchild, eds., *The International Spread of Ethnic Conflict: Fear, Diffusion, and Escalation.* Princeton, N.J.: Princeton University Press.

Lamont, Michèle (2001): "Culture and Identity," in Jonathan H. Turner, ed., *Handbook of Sociological Theory.* New York: Kluwer-Plenum.

Lamont, Michèle, and Virág Molnár (2002): "The Study of Boundaries in the Social Sciences," *Annual Review of Sociology* 28: 167–95.

Landa, Janet Tai (1994): *Trust, Ethnicity, and Identity: Beyond the New Institutional Economics of Ethnic Trading Networks, Contract Law, and Gift-Exchange.* Ann Arbor: University of Michigan Press.

Lang, James (2001): *Notes of a Potato Watcher.* College Station, Texas: A&M University Press.

Lebovics, Herman (1995): "Une 'nouvelle histoire culturelle'? La politique de la différence chez les historiens américains," *Genèses* 20: 116–25.

Ledeneva, Alena V. (1998): *Russia's Economy of Favours: Blat, Networking and Informal Exchange.* Cambridge: Cambridge University Press.

——— (2004): "Genealogy of *krugovaya poruka:* Forced Trust as a Feature of Russian Political Culture," *Proceedings of the British Academy* 123: 85–108.

Levi, Margaret (1988): *Of Rule and Revenue.* Berkeley: University of California Press.

——— (1997): *Consent, Dissent, and Patriotism.* Cambridge: Cambridge University Press.

Levi, Margaret, and Laura Stoker (2000): "Political Trust and Trustworthiness," *Annual Review of Political Science* 3: 475–508.

Levy, Yagil (1997): *Trial and Error: Israel's Route from War to De-Escalation.* Albany: State University of New York Press.

Lichbach, Mark Irving (1987): "Deterrence or Escalation? The Puzzle of Aggregate Studies of Repression and Dissent," *Journal of Conflict Resolution* 31: 266–97.

Light, Ivan (1984): "Immigrant and Ethnic Enterprise in North America," *Ethnic and Racial Studies* 7: 195–216.

Lin, Nan (1982): "Social Resources and Instrumental Action," in Peter V. Marsden and Nan Lin, eds., *Social Structure and Network Analysis.* Beverly Hills, Calif.: Sage.

Lin, Nan, and Mary Dumin (1986): "Access to Occupations Through Social Ties," *Social Networks* 8: 365–85.

Linard, André (1996): "La pêche, enjeu de toutes les convoîtises," in Ignacio Ramonet, Christian de Brie, and Alain Gresh, eds., *Conflits fin de siècle*. Paris: Le Monde Diplomatique; Manière de Voir, no. 29.

Lindenberger, Thomas (1993): "Politique de rue et action de classe à Berlin avant la Première Guerre mondiale," *Genèses* 12: 47–68.

——— (1995): *Strassenpolitik: Zur Sozialgeschichte der öffentlichen Ordnung in Berlin 1900 bis 1914*. Bonn: Dietz.

Little, Daniel (1991): *Varieties of Social Explanation: An Introduction to the Philosophy of Social Science*. Boulder, Colo.: Westview.

——— (1998): *On the Philosophy of the Social Sciences: Microfoundations, Method, and Causation*. New Brunswick, N.J.: Transaction.

Lonkila, Markku (1999): *Social Networks in Post-Soviet Russia*. Helsinki: Kikimora Publications.

López-Alves, Fernando (2000): *State Formation and Democracy in Latin America, 1810–1900*. Durham, N.C.: Duke University Press.

Loveman, Mara (1998): "High-Risk Collective Action: Defending Human Rights in Chile, Uruguay, and Argentina," *American Journal of Sociology* 104: 477–525.

Lowe, Philip D., and Wolfgang Rüdig (1986): "Political Ecology and the Social Sciences—The State of the Art," *British Journal of Political Science* 16: 513–50.

Ludden, David, ed. (1996): *Contesting the Nation: Religion, Community, and the Politics of Democracy in India*. Philadelphia: University of Pennsylvania Press.

Lundqvist, Sven (1977): *Folkrörelserna i det svenska samhället, 1850–1920*. Stockholm: Almqvist and Wiksell.

Lynn, John (1997): *Giant of the Grand Siècle: The French Army 1610–1715*. Cambridge: Cambridge University Press.

Malcolm, Noel (1996): *Bosnia: A Short History*. Rev. ed. New York: New York University Press. First published in 1994.

Malkki, Liisa H. (1995): *Purity and Exile: Violence, Memory, and National Cosmology among Hutu Refugees in Tanzania*. Chicago: University of Chicago Press.

Mamdani, Mahmood (1996): *Citizen and Subject: Contemporary Africa and the Legacy of Late Colonialism*. Princeton, N.J.: Princeton University Press.

——— (2001a): "Beyond Settler and Native as Political Identities: Overcoming the Political Legacy of Colonialism," *Comparative Studies in Society and History* 43: 651–64.

——— (2001b): *When Victims Become Killers: Colonialism, Nativism, and the Genocide in Rwanda*. Princeton, N.J.: Princeton University Press.

Mann, Michael (2005): *The Dark Side of Democracy*. Cambridge: Cambridge University Press.

Markoff, John (1996a): *The Abolition of Feudalism: Peasants, Lords, and Legislators in the French Revolution*. University Park: Pennsylvania State University Press.

——— (1996b): *Waves of Democracy: Social Movements and Political Change*. Thousand Oaks, Calif.: Pine Grove Press.

———— (1999): "Where and When Was Democracy Invented?" *Comparative Studies in Society and History* 41: 660–90.

Marsden, Peter V., and Jeanne S. Hurlbert (1988): "Social Resources and Mobility Outcomes: A Replication and Extension," *Social Forces* 66: 1038–59.

Marston, Sallie A. (1989): "Public Rituals and Community Power: St. Patrick's Day Parades in Lowell, Massachusetts, 1841–1874," *Political Geography Quarterly* 8: 255–69.

Martin, Terry (2001): *The Affirmative Action Empire: Nations and Nationalism in the Soviet Union, 1923–1939.* Ithaca, N.Y.: Cornell University Press.

Marx, Anthony (1998): *Making Race and Nation: A Comparison of the United States, South Africa, and Brazil.* Cambridge: Cambridge University Press.

———— (2003): *Faith in Nation: Exclusionary Origins of Nationalism.* Oxford: Oxford University Press.

Marx, Karl, and Friedrich Engels (1958): *Selected Works in Two Volumes.* Moscow: Foreign Languages Publishing House.

Mason, T. David (1989): "Nonelite Response to State-Sanctioned Terror," *Western Political Quarterly* 42: 467–92.

———— (2004): *Caught in the Crossfire: Revolution, Repression, and the Rational Peasant.* Lanham, Md.: Rowman & Littlefield.

Mason, T. David, and Dale A. Krane (1989): "The Political Economy of Death Squads: Toward a Theory of the Impact of State-Sanctioned Terror," *International Studies Quarterly* 33: 175–98.

Mayer, Margit (1997): "Les mouvements sociaux comme acteurs politiques dans les villes européennes: leur évolution entre les années soixante-dix et quatre-vingt-dix," in Arnaldo Bagnasco and Patrick Le Galès, eds., *Villes en Europe.* Paris: La Découverte.

Mazower, Mark (2000): *The Balkans: A Short History.* New York: Modern Library.

McAdam, Doug (1988): *Freedom Summer.* New York: Oxford University Press.

———— (1999): *Political Process and the Development of Black Insurgency, 1930–1970.* 2nd ed. Chicago: University of Chicago Press.

McAdam, Doug, and Ronnelle Paulsen (1993): "Specifying the Relationship Between Social Ties and Activism," *American Journal of Sociology* 99: 640–67.

McAdam, Doug, Sidney Tarrow, and Charles Tilly (2001): *Dynamics of Contention.* Cambridge: Cambridge University Press.

McCall, Leslie (2001): *Complex Inequality: Gender, Class, and Race in the New Economy.* New York: Routledge.

McPhee, Peter (1988): "Les formes d'intervention populaire en Roussillon: L'exemple de Collioure, 1789–1815," in *Centre d'Histoire Contemporaine du Languedoc Méditerranéen et du Roussillon: Les pratiques politiques en province à l'époque de la Révolution française.* Montpellier: Publications de la Recherche, Université de Montpellier.

Mertes, Tom, ed. (2004): *A Movement of Movements: Is Another World Really Possible?* London: Verso.

Merton, Robert K. (1968): "The Self-Fulfilling Prophecy," in *Social Theory and Social Structure.* New York: The Free Press.

Meyer, David S., and Sidney Tarrow, eds. (1998): *The Social Movement Society: Contentious Politics for a New Century.* Lanham, Md.: Rowman & Littlefield.

Midlarsky, Manus I. (1999): *The Evolution of Inequality: War, State Survival, and Democracy in Comparative Perspective.* Cambridge, Mass.: Harvard University Press.

Mirala, Petri (2000): "'A Large Mob, Calling Themselves Freemasons': Masonic Parades in Ulster," in Peter Jupp and Eoin Magennis, eds., *Crowds in Ireland, c. 1720–1920.* London: Macmillan.

Model, Suzanne (1985): "A Comparative Perspective on the Ethnic Enclave: Blacks, Italians, and Jews in New York City," *International Migration Review* 19: 64–81.

——— (1992): "The Ethnic Economy: Cubans and Chinese Reconsidered," *Sociological Quarterly* 33: 63–82.

——— (1996): "An Occupational Tale of Two Cities: Minorities in London and New York," paper presented to Conference on Social Stratification in Modern Welfare States, Stockholm University.

Mohr, John, ed. (2000): "Relational Analysis and Institutional Meanings: Formal Models for the Study of Culture," special issue of *Poetics* 27, nos. 2 and 3.

Mohr, John W., and Roberto Franzosi, eds. (1997): "Special Double Issue on New Directions in Formalization and Historical Analysis," *Theory and Society* 28, nos. 2 and 3.

Mokyr, Joel (2002): *The Gifts of Athena: Historical Origins of the Knowledge Economy.* Princeton, N.J.: Princeton University Press.

Monroe, Kristen Renwick, James Hankin, and Renée Bukovchik Van Vechten (2000): "The Psychological Foundations of Identity Politics," *Annual Review of Political Science* 3: 419–47.

Montgomery, David (1993): *Citizen Worker: The Experience of Workers in the United States with Democracy and the Free Market During the Nineteenth Century.* Cambridge: Cambridge University Press.

Montgomery, James D. (1994): "Weak Ties, Employment, and Inequality: An Equilibrium Analysis," *American Journal of Sociology* 99: 1212–36.

Moore, Barrington, Jr. (1979): *Injustice. The Social Bases of Obedience and Revolt.* White Plains, N.Y.: M. E. Sharpe.

——— (1993): *Social Origins of Dictatorship and Democracy.* Boston: Beacon. First published in 1966.

Morawska, Ewa (1985): *For Bread with Butter: Life-Worlds of East Central Europeans in Johnstown, Pennsylvania, 1890–1940.* Cambridge: Cambridge University Press.

——— (1990): "The Sociology and Historiography of Immigration," in Virginia Yans-McLaughlin, ed., *Immigration Reconsidered: History, Sociology, and Politics.* New York: Oxford University Press.

——— (1994): "Afterword: America's Immigrants in the 1910 Census Monograph: Where Can We Who Do It Differently Go From Here?" in Susan Cotts Watkins, ed., *After Ellis Island: Newcomers and Natives in the 1910 Census*. New York: Russell Sage Foundation.

—— (1996): *Insecure Prosperity: Small-Town Jews in Industrial America, 1890–1940*. Princeton, N.J.: Princeton University Press.

Morgan, David (1990): *The Mongols*. Oxford: Blackwell.

Mueller, Carol (1997): "International Press Coverage of East German Protest Events, 1989," *American Sociological Review* 62: 820–32.

—— (1999): "Escape from the GDR, 1961–1989: Hybrid Exit Repertoires in a Disintegrating Leninist Regime," *American Journal of Sociology* 105: 697–735.

Muldrew, Craig (1993): "Interpreting the Market: The Ethics of Credit and Community Relations in Early Modern England," *Social History* 18: 163–83.

—— (1998): *The Economy of Obligation: The Culture of Credit and Social Relations in Early Modern England*. London: Macmillan.

Munger, Frank (1981): "Suppression of Popular Gatherings in England, 1800–1830," *American Journal of Legal History* 25: 111–40.

Murray, Stephen O., Joseph H. Rankin, and Dennis W. Magill (1981): "Strong Ties and Job Information," *Sociology of Work and Occupations* 8: 119–36.

Nagi, Saad Z. (1992): "Ethnic Identification and Nationalist Movements," *Human Organization* 51: 307–17.

Naimark, Norman M. (2001): *Fires of Hatred: Ethnic Cleansing in Twentieth-Century Europe*. Cambridge, Mass.: Harvard University Press.

Nesse, Randolph M. (1999): "The Evolution of Hope and Despair," *Social Research* 66: 429–70.

Nicolas, Jean (2002): *La Rébellion française: Mouvements populaires et conscience sociale (1661–1789)*. Paris: Seuil.

O'Donnell, Guillermo (1999): *Counterpoints: Selected Essays on Authoritarianism and Democratization*. Notre Dame, Ind.: University of Notre Dame Press.

Öhngren, Bo (1974): *Folk i rörelse: Samhällsutveckling, flyttningsmonster och folkrörelser i Eskilstuna 1870–1900*. Uppsala: Almqvist and Wicksell.

Olcott, Martha Brill (1997): "Democratization and the Growth of Political Participation in Kazakstan," in Karen Dawisha and Bruce Parrott, eds., *Conflict, Cleavage, and Change in Central Asia and the Caucasus*. Cambridge: Cambridge University Press. Democratization and Authoritarianism in Postcommunist Societies: 4.

—— (2002): *Kazakhstan: Unfulfilled Promise*. Washington, D.C.: Carnegie Endowment for International Peace.

Oliver, Pamela E., and Daniel J. Myers (1999): "How Events Enter the Public Sphere: Conflict, Location, and Sponsorship in Local Newspaper Coverage of Public Events," *American Journal of Sociology* 105: 38–87.

Olivier, Johan (1991): "State Repression and Collective Action in South Africa, 1970–84," *South African Journal of Sociology* 22: 109–17.

Olzak, Susan (1989): "Analysis of Events in the Study of Collective Action," *Annual Review of Sociology* 15: 119–41.

———— (1992): *The Dynamics of Ethnic Competition and Conflict.* Stanford, Calif.: Stanford University Press.

Olzak, Susan, and S. C. Noah Uhrig (2001): "The Ecology of Tactical Overlap," *American Sociological Review* 66: 694–717.

Omi, Michael, and Howard A. Winant (1994): *Racial Formation in the United States: From the 1960s to the 1990s.* 2nd ed. New York: Routledge.

Ong, Aihwa (1996): "Cultural Citizenship as Subject-Making: Immigrants Negotiate Racial and Cultural Boundaries in the United States," *Current Anthropology* 37: 737–62.

Ostrom, Elinor (1990): *Governing the Commons: The Evolution of Institutions for Collective Action.* Cambridge: Cambridge University Press.

———— (1998): "A Behavioral Approach to the Rational Choice Theory of Collective Action," *American Political Science Review* 92: 1–22.

Padgett, John F., and Christopher K. Ansell (1993): "Robust Action and the Rise of the Medici, 1400–1434," *American Journal of Sociology* 98: 1259–1319.

Paige, Jeffery M. (1997): *Coffee and Power: Revolution and the Rise of Democracy in Central America.* Cambridge, Mass.: Harvard University Press.

Palmer, R. R. (1959, 1964): *The Age of the Democratic Revolution.* 2 vols. Princeton, N.J.: Princeton University Press.

Parkin, Frank (1979): *Marxism and Class Theory: A Bourgeois Critique.* London: Tavistock.

Passy, Florence (1998): *L'Action altruiste: Contraintes et opportunités de l'engagement dans les mouvements sociaux.* Geneva: Droz.

Paxton, Pamela (1999): "Is Social Capital Declining in the United States? A Multiple Indicator Assessment," *American Journal of Sociology* 108: 88–127.

Payne, Charles M. (1995): *I've Got the Light of Freedom: The Organizing Tradition and the Mississippi Freedom Struggle.* Berkeley: University of California Press.

Pérez Firmat, Gustavo (1994): *Life on the Hyphen: The Cuban-American Way.* Austin: University of Texas Press.

Petersen, Roger D. (2002): *Understanding Ethnic Violence: Fear, Hatred, and Resentment in Twentieth-Century Eastern Europe.* Cambridge: Cambridge University Press.

Peterson, Paul E., ed. (1995): *Classifying by Race.* Princeton, N.J.: Princeton University Press.

Pettifor, Ann (2001): "Why Jubilee 2000 Made an Impact," in Helmut Anheier, Marlies Glasius, and Mary Kaldor, eds., *Global Civil Society 2001.* Oxford: Oxford University Press.

Pickel, Andreas, ed. (2004a): "Systems and Mechanisms: A Symposium on Mario Bunge's Philosophy of Social Science," *Philosophy of the Social Sciences* 34 (no. 2, June 2004), entire issue.

———— (2004b): "Systems and Mechanisms: A Symposium on Mario Bunge's Philosophy of Social Science, Part II," *Philosophy of the Social Sciences* 34 (no. 3, September 2004), entire issue.

Pigenet, Michel, and Danielle Tartakowsky, eds. (2003): "Les marches," *Le mouvement social* 202 (January–March), entire issue.

Polletta, Francesca (1998a): "'It Was Like A Fever . . .' Narrative and Identity in Social Protest," *Social Problems* 45: 137–59.

———— (1998b): "Contending Stories: Narrative in Social Movements," *Qualitative Sociology* 21: 419–46.

———— (2005): *It Was Like a Fever: Storytelling in Protest and Politics.* Chicago: University of Chicago Press.

Pomeranz, Kenneth (2000): *The Great Divergence: China, Europe, and the Making of the Modern World Economy.* Princeton, N.J.: Princeton University Press.

della Porta, Donatella (1995): *Social Movements, Political Violence, and the State: A Comparative Analysis of Italy and Germany.* Cambridge: Cambridge University Press.

della Porta, Donatella, and Herbert Reiter, eds. (1998): *Policing Protest: The Control of Mass Demonstrations in Western Democracies.* Minneapolis: University of Minnesota Press.

Portes, Alejandro, ed. (1995): *The Economic Sociology of Immigration: Essays on Networks, Ethnicity, and Entrepreneurship.* New York: Russell Sage Foundation.

Portes, Alejandro, and Min Zhou (1992): "Gaining the Upper Hand: Economic Mobility Among Immigrant and Domestic Minorities," *Ethnic and Racial Studies* 15: 491–522.

Portes, Alejandro, and Rubén Rumbaut (1990): *Immigrant America: A Portrait.* Berkeley: University of California Press.

Postel-Vinay, Gilles (1998): *La terre et l'argent: L'agriculture et le crédit en France du XVIIIe au début du Xxe siècle.* Paris: Albin Michel.

Przeworski, Adam (1997): "The State in a Market Economy," in Joan M. Nelson, Charles Tilly, and Lee Walker, eds., *Transforming Post-Communist Political Economies.* Washington, D.C.: National Academies Press.

Przeworski, Adam, Michael Alvarez, José Antonio Cheibub, and Fernando Limongi (1997): "What Makes Democracies Endure?" in Larry Diamond, Marc F. Plattner, Yun-han Chu, and Hung-mao Tien, eds., *Consolidating the Third Wave Democracies.* Baltimore, Md.: Johns Hopkins University Press.

———— (2000): *Democracy and Development: Political Institutions and Well-Being in the World.* Cambridge: Cambridge University Press.

Rae, Heather (2002): *State Identities and the Homogenisation of Peoples.* Cambridge: Cambridge University Press.

Ragin, Charles C. (2000): *Fuzzy-Set Social Science.* Chicago: University of Chicago Press.

Ragin, Charles C., and Howard S. Becker, eds. (1992): *What Is a Case? Exploring the Foundations of Social Inquiry.* Cambridge: Cambridge University Press.

Rajagopal, Balakrishnan (2003): *International Law from Below: Development, Social Movements and Third World Resistance.* Cambridge: Cambridge University Press.

Ramirez, Franciso O., Yasemin Soysal, and Suzanne Shanahan (1997): "The Changing Logic of Political Citizenship: Cross-National Acquisition of Women's Suffrage Rights, 1890 to 1990," *American Sociological Review* 62: 735–45.

Reskin, Barbara F., Debra B. McBrier, and Julie A. Kmec (1999): "The Determinants and Consequences of Workplace Sex and Race Composition," *Annual Review of Sociology* 25: 335–61.

Reskin, Barbara, and Irene Padavic (1994): *Women and Men at Work.* Thousand Oaks, Calif.: Pine Forge.

Robert, Vincent (1996): *Les chemins de la manifestation, 1848–1914.* Lyon: Presses Universitaires de Lyon.

Roemer, John (1982): *A General Theory of Exploitation and Class.* Cambridge, Mass.: Harvard University Press.

Rokkan, Stein (1969): "Models and Methods in the Comparative Study of Nation Building," *Acta Sociologica* 12: 52–73.

——— (1970): *Citizens, Elections, Parties.* Oslo: Universitetsforlaget.

Rollison, David (1992): *The Local Origins of Modern Society: Gloucestershire 1500–1800.* London: Routledge.

Ron, James (2003): *Frontiers and Ghettos: State Violence in Serbia and Israel.* Berkeley: University of California Press.

Rosenberg, Janet, Harry Perlstadt, and William R. F. Phillips (1993): "Now That We Are Here: Discrimination, Disparagement, and Harassment at Work and the Experience of Women Lawyers," *Gender and Society* 7: 415–33.

Rotberg, Robert, ed. (1999): "Patterns of Social Capital: Stability and Change in Comparative Perspective," *Journal of Interdisciplinary History* 29: nos. 3 and 4, Winter and Spring 1999, two entire issues.

Roy, Beth (1994): *Some Trouble with Cows: Making Sense of Social Conflict.* Berkeley: University of California Press.

Rucht, Dieter, and Ruud Koopmans, eds. (1999): "Protest Event Analysis," *Mobilization* 4, no. 2, entire issue.

Rucht, Dieter, Ruud Koopmans, and Friedhelm Neidhardt, eds. (1998): *Acts of Dissent: New Developments in the Study of Protest.* Berlin: Sigma Rainer Bohn Verlag.

Rudé, George (1962): *Wilkes and Liberty.* Oxford: Clarendon Press.

——— (1971): *Hanoverian London, 1714–1808.* London: Secker and Warburg.

Rueschemeyer, Dietrich, Evelyne Huber Stephens, and John D. Stephens (1992): *Capitalist Development and Democracy.* Chicago: University of Chicago Press.

——— (1993): "The Impact of Economic Development on Democracy," *Journal of Economic Perspectives* 7: 71–85.

Rutten, Rosanne (1994): "Courting the Workers' Vote in a Hacienda Region: Rhetoric and Response in the 1992 Philippine Elections," *Pilipinas* 22: 1–34.

Sahlins, Peter (1989): *Boundaries: The Making of France and Spain in the Pyrenees.* Berkeley: University of California Press.

——— (2004): *Unnaturally French: Foreign Citizens in the Old Regime and After.* Ithaca, N.Y.: Cornell University Press.

Sandell, Rickard (1998): *Social Movements and Social Networks.* Stockholm: Department of Sociology, Stockholm University. Stockholm Series on Social Mechanisms, No. 1.

Sanders, Jimy (2002): "Ethnic Boundaries and Identity in Plural Societies," *Annual Review of Sociology* 28: 327–57.

Sant Cassia, Paul (1993): "Banditry, Myth, and Terror in Cyprus and Other Mediterranean Societies," *Comparative Studies in Society and History* 35: 773–95.

Sawyer, R. Keith (2001): *Creating Conversations. Improvisation in Everyday Discourse.* Cresskill, N.J.: Hampton Press.

Scalmer, Sean (2000): "Translating Contention: Culture, History, and the Circulation of Collective Action," *Alternatives* 25: 491–514.

——— (2002a): *Dissent Events: Protest, the Media and the Political Gimmick in Australia.* Sydney: University of New South Wales Press.

——— (2002b): "The Labor of Diffusion: The Peace Pledge Union and the Adaptation of the Gandhian Repertoire," *Mobilization* 7: 269–85.

Schama, Simon (1977): *Patriots and Liberators: Revolution in the Netherlands 1780–1813.* London: Collins.

Schneider, Eric C. (1999): *Vampires, Dragons, and Egyptian Kings: Youth Gangs in Postwar New York.* Princeton, N.J.: Princeton University Press.

Schroedel, Jean Reith (1985): *Alone in a Crowd: Women in the Trades Tell Their Stories.* Philadelphia: Temple University Press.

Schumpeter, Joseph A. (1947): *Capitalism, Socialism, and Democracy.* 2nd ed. New York: Harper and Brothers. First published in 1942.

Schweitzer, R. A., and Charles Tilly (1982): "How London and Its Conflicts Changed Shape, 1758–1834," *Historical Methods* 5: 67–77.

Scott, James C. (1985): *Weapons of the Weak: Everyday Forms of Peasant Resistance.* New Haven, Conn.: Yale University Press.

——— (1990): *Domination and the Arts of Resistance: Hidden Transcripts.* New Haven, Conn.: Yale University Press.

——— (1998): *Seeing Like a State: How Certain Schemes to Improve the Human Condition Have Failed.* New Haven, Conn.: Yale University Press.

Scott, James C., John Tehranian, and Jeremy Mathias (2002): "The Production of Legal Identities Proper to States: The Case of the Permanent Family Surname," *Comparative Studies in Society and History* 44: 4–44.

Scott, Joan W. (1974): *The Glassworkers of Carmaux: French Craftsmen and Political Action in a Nineteenth-Century City.* Cambridge, Mass.: Harvard University Press.

Seidman, Gay W. (1993): "'No Freedom without the Women': Mobilization and Gender in South Africa, 1970–1992," *Signs* 18: 291–320.

——— (1999): "Gendered Citizenship: South Africa's Democratic Transition and the Construction of a Gendered State," *Gender and Society* 13: 287–307.

Seip, Jens Arup (1974, 1981): *Utsikt over Norges Historie.* 2 vols. Oslo: Gylendal Norsk Forlag.

Seligman, Adam (1997): *The Problem of Trust.* Princeton, N.J.: Princeton University Press.

Sen, Amartya (1992): *Inequality Reexamined.* New York: Russell Sage Foundation and Cambridge, Mass.: Harvard University Press.

Shapiro, Gilbert, and John Markoff (1998): *Revolutionary Demands: A Content Analysis of the Cahiers de Doléances of 1789.* Stanford, Calif.: Stanford University Press.

Shapiro, Susan P. (1987): "The Social Control of Impersonal Trust," *American Journal of Sociology* 93: 623–58.

Shklar, Judith N. (1990): *The Faces of Injustice.* New Haven, Conn.: Yale University Press.

Shubik, Martin (1993): "Models of Strategic Behavior and Nuclear Deterrence," in Philip E. Tetlock et al., eds., *Behavior, Society, and International Conflict.* Vol. III. New York: Oxford University Press.

Simon, Curtis J., and John T. Warner (1992): "Matchmaker, Matchmaker: The Effect of Old Boy Networks on Job Match Quality, Earnings, and Tenure," *Journal of Labor Economics* 10: 306–31.

Skocpol, Theda, ed. (1998): *Democracy, Revolution, and History.* Ithaca, N.Y.: Cornell University Press.

Smith, Jackie (1997): "Characteristics of the Modern Transnational Social Movement Sector," in Jackie Smith, Charles Chatfield, and Ron Pagnucco, eds., *Transnational Social Movements and Global Politics: Solidarity Beyond the State.* Syracuse: Syracuse University Press.

——— (2002): "Globalizing Resistance: The Battle of Seattle and the Future of Social Movements," in Jackie Smith and Hank Johnston, eds., *Globalization and Resistance: Transnational Dimensions of Social Movements.* Lanham, Md.: Rowman & Littlefield.

Sober, Elliott, and David Sloan Wilson (1998): *Unto Others: The Evolution and Psychology of Unselfish Behavior.* Cambridge, Mass.: Harvard University Press.

Solnick, Steven L. (1998): *Stealing the State: Control and Collapse in Soviet Institutions.* Cambridge, Mass.: Harvard University Press.

Somers, Margaret R. (1992): "Narrativity, Narrative Identity, and Social Action: Rethinking English Working-Class Formation," *Social Science History* 16: 591–630.

——— (1994): "The Narrative Constitution of Identity: A Relational and Network Approach," *Theory and Society* 23: 605–50.

Sommier, Isabelle (1993): "La CGT: du service d'ordre au service d'accueil," *Genèses* 12: 69–88.

Sørensen, Aage B. (1996): "The Structural Basis of Social Inequality," *American Journal of Sociology* 101: 1333–65.

Spilerman, Seymour (2000): "Wealth and Stratification Processes," *Annual Review of Sociology* 26: 497–524.

Squatriti, Paolo (2002): "Digging Ditches in Early Medieval Europe," *Past and Present* 176: 11–65.

Stanley, William (1996): *The Protection Racket State: Elite Politics, Military Extortion, and Civil War in El Salvador.* Philadelphia: Temple University Press.

Stark, Oded (1995): *Altruism and Beyond: An Economic Analysis of Transfers and Exchanges within Families and Groups.* Cambridge: Cambridge University Press.

Steinberg, Marc W. (1999): *Fighting Words: Working-Class Formation, Collective Action, and Discourse in Early Nineteenth-Century England.* Ithaca, N.Y.: Cornell University Press.

Steinmetz, George (1993): "Reflections on the Role of Social Narratives in Working-Class Formation: Narrative Theory in the Social Sciences," *Social Science History* 16: 489–516.

Stenius, Henrik (1987): *Frivilligt, Jämlikt, Samfällt: Föreningsväsendets utveckling I Finland fram till 1900–talets början med speciell hänsyn till massorganisationsprincipens genombrott.* Helsinki: Svenska Litteratursällskapet I Finland.

Stephens, John D. (1989): "Democratic Transition and Breakdown in Western Europe, 1870–1939: A Test of the Moore Thesis," *American Journal of Sociology* 94: 1019–77.

Stinchcombe, Arthur L. (1990): "Work Institutions and the Sociology of Everyday Life," in Kai Erikson and Steven Peter Vallas, eds., *The Nature of Work. Sociological Perspectives.* New Haven, Conn.: Yale University Press.

——— (1991): "The Conditions of Fruitfulness of Theorizing About Mechanisms in Social Science," *Philosophy of the Social Sciences* 21: 367–88.

——— (1995): *Sugar Island Slavery in the Age of Enlightenment: The Political Economy of the Caribbean World.* Princeton, N.J.: Princeton University Press.

——— (2005): *The Logic of Social Research.* Chicago: University of Chicago Press.

Suny, Ronald Grigor (1993): *The Revenge of the Past: Nationalism, Revolution, and the Collapse of the Soviet Union.* Stanford, Calif.: Stanford University Press.

Swedberg, Richard (1999): "Civil Courage (*Zivilcourage*). The Case of Knut Wicksell," *Theory and Society* 28: 501–28.

Tambiah, Stanley J. (1996): *Leveling Crowds: Ethnonationalist Conflicts and Collective Violence in South Asia.* Berkeley: University of California Press.

——— (1997): "Friends, Neighbors, Enemies, Strangers: Aggressor and Victim in Civilian Ethnic Riots," *Social Science and Medicine* 45: 1177–88.

Tarrow, Sidney (1998): *Power in Movement.* 2nd ed. Cambridge: Cambridge University Press.

——— (2001): "Transnational Politics: Contention and Institutions in International Politics," *Annual Review of Political Science* 4: 1–20.

——— (2002): "From Lumping to Splitting: Specifying Globalization and Resistance," in Jackie Smith and Hank Johnston, eds., *Globalization and Resistance: Transnational Dimensions of Social Movements.* Lanham, Md.: Rowman & Littlefield.

——— (2003): "The New Transnational Contention: Social Movements and Institutions in Complex Internationalism," Working Paper 2003.1, Transnational Contention Project, Cornell University.

Tarrow, Sidney, and Doug McAdam (2004): "Scale Shift in Transnational Contention," in Donatella della Porta and Sidney Tarrow, eds., *Transnational Protest and Global Activism.* Lanham, Md.: Rowman & Littlefield.

Tartakowsky, Danielle (1997): *Les Manifestations de rue en France, 1918–1968.* Paris: Publications de la Sorbonne.

——— (1999): *Nous irons chanter sur vos tombes:. Le Père-Lachaise, XIXe–XXe siècle.* Paris: Aubier.

——— (2004): *La Manif en éclats.* Paris: La Dispute.

Taubman, Paul J. (1991): "Discrimination Within the Family. The Treatment of Daughters and Sons," in Emily P. Hoffman, ed., *Essays on the Economics of Discrimination.* Kalamazoo, Mich.: W. E. Upjohn Institute for Employment Research.

Temperley, Howard (1981): "The Ideology of Antislavery," in David Eltis and James Walvin, eds., *The Abolition of the Atlantic Slave Trade: Origins and Effects in Europe, Africa, and the Americas.* Madison: University of Wisconsin Press.

Thorne, Barrie (1993): *Gender Play: Girls and Boys in School.* New Brunswick, N.J.: Rutgers University Press.

Tilly, Charles (1975): "Food Supply and Public Order in Modern Europe," in Charles Tilly, ed., *The Formation of National States in Western Europe.* Princeton, N.J.: Princeton University Press.

——— (1982): "Proletarianization and Rural Collective Action in East Anglia and Elsewhere, 1500–1900," *Peasant Studies* 10: 5–34.

——— (1984): "Demographic Origins of the European Proletariat," in David Levine, ed., *Proletarianization and Family Life.* Orlando, Fla.: Academic Press.

——— (1986): *The Contentious French.* Cambridge, Mass.: Harvard University Press.

——— (1992): "Conclusions," in Leopold Haimson and Giulio Sapelli, eds., *Strikes, Social Conflict and the First World War: An International Perspective.* Milan: Feltrinelli. Fondazione Giangiacomo Feltrinelli, *Annali* 1990/1991.

——— (1993a): *European Revolutions, 1492–1992.* Oxford: Blackwell.

——— (1993b): "Contentious Repertoires in Great Britain, 1758–1834," *Social Science History* 17: 253–80.

——— (1995): "The Emergence of Citizenship in France and Elsewhere," in Charles Tilly, ed., *Citizenship, Identity and Social History.* Cambridge: Cambridge University Press.

——— (1996): "Invisible Elbow," *Sociological Forum* 11: 589–601.

——— (1998a): "Social Movements and (All Sorts of) Other Political Interactions—Local, National, and International—Including Identities. Several Divagations from a Common Path, Beginning with British Struggles over Catholic Emancipation, 1780–1829, and Ending with Contemporary Nationalism," *Theory and Society* 27: 453–80.

——— (1998b): "Contentious Conversation," *Social Research* 65: 491–510.

——— (1998c): *Durable Inequality.* Berkeley: University of California Press.

——— (1998d): "Political Identities," in Michael P. Hanagan, Leslie Page Moch, and Wayne te Brake, eds., *Challenging Authority: The Historical Study of Contentious Politics.* Minneapolis: University of Minnesota Press.

——— (1999a): "The Trouble with Stories," in Ronald Aminzade and Bernice Pescosolido, eds., *The Social Worlds of Higher Education: Handbook for Teaching in a New Century.* Thousand Oaks, Calif.: Pine Forge Press.

—— (1999b): "Power—Top Down and Bottom Up," *Journal of Political Philosophy* 7: 306–28.

—— (1999c): "Why Worry about Citizenship?" in Michael P. Hanagan and Charles Tilly, eds., *Expanding Citizenship, Reconfiguring States.* Lanham, Md.: Rowman & Littlefield.

—— (2000a): "Errors, Durable and Otherwise," *Comparative Studies in Society and History* 42: 487–93.

—— (2000b): "Relational Studies of Inequality," *Contemporary Sociology* 29: 782–85.

—— (2001a): "Mechanisms in Political Processes," *Annual Review of Political Science* 4: 21–41.

—— (2001b): "Relational Origins of Inequality," *Anthropological Theory* 1: 355–72.

—— (2001c): "Do Unto Others," in Marco Giugni and Florence Passy, eds., *Political Altruism? The Solidarity Movement in International Perspective.* Lanham, Md.: Rowman & Littlefield.

—— (2001d): "Past and Future Inequalities," *Hagar* 2: 5–18.

—— (2002a): *Stories, Identities, and Political Change.* Lanham, Md.: Rowman & Littlefield.

—— (2002b): "Event Catalogs as Theories," *Sociological Theory* 20: 248–54.

—— (2003): *The Politics of Collective Violence.* Cambridge: Cambridge University Press.

—— (2004a): "Social Boundary Mechanisms," *Philosophy of the Social Sciences* 34: 211–36.

—— (2004b): *Contention and Democracy in Europe, 1650–2000.* Cambridge: Cambridge University Press.

—— (2004c): *Social Movements, 1768–2004.* Boulder, Colo.: Paradigm Press, 2004.

—— (2004d): "Trust and Rule," *Theory and Society* 33: 1–30.

—— (2004e): "Terror, Terrorism, Terrorists," *Sociological Theory* 22: 5–13.

Tilly, Chris, and Charles Tilly (1998): *Work Under Capitalism.* Boulder, Colo.: Westview.

Tishkov, Valery (1997): *Ethnicity, Nationalism and Conflict in and After the Soviet Union: The Mind Aflame.* London: Sage.

—— (1999): "Ethnic Conflicts in the Former USSR: The Use and Misuse of Typologies and Data," *Journal of Peace Research* 36: 571–91.

—— (2004): *Chechnya: Life in a War-Torn Society.* Berkeley: University of California Press.

Torsvik, Per, ed. (1981): *Mobilization, Center-Periphery Structures and Nation-Building.* Bergen: Universitetsforlaget.

Turner, Victor (1982): *From Ritual to Theatre: The Human Seriousness of Play.* New York: Performing Arts Journal Publications.

UNDP (2001): United Nations Development Program, *Human Development Report 2001.* New York: Oxford University Press.

United Nations (1995): *Kazakstan: The Challenge of Transition. Human Development Report 1995. www.undp.org/undp/rbec/nhdr/kazakstan.*

Van Dyke, Nella (2003): "Crossing Movement Boundaries: Factors that Facilitate Coalition Protest by American College Students, 1930–1990," *Social Problems* 50: 226–50.

Varshney, Ashutosh (2002): *Ethnic Conflict and Civic Life: Hindus and Muslims in India.* New Haven, Conn.: Yale University Press..

Verdery, Katherine (1991): *National Identity Under Socialism: Identity and Cultural Politics in Ceausescu's Romania.* Berkeley: University of California Press.

———— (2003): *The Vanishing Hectare: Property and Value in Postsocialist Transylvania.* Ithaca, N.Y.: Cornell University Press.

Vermunt, Riël, and Herman Steensma, eds. (1991): *Social Justice in Human Relations.* 2 vols. New York: Plenum.

Wåhlin, Vagn (1986): "Opposition og statsmagt," in Flemming Mikkelen, ed., *Protest og Oprør. Kollektive aktioner I Danmark 1700–1985.* Aarhus: Modtryk.

Waldinger, Roger D. (1986): *Through the Eye of the Needle: Immigrants and Enterprise in New York's Garment Trades.* New York: New York University Press.

———— (1996): *Still the Promised City? African-Americans and New Immigrants in Postindustrial New York.* Cambridge, Mass.: Harvard University Press.

Walter, E. V. (1969): *Terror and Resistance: A Study of Political Violence.* New York: Oxford University Press.

Walton, John (2001): *Storied Land: Community and Memory in Monterey.* Berkeley: University of California Press.

Walvin, James (1980): "The Rise of British Popular Sentiment for Abolition, 1787–1832," in Christine Bolt and Seymour Drescher, eds., *Anti-Slavery, Religion, and Reform: Essays in Memory of Roger Anstey.* Folkestone, U.K.: Dawson/Archon.

———— (1981): "The Public Campaign in England against Slavery, 1787–1834," in David Eltis and James Walvin, eds., *The Abolition of the Atlantic Slave Trade: Origins and Effects in Europe, Africa and the Americas.* Madison: University of Wisconsin Press.

Warren, Mark E. , ed. (1999): *Democracy and Trust.* Cambridge: Cambridge University Press.

Watkins-Owens, Irma (1996): *Blood Relations: Caribbean Immigrants and the Harlem Community, 1900–1930.* Bloomington: Indiana University Press.

Weber, Linda R., and Allison I. Carter (2003): *The Social Construction of Trust.* New York: Kluwer/Plenum.

Weber, Max (1968): Guenther Roth, and Claus Wittich, eds., *Economy and Society: An Outline of Interpretive Sociology.* 3 vols. New York: Bedminster.

Wendt, Alexander E. (1994): "Collective Identity Formation and the International State," *American Political Science Review* 88: 384–98.

White, Harrison (2002): "Strategies and Identities by Mobilization Context," *Soziale Systeme* 8: 231–47.

White, Robert W. (1993): "On Measuring Political Violence: Northern Ireland, 1969 to 1980," *American Sociological Review* 58: 575–85.

Whitehead, Laurence, ed. (2001): *The International Dimensions of Democratization. Europe and the Americas.* Oxford: Oxford University Press.

Williams, Brackette (1989): "A Class Act: Anthropology and the Race to Nation Across Ethnic Terrain," *Annual Review of Anthropology* 18: 401–44.

Williams, Brett, ed. (1991): *The Politics of Culture.* Washington, D.C.: Smithsonian Institution Press.

Williams, Lena (1997): "The Battle of the Braid Brigade," *New York Times,* January 26, 1997, City, p. 4.

Wilson, John, and Marc A. Musick (1999): "Attachment to Volunteering," *Sociological Forum* 14: 243–72.

Wolf, Eric R. (1982): *Europe and the People Without History.* Berkeley: University of California Press.

——— (1999): *Envisioning Power:. Ideologies of Dominance and Crisis.* Berkeley: University of California Press.

Wolff, Edward N. (1995): "How the Pie Is Sliced: America's Growing Concentration of Wealth," *The American Prospect* 22: 58–64.

Woloch, Isser (1970): *Jacobin Legacy: The Democratic Movement under the Directory.* Princeton, N.J.: Princeton University Press.

——— (1994): *The New Regime:. Transformations of the French Civic Order, 1789–1820s.* New York: Norton.

Wong, R. Bin (1997): *China Transformed: Historical Change and the Limits of European Experience.* Ithaca, N.Y.: Cornell University Press.

——— (1999): "Citizenship in Chinese History," in Michael Hanagan and Charles Tilly, eds., *Extending Citizenship, Reconfiguring States.* Lanham, Md.: Rowman & Littlefield.

Wood, Andrew Grant (2001): *Revolution in the Street: Women, Workers, and Urban Protest in Veracruz, 1870–1927.* Wilmington, Del.: Scholarly Resources.

Wood, Lesley J. (2004): "Breaking the Bank and Taking to the Streets—How Protesters Target Neoliberalism," *Journal of World Systems Research* 10: 69–89.

Woolcock, Michael (1998): "Social Capital and Economic Development: Toward a Theoretical Synthesis and Policy Framework," *Theory and Society* 27: 151–208.

World Bank (2002): *Building Institutions for Markets: World Development Report 2002.* New York: Oxford University Press.

Wright, Erik Olin (1997): *Class Counts: Comparative Studies in Class Analysis.* Cambridge: Cambridge University Press.

Wrightson, Keith (1982): *English Society 1580–1680.* London: Hutchinson.

Wrightson, Keith, and David Levine (1979): *Poverty and Piety in an English Village. Terling, 1525–1700.* New York: Academic Press.

——— (1991): *The Making of an Industrial Society. Whickham 1560–1765.* Oxford: Clarendon Press.

Wuthnow, Robert (1991): *Acts of Compassion: Caring for Others and Helping Ourselves.* Princeton, N.J.: Princeton University Press.

——— (2004): "Trust as an Aspect of Social Structure," in Jeffrey C. Alexander, Gary T. Marx, and Christine L. Williams, eds., *Self, Social Structure, and Beliefs: Explorations in Sociology.* Berkeley: University of California Press.

Yamagishi, Toshio, and Midori Yamagishi (1994): "Trust and Commitment in the United States and Japan," *Motivation and Emotion* 18: 129–66.

Yashar, Deborah J. (1997): *Demanding Democracy: Reform and Reaction in Costa Rica and Guatemala, 1870s–1950s.* Stanford, Calif.: Stanford University Press.

Young, Iris Marion (1990): *Justice and the Politics of Difference.* Princeton, N.J.: Princeton University Press.

Zablocki, Benjamin D. (1980): *Alienation and Charisma: A Study of Contemporary American Communes.* New York: Free Press.

Zald, Mayer N., and John D. McCarthy (1977): "Resource Mobilization and Social Movements: A Partial Theory," *American Journal of Sociology* 82: 1212–41.

Zelizer, Viviana (1994): *The Social Meaning of Money.* New York: Basic Books.

——— (1999): "Multiple Markets, Multiple Cultures," in Neil Smelser and Jeffrey Alexander, eds., *Diversity and Its Discontents: Cultural Conflict and Common Ground in Contemporary American Society.* Princeton, N.J.: Princeton University Press.

——— (2005a): "Circuits within Capitalism," in Victor Nee and Richard Swedberg, eds. *The Economic Sociology of Capitalism.* Princeton, N.J.: Princeton University Press.

——— (2005b): "Culture and Consumption," in Neil Smelser and Richard Swedberg, eds. *Handbook of Economic Sociology.* Rev. ed. Princeton, N.J.: Princeton University Press and New York: Russell Sage Foundation.

——— (2005c): *The Purchase of Intimacy.* Princeton, N.J.: Princeton University Press.

Zerubavel, Eviatar (1991): The Fine Line: Making Distinctions in Everyday Life. New York: Free Press.

Index

Credits

E ARLIER VERSIONS OF THE BOOK'S MAIN CHAPTERS APPEARED AS:

Violent Conflict, Social Relations, and Explanation of Social Processes," paper for conference in memory of Roger Gould, Yale University, October 2003.

"Mechanisms in Political Processes," *Annual Review of Political Science* 4 (2001), 21–41.

"Do Unto Others," in Marco Giugni and Florence Passy, eds., *Political Altruism? The Solidarity Movement in International Perspective.* Lanham, Md.: Rowman & Littlefield, 2001.

"Durable Inequality," in Phyllis Moen, Donna Dempster-McClain, and Henry Walker, eds., *A Nation Divided: Diversity, Inequality, and Community in American Society,* Cornell University Press, 1999.

"Relational Origins of Inequality," pp. 355–72 in Charles Tilly, ed., special issue on inequality, *Anthropological Theory,* vol. 1, no. 3, 2001.

"Changing Forms of Inequality," *Sociological Theory* 21 (2003), 31–36.

"Unequal Knowledge," *Graduate Researcher. Journal for the Arts, Sciences and Technology* 1 (2003), 11–17.

"Social Boundary Mechanisms," *Philosophy of the Social Sciences* 34 (2004), 211–36.

"Chain Migration and Opportunity Hoarding," in Janina W. Dacyl and Charles Westin, eds., *Governance of Cultural Diversity.* Stockholm: CEIFO [Centre for Research in International Migration and Ethnic Relations], 2000.

"Boundaries, Citizenship, and Exclusion," lecture, Harvard University, September 2004.

"Why Worry About Citizenship?" in Michael P. Hanagan and Charles Tilly, eds., *Expanding Citizenship, Reconfiguring States.* Lanham, Md.: Rowman & Littlefield, 1999.

"Inequality, Democratization, and De-Democratization," *Sociological Theory* 21 (2003), 37–43.

"Political Identities in Changing Polities," *Social Research* 70 (2003), 1301–15.

"Invention, Diffusion, and Transformation of the Social Movement Repertoire," keynote address for Conference on Political Transfer, Groningen University, February 2004.

In editing previously published chapters for this volume, I added a few clarifying passages and brought some references up to date, but otherwise retained the original texts. (Exception: despite the defense of autoplagiarism in this book's preface, I have cut, curtailed, corrected, or camouflaged a few egregious repetitions from one essay to another.) I have, however, made extensive revisions to the previously unpublished chapters.

About the Author

After long-term teaching and research appointments at Delaware, Harvard, MIT, Toronto, Michigan, and the New School for Social Research, since 1996 Charles Tilly has been Joseph L. Buttenwieser Professor of Social Science at Columbia University in New York City. He has held shorter-term teaching and research appointments at Princeton University, Sir George Williams University, the Center for Advanced Study in the Behavioral Sciences (Stanford), the Ecole des Hautes Etudes en Sciences Sociales, the Institute for Advanced Study (Princeton), the University of Paris I (Sorbonne), University of Paris VII (Jussieu), the Collège de France, the Postgraduate Institute of Social Science (Amsterdam), the Institut d'Etudes Politiques (Paris), Stanford University, and the Russell Sage Foundation. He is a member of the National Academy of Sciences, the American Academy of Arts and Sciences, and the American Philosophical Society, as well as a Fellow of the American Association for the Advancement of Science and a Chevalier des Palmes Académiques. He has received honorary doctorates in social sciences from Erasmus University (Rotterdam), the Institut d'Etudes Politiques (Paris), the University of Toronto, the University of Strasbourg, the University of Geneva , the University of Crete, and the University of Québec at Montréal.

Tilly's recent books include *Stories, Identities, and Political Change* (2002), *The Politics of Collective Violence* (2003), *Contention and Democracy in Europe, 1650–2000* (2004), *Trust and Rule* (2005), *Why?* (2006), and the *Oxford Handbook of Contextual Political Analysis* (co-authored and co-edited with Robert Goodin, 2006). With Paradigm Press, he has also published *Social Movements, 1768–2004* (2004), *Economic and Political Contention in Comparative Perspective* (co-authored and co-edited with Maria Kousis, 2005), and a new edition of *Popular Contention in Great Britain, 1758–1834* (2005). He is currently writing *Contentious Politics* (with Sidney Tarrow, to be published by Paradigm) and *Regimes and Repertoires.*